BETWEENER TALK

Qualitative Inquiry and Social Justice

Series Editors:
Norman K. Denzin (University of Illinois, Champaign-Urbana) and
Yvonna S. Lincoln (Texas A&M University)

Books in this series address the role of critical qualitative research in an era that cries out for emancipatory visions that move people to struggle and resist oppression. Rooted in an ethical framework that is based on human rights and social justice, the series publishes exemplary studies that advance this transformative paradigm.

Volumes in this series:

Betweener Talk, Decolonizing Knowledge Production, Pedagogy, and Praxis, Marcelo Diversi and Cláudio Moreira

BETWEENER TALK

DECOLONIZING KNOWLEDGE PRODUCTION, PEDAGOGY, AND PRAXIS

Marcelo Diversi
Cláudio Moreira

Walnut Creek, California

LEFT COAST PRESS, INC.
1630 North Main Street, #400
Walnut Creek, CA 94596
http://www.LCoastPress.com

Copyright © 2009 by Left Coast Press, Inc.

All rights reserved. No part of this publication may be reproduced, stored in a retrieval system, or transmitted in any form or by any means, electronic, mechanical, photocopying, recording, or otherwise, without the prior permission of the publisher.

ISBN 978-1-59874-359-3 hardcover
ISBN 978-1-59874-360-9 paperback

Library of Congress Cataloging-in-Publication Data

Diversi, Marcelo.
Betweener talk: decolonizing knowledge production, pedagogy, and praxis / Marcelo Diversi, Cláudio Moreira.
   p. cm.—(Qualitative inquiry and social justice)
Includes bibliographical references and index.
ISBN 978-1-59874-359-3 (hardcover : alk. paper)—ISBN 978-1-59874-360-9 (pbk. : alk. paper)
 1. Knowledge, Sociology of—Brazil. 2. Social epistemology—Brazil. 3. Social justice—Brazil. 4. Communication and culture—Brazil. 5. Ethnicity—Brazil. 6. Ethnoscience—Brazil. 7. Postcolonialism—Brazil. 8. Decolonization—Brazil. 9. Brazil—Social conditions. I. Moreira, Cláudio II. Title.
HM651.D58 2009
306.4'20981—dc22 2009021215

Printed in the United States of America

∞™ The paper used in this publication meets the minimum requirements of American National Standard for Information Sciences—Permanence of Paper for Printed Library Materials, ANSI/NISO Z39.48–1992.

09 10 11 12 13   5 4 3 2 1

Special thanks to Renner Larson for drawing the chapter-opening art, the art on the last page of Chapter 10, and the cover image. All the photos are the authors'.

Contents

Foreword		7
Acknowledgments		9
Part I	**Betweenness and Decolonizing Resistance**	11
Chapter 1	The Beginnings of a Critical Postcolonial Duo	13
	Betweener Talk	13
	Things We Talk about When Sitting at the Curb	14
	Crossing Paths, Making Bridges	17
	Central Metaphor: Betweeners, Life In-Between	18
	On Oppression	25
	Who Gives the Authority to Ask Questions?	27
	On Why We Wrote Together	28
	Nurturing New Battlegrounds	28
	Outline of the Rest of the Book	28
Chapter 2	Onto-Epistemological Stance	31
Part II	**Stories from the Margins**	35
Chapter 3	Betweenness in Identity	37
	Street Life	37
	Fragments	45
	Back on the Streets	61
	The Streets or Not the Streets	65
	Off the Streets	68
Chapter 4	Betweenness in Class	71
	With Grace	71
	My Bad English	73
	Bathroom	84
	Newspaper Picture	86
Chapter 5	Betweenness in Race	89
	Words	89
	Too Blond Too White	92

	The Tales of Conde, Zezao, Master Cláudio, and Cláudio	98
	No More Soccer	115
Chapter 6	Betweenness in Sexuality	119
	A Place for Recovery	119
	Made for Sex	128
	Stolen Romance	133
Chapter 7	Betweenness in Indigenousness and Postcolonialism	137
	Old-Fashioned Nikes	137
	"She Could Be Living in Italy Now..."	138
	Unspeakable Transgressions	142
	Nike Cap	155
Chapter 8	Betweenness in Knowledge Production	157
	Fire in the Mission	157
	Life in So Many Acts	161
Part III	Methodological Acts/Detours and Postcolonial Resistance: Decolonizing Scholarship for Social Justice in the 21st Century	181
Chapter 9	Methodological Acts and Detours	183
	A Dialogue on (Auto)Ethnography	187
Chapter 10	Words to End With: Decolonizing Praxis and Social Justice	205
	Decolonizing Praxis	208
	Parting Thoughts...	218
References		225
Index		233
About the Authors		236

FOREWORD

> "From the vantage point of the colonized . . . the word 'research' . . . is probably one of the dirtiest words in the indigenous world's vocabulary." (Linda Tuhiwai Smith, 1999, p. 1)

> "I used . . . social justice theatre . . . Augusto Boal's. . . . Theatre of the Oppressed . . . to help my students make the connection between critical thinking and critical consciousness." (Michael Yellow Bird, 2005, p. 13)

The Decade of the World's Indigenous Peoples (1994–2004) ended over a decade ago. Non-indigenous scholars have yet to learn from it, to learn that it is time to dismantle, deconstruct, and decolonize Western epistemologies from within, to learn that research does not have to be a dirty word, to learn that research can be moral and political. It is time to chart a new dialogue of decolonizing resistance, a new Decade of Critical, Indigenous Inquiry. This brilliant book by two young Brazilian scholars is dedicated to this charge.

Betweener Talk: Decolonizing Knowledge Production, Pedagogy, and Praxis embraces the dialogical, performative turn in the human disciplines. Thoroughly grounded in the worlds of both the colonizer and colonized, the dialogue works back and forth across Paulo Freire, Gloria Anzaldúa, Soyini Madison, Dwight Conquergood, and various Third World feminisms. This book is written in the form of a manifesto, an invitation to both indigenous and non-indigenous scholars to think through the implications of connecting indigenous epistemologies (and theories of decolonization and the postcolonial) with emancipatory discourses, critical theory, and critical pedagogy. The authors, situated between the world of northern academe and their southern origins, are uniquely placed to address this.

Marcelo and Cláudio bring their dialogical notions of betweenness and decolonizing discourse into the spaces of identity, race, class, sexuality, and the classroom. They offer the reader a progressive politics of performative inquiry. Working out of their intertwined biographies, they offer new ways of reading, writing, and performing global and local culture. The stories move from street life in Brazil and dirty work in colonizers' bathrooms to the problems of illiteracy in local cultures riddled with sexual violence, rape, and crushing poverty. Each page is marked with the traces of death and pain. Images of tattered T-shirts, dirty Nike sneakers, and tear stains on sad faces leap off the page.

In this new century, how do qualitative scholars realize Freire's progressive dreams in the wake of a host of global crises, both natural and human-made—hurricanes, tsunamis, wars, post-9/11 atrocities, genocide, jihadist attacks, human rights violations? Marcelo and Cláudio show us how to do this. With their liberatory, emancipatory commitments, they believe that critical methodologists, can—in concert with indigenous methodologies—speak to oppressed, colonized persons living in postcolonial situations of injustice: women of all colors, situations, and ethnicities; queer, lesbian, transgendered individuals; Aboriginal, First Nation, Native American, South African, Latin American, Pacific and Asian Islander persons. They seek the utopia of social justice. Their dialogical texts model forms of decolonizing praxis that empower persons by honoring their voices, their experiences, and their struggles for dignity.

This powerful book opens the door for a new generation of critical inquiry. We are honored to have it as the inaugural volume in our Qualitative Inquiry and Social Justice series with Left Coast Press, Inc.

Norman K. Denzin
Yvonna S. Lincoln

ACKNOWLEDGMENTS

The pleasure of feeling grateful . . .

We couldn't have done it alone
    Norman Denzin, Yvonna Lincoln, Mitch Allen

Together we are a force
    Dan Cook, Jim Denison, João Batista Freire, Margareth Morelli, Bob Rinehart, Silvana Venâncio, Katie Peña

Inspired by Anzaldúa
    and Paulo Freire, bell hooks, Richard Rorty, Joe Kincheloe, Peter McLaren, Laurel Richardson, Carolyn Ellis, Denzin and Lincoln

By those who honor differences
    Reed Larson, Syndy Sydnor, Eva Maria Oxelson, Vonda Jump, Cole, Cameron McCarthy, Lino Castellani Filho, Michael Giardina, Stacey C. Sawyer

Bodies that make impossibilities possible
    Audre Lorde, Harvey Milk, Zumbi dos Palmares, D. Soyini Madison, Dwight Conquergood

People who have touched our lives
    Dani, Analua, Francisco, Cláudio Augusto de Castro Paiva, Sylvia Alves Diversi, Adriana Diversi, Emily Mills, Silvia Guapita Sobral, Nate Norman, Martinho and Elisa, Lidia and Luiz, Elio and Laura, Ana Rosa and Wagner

Other Betweeners
> Islara, Lindalva, Tatu, Jorge Diversi, Carolyn E. Taylor, Carla Crócomo, João Henrique Lavor, Lalá, Suzi Wilson, Desiree, Aisha, Himika, Sukki, Roni, Mariolga

Advancing decolonizing pedagogies
> Susan Finley, Sam Veissiere, Ferréz, Linda Tuhiwai Smith, Bryant Keith Alexander, Tami Spry, Stacey Holman Jones, Cherrie Moraga, Paula Gunn Allen, Arthur P. Bochner, Ronald Pelias, Elyse Pineau

Challenging knowledge production
> Dojão, Dorothy Smith, Ney Moraes Filho, Michel, Noam, "Boss"

Offering possibilities
> Chico Buarque, Jorge Amado, Augusto Boal, and Norman

To my brother Marcelo
To my brother Cláudio
To all interested in expanding a sense of Us
Betweeners for inclusive dreams of social justice, democracy, liberty
As our muse says
Onward!

Part I

BETWEENNESS AND DECOLONIZING RESISTANCE

Chapter 1

THE BEGINNINGS OF A CRITICAL POSTCOLONIAL DUO

BETWEENER TALK

We can't press the keys at the same time. But this introduction and the entire book are ours. Equally ours. Even as I type this sentence, 2,000 miles away from my writing partner, I know that these words, meanings, intentions, and emotions reside not in me but in *us*. Most of what we have written in this book inhabits the memories of our conversations, discussions, and occasional disagreements. We already do not remember who first brought up a significant number of ideas and concepts central to this book. And after a few attempts at keeping the story straight, we gave in and embraced the exhilarating experience of truly co-constructing a book together. We have found a dialogic voice that has made our individual work more meaningful, grounded, and, yes, fulfilling. We have found a voice we did not have in our work alone, a voice that seems, to both of us, more vibrant, truer to our experiences as betweeners and decolonizing scholars. Indeed, because of our collaboration in every line of this book, we feel we have achieved a higher understanding of what it means to be a betweener and a postcolonial scholar. Even when each of our voices is clear, as in the stories in Part III, we can see the questions, suggestions, and approving nods from each other that form the canvas on which these slices of lived experiences were drawn.

But because we experienced growing up and doing research in Brazil from significantly different perspectives, we also attempt to present our *individual* views on the central themes of this book: social justice, betweeners, oppression, the classroom as a site for struggle against ideologies of domination, methodology, and the role of decolonizing inquiry in knowledge production in the 21st century. We have decided to present our perspectives in the form of dialogue in order to recapture, as closely as we can, the very dialogic process that gave birth to this book.

We see this book as a stage where we perform our dialogue over social justice in the world we inhabit. In this stage, you will find three authorial voices: the co-constructed dialogical narration, as explained above, then Cláudio's, then Marcelo's. We hope you will find other voices as well as you read about our encounters with humans living at the margins of Brazilian society and knowledge production. We are not elected representatives of the worlds we describe and act on. But we have been shaped and marked by these worlds. And it is from these worlds that we speak and write.

THINGS WE TALK ABOUT WHEN SITTING AT THE CURB

"Why did you have to go to an American university to study Brazilian street children?" my friend Cláudio asked as we sat down on the curb in front of my parents' home in Brazil.

I didn't answer right away. I perceived the question as loaded with a postcolonial critique, partially because I had been asking myself the same question, but mostly because I was familiar with Cláudio's incisive challenges of the arrogance with which academics construct knowledge about oppression from the comfort of a privileged life. I also hesitated in my answer because of the sudden seriousness his question had brought to our long night of music, drinking, and delicious conversations about everything and nothing much—the things of our friendship throughout the years.

Not wanting to do the work, I joked about being a colonizer wanting to document the lives of the natives. Cláudio kept his eyes on mine, silent, smiling yet serious. He wasn't going to let me off the hook the easy way.

"I didn't learn the theories and methods to do this type of work until I started grad school," I said feeling a bit self-conscious about those two words—theories and methods.

"But how can you understand what these kids go through living so far away, in a safe place, taking classes from folks who know nothing about the hardships of Brazilian streets?" Cláudio pressed on.

"Exactly! These theories and methods are not saying I can completely understand these kids' lives but that I can examine the social forces shaping their lives and portray their experiences in comparison and contrast with my own privileged upbringing here in Brazil."

"I don't know about that. Look, I know you mean well. I believe you care about these kids and their condition. But how can your study help these kids? You come, enter their lives, collect your stories, then you leave and go back to the beauty of your American campus. You get a degree and advance your career. But these kids will continue to get shot at."

I knew Cláudio too well to take his comments as a personal accusation. Not to mention that his points rang true whichever way I turned them. Yes, I wanted to be doing something meaningful, but I believed there was more to it than my personal advancement. I have since wavered at times in my dialogic conviction, but during those days of street fieldwork I felt as strongly as ever that the only way to more inclusive systems of social justice was through the expansion of the dominant discourse about the Other. And this discursive expansion had to be done by challenging binary systems of either/or, normal childhood/abnormal childhood, good kid/bad kid, us/them, more human/less human, children/little criminals. Ideologies of domination, such as the one behind street children, depend on people accepting that humans can be summed up by essentializing dichotomies of self.

"Emic narratives about life in the streets can help others see these kids as more than little criminals," I finally said in rapid fire.

"Emic what?"

There. I had used jargon that carried a whole library of scholarship meaningful to me, but not to Cláudio at the time.

"Look, it's not a new idea. And it's certainly not my own. Think about it this way. How do most people know about street kids?" I asked.

"From what they see in the streets, the news, the movies," Cláudio replied.

"Right! So people form their views of street kids from the narratives available to them. And these narratives are very one-sided, told from the point of view of the privileged, the ones with space to circulate their stories in the main channels that inform public opinion in our society. This is what the theories I am studying call dominant discourse. And in my view, the dominant discourse about street kids present them in only two ways, as victims and as little criminals. The emic perspective that I mentioned attempts to add the stories from the inside, from the kids and those working with them on a daily basis. These voices are missing from the dominant discourse, and this omission does great damage to all, especially to street kids, for they are among the most vulnerable in our society."

"Aren't you saying the same thing, that they are victims of society?"

"What I am trying to say is that their vulnerability is what makes them victims so often, victims to violence, abuse, and neglect. These kids are poor, darker-skinned, homeless, hungry, all of which would make the beginning of life pretty hard. And to top it off, these kids don't have parents, relatives, or any other caring and invested adults around to protect, guide, discipline, or supervise. Anyway, that is the sort of thing that these theories and methods are trying to examine and incorporate into the dominant discourse. They are lenses, tools, angles, etc. that point researchers to parts of experience that are missing from artificial yet pervasive dichotomous representations of the Other. In the case of street kids, these theories and methods might help me fill in some of the missing parts, like how do these kids make sense of their lives in the streets? What are their views about hunger, drugs, crime, justice, identity, choice, and future? What are their fears, joys, and dreams? How did they leave home? Why don't they go back? How come they prefer the streets to the shelters in town? *E por ai vai,* and on it goes."

"Hum."

"It's not a formula or magic power. It's about trying hard to listen to the Other with maximum attention and the least amount of prejudgment I can, even as I try just as hard to be aware of what my prejudgments may be."

"And how can all this, with the big words I don't understand, and that I am sure the street kids don't understand, how can all of this help these kids?" Cláudio asked.

"I don't think my research can help these kids very much," I said.

"So why do you do it, then?"

"Because I believe future lives can be improved by this kind of work. Once more people begin to see themselves in these kids' life stories, once these kids become less strange and more familiar to the critical mass, then there will be more political and systemic pressure for society at large to intervene in more humanizing ways. I don't have hard evidence to back up this belief. But I think it's a reality-grounded belief anyway. It is said that Victor Hugo's writings on the street urchins of Paris in the early 1800s, especially his writings about Gavroche, 'le Gamin de Paris,' the street kid of Paris, in *Les Misérables,* touched the popular thinking about Parisian street kids to the point of positive change. George Orwell wrote that he thought Charles Dickens changed the way people saw childhood and street urchins through his novels about the conditions of the urban poor in England. I don't mean to compare myself with such genius. It's possible my writings about street kids will never amount to much. But that is the idea behind my project. Get the unheard stories of lived experience out there. Expand the dominant discourse about street kids. Hopefully get people to see them beyond the little criminal image of today. Offer glimpses into these kids' lives. Move people to do something to change the current system. Perhaps this type of research and writing can help fuel some of that."

"I've never read these authors, but now I think I understand your point better. It's like what Chico Buarque has done here in Brazil through his music and poetry. It seems like a lot of people have become more aware about the struggle of the poor through his songs, especially because most of his audience is middle and upper class folk, formally educated and with more power to change things," Cláudio said.

"Yes, of course, like Chico Buarque! I hadn't thought about him," I said, now glad Cláudio had started this conversation.

"Look at what Chico Buarque did for the resistance against the military regime. His songs, so full of symbolic nuance and double-meaning, allowed a whole generation of youth and adults to express their discontent with the military regime's censorship, oppression of civil rights, and political dictatorship. He did help change the *dominant discourse*, as you say," Cláudio said giving me a teasing smile.

I was grateful to him, Cláudio, my good friend, for helping me make another important connection between resistance theory and practice of resistance, between art and social sciences.

"It will be interesting to talk about this again in 10 or 20 years," Cláudio said as we got up from the curb to go inside the house.

Crossing Paths, Making Bridges

Glimpses

Glimpse 1, around 1987

It was a long time ago, around the time I met Marcelo. Marcelo and I were talking and then he opened his wallet. Could not help myself. Never saw so many bills inside a wallet before. It's the thug in me. Marcelo, I am sure, did not notice a thing.

Glimpse 2, around 2005

Marcelo is now a construction worker with a drunken boss in Utah. I am trying to figure out how I can get out of my mess in Champaign. I don't want be a grad student for much longer.

Glimpse 3, around 1994

CLÁUDIO: "Hey, I'm only joking. I'm not racist. I make jokes about everybody. Blacks, blondes, gays. . . . I make jokes about myself all the time."
MARCELO: "So stop making them. Hope you understand one day."

Glimpse 4, around 2007

With my moving fingers in front of my computer at home:

I am understanding
Learning
Becoming
The Brazilian white
Hybrid
The Bastard male product of the colonial rape
Somehow the product of the European fucker sounds okay
Thank you my brother.

Glimpse 5, around 2000

A day at the lake. Marcelo and I, other friends with us, walking along Michigan Avenue, Chicago, singing the Brazilian national anthem.

Glimpse 6, around 2001

Lost, I'm totally lost. I just came back from my fieldwork with soccer fans in Brazil. Now, I have to write a master thesis, and I don't know how. It's very confusing. I open Marcelo's dissertation. It's all there. I feel empowered. My good friend did a beautiful job. I start to understand his work and also to find my way. Marcelo is not the colonizing ethnographer.
This glimpse takes me to . . .

Glimpse 7, June 1994

After a long night and many beers, Marcelo and I sit down on the curb in front of a bar that just closed. It is already dawn. It's gonna be a beautiful day. Putting my hand in front of my eyes to shade the first sunlight, I say to Marcelo: "So, now you are one of them. You come here," I say with a hint of irony, "study the street kids, and then go back to that beautiful university of yours. What's the name of the town, Champaign? Like the fancy French drink? You go back to your good life in the States. What about the street kids?"

CENTRAL METAPHOR: BETWEENERS, LIFE IN-BETWEEN

This book is about living at the margins, written from the standpoint of two betweeners. It is a book about our encounters with Brazilian street kids, sugar cane workers, organized soccer fan clubs, the production of knowledge, and, of course, the self. We are Brazilians living as academics in the

United States, studying back-alley lives in Brazil. In our ethnographic fieldwork in Brazil, we are insiders as fellow nationals yet outsiders as researchers. We move from the poor inequality of the streets to the rich inequality of our families' homes. We are two friends from European-colonized Brazil who had to come to the United States to learn about Paulo Freire's conscientization and postcolonial inquiry. We are treated as white in Brazil and as colored in the United States of America. We can speak street vernacular as Brazilian natives yet have trouble discussing Pedagogy of the Oppressed in its original language—our own mother tongue, Portuguese. In Brazil, where we were born, we are called *gringos* by the folks we work with. In the U.S.A., where we live, the establishment calls us *aliens*. We call ourselves *betweeners*: (un)conscious bodies experiencing life in and between two cultures.

We are claiming this position, betweener, not to fix our identities but to situate ourselves in the socially constructed, fluid space from which we are writing, thinking, and giving meaning to the experiences represented in this book. This name does not tell the whole story about who we are and the type of scholarship we are trying to advance in this book, but we believe it gives us a starting point for the dialogic thinking in which we want to engage with readers. It also forecasts, we believe, other layers of betweenness informing the praxis and writing at play in this book: interdisciplinarity, representational blurriness, and the politics of knowledge production.

As you move into the more theoretical parts of this book, you will notice that we believe all humans experience this betweenness, although at varying degrees of intensity and cost. Living between the modern assumptions of childhood innocence and delinquent behavior, as street kids do, is certainly more intense and costly than, say, living as privileged foreigners in the U.S.A. In advancing this common assumption of betweenness, we are not attempting to level out or trivialize experiences of lived oppression. We do not all suffer the same way, with the same intensity, or under similar systems of (in)justice. We realize that certain individuals and groups are more vulnerable to systems of domination, oppression, and misrepresentation than others are. Such power differential between and among humans is, indeed, the target of the central critique of our work.

We nevertheless want to use the notion of shared betweenness as a point of communality in our journey on earth. There is not a human who has always been on the "right" side, in the "cool" crowd, loved by all, disliked by none. Even the most privileged, however they may be defined, among us has suffered the sting of rejection, the uncertainty of the future, the anxiety of feeling socially awkward, the indignity of unjust treatment, the insignificance in relation to time and space, and the pain of the fleeting nature of identity.

In a Bakhtinian sense, discussed in greater detail in Chapter 9, we are all engaged in an endless negotiation of identities, furiously pursuing identities we value and dodging the ones we abhor. Identities are not inside individuals but in the space between interacting individuals. Identity does not reside neatly and dormant inside people until truth can awaken and reveal its original design and plan. Instead, identity is forever mutant and relational, adapting to the contextual pressures of making oneself feel worthwhile—by saving face, advancing images of self that one perceives to be advantageous, resisting negative identity-framing commentary by others (real and imaginary), to mention a few of the image management expressions involved in identity matters.

Obviously, power relations are paramount to the inevitable co-construction of identity. We have all been dissatisfied with identity labels slapped onto us against our will by those with more power of definition in a particular negotiation or interaction. This power differential can be rather subtle and fluid, as in a group of friends, unmistakable and benign, as in idealized adult-child relations, or brutal and omnipotent, as in the case of dehumanizing acts. Most of us experience all these types of power differential along the way. But there is a large number of humans who continue to exist mostly under the crushing fist of brutality and omnipotence. Any sensible person, in our view, would agree that children and youth who come of age without the care and guidance of invested adults are particularly vulnerable to physical and symbolic brutality.

Growing up in Brazil is the center stage of our performance here. We bring our personal experiences to this performative stage and weave our memories, histories, and methodologies to reconstruct encounters with and lived experiences of oppression in the context of Brazilian childhood at the end of the 20th century. Also, we do so in order to create narrative space in the enduring struggle to resist and challenge the colonizing ways of knowing about the Other that, in our view, continues to dictate the acceptable voices, representational styles, and technologies of justification—whereby the talking-head expert humbly trumps the oppressed body, verbatim phrases trump recollections of encounters, and theory trumps the marked body. We bring to this book, to this performative stage, our desire to push the postcolonial movement toward epistemologies ever more inclusive of those who are actually getting caned for wanting dignity and social equality. This desire does not come from a "do-it-like-us" position but from our collaborative attempt at learning how to think, act, and represent inclusively. We know we are not pioneers in this attempt. Yet we think we can offer a unique angle because of our commitment to write this book to the best of our dialogic abilities. Instead of a solo dance, we perform a duet on this stage, hoping that our representational style mirrors our attempts at decolonizing ways of knowing. As we compose our choreography, we hope you can see the many levels of our betweenness as private folks and public scholars. And we hope you can feel your own betweenness in the process.

In this book we explore this betweenness in several layers. We put forth a unified work that was largely created between two authors, us, while standing on the shoulders of thinkers who have called for reciprocal empowering collaboration in the production of knowledge about the human experience. We situate our differing epistemologies in relation to the in-between academic spaces we inhabit: indigenous postcolonial scholars criticizing dominant modes of knowledge production who make a living from within the dominant educational system. We write about children who live in the space between pity and hatred, between childhood and marginalization, between wanting to be accepted and being essentialized and treated as *trombadinhas* (pickpockets) by adults. And we write about the inclusion of the missing bodies of the oppressed who continue to appear as subjects in the "center" of knowledge production while being kept at the peripheries of sociological meaning-making by hegemonic rules of language use, theoretical sophistication, and representational authority—missing bodies that inhabit the space between compassion on one hand (as subject of knowledge production) and condescension on the other (as producer of knowledge).

We will try to make the case that conscientization and notions of inclusive social justice—states of mind often associated with positive feelings of connectedness with others—result from the experience of seeing ourselves in Others and vice-versa. Later in the book, we try to ground our views of experiential betweenness in relation to our reading of the field of qualitative inquiry and its allied paradigms. For now, as way of introduction, we wish to convey the idea that this resonance with life in-between is behind every idea and story in this book. We have felt the joys and guilt of being included in "us." We have felt the anger, fear, and anxiety of being "them." And our accented, off-white, privileged lives bring us back to the space in between "us" and "them" on a daily basis.

We often inhabit in-between spaces in Brazil, the United States, the streets of Brazil, and in academia. It is in this in-between space that we resonate with the lives we investigate, interpret, and represent here. We feel that, at one time or another, we all have been "us" or "them" merely by virtue of perspective, not of personal value. We believe things will be better for more people when the rings around notions of "us" get bigger, and as the impulse to call strangers "them" is rendered less meaningful, as the category of Other becomes too empty compared to the shared desire for acceptance in larger cause of humanity. This book is our way of adding to the movement against ideological systems based on the dichotomous, binary, either/or, us/them view of the world. Most of us know, by experience and reflection, that this view is dehumanizing and oppressive, not objective or factual. Yet it is exasperatingly persistent. We think our contribution to the cause of conscientization and inclusive social justice is our insistence in scholarship that instantiates texts that are *both* situated *and* polyvocal, singular *and* universal, analytical *and* emotional, critical *and* constructive, challenging *and* peaceful.

But we have reached the understanding of being a betweener also from different personal paths.

"Where did you first come up with the idea of calling yourself a betweener?" Marcelo asks.

"I was in a conference for grad students of the communication programs in the UIUC and UIC. I was the last presenter of the day, and when I finished, in the confusion of many people talking to me at once, another grad student, Marina Levina, told me: 'You live life in betweenness; read Anzaldúa.' That was the start," Cláudio says.

"But why was her notion of betweenness more powerful for you than other minority scholars' similar theories? Michelle Fine writes about the hyphenated self that lives between two sides of essentializing signifiers. Patricia Collins writes about the outsider within, the person of color who becomes an insider of the colonizing order yet remains, forever, an outsider. What was it about Anzaldúa's concept of life in-between that made you resonate so viscerally with her writing?" Marcelo asks.

"There are so many things that make Anzaldúa's writings so appealing to me. First, there is the presence of the body, the viscera. Her theory brings the body into place . . . the body that does not fit . . . does not fall in the binaries of colonization. . . . It's the story of the body told through the body. As I've been told, a Brazilian with a chip in his shoulder is scary. With Anzaldúa, I learned that I am a threat, because I do not fit. Reading Anzaldúa meant empowerment for me. She helps me come to terms with my own liminal body. I was able to find the tools to address the color of my skin, social class, and gender in relation to other bodies that have not fitted or fulfilled the available binaries, that was when I started to call myself a betweener.

"Oh, she said that when she writes 'she feels like a carving bone . . . writing is a constantly remaking and giving birth to itself through my [her] body,' or something like that. Anzaldúa's *autohistória-teoría* cannot exist without the body.

"Anzaldúa speaks to the process of colonization. In my opinion, she brings the postcolonial to the table. Her in-between is in dialogue with, for example, Homi Bhabha's concept of hybridity. I'm not that familiar with Fine, but Collin's concept works, in my opinion, with an American construction of race in Black and White. I think my point here is, for example, when Collins analyzes the domination of the white man/slave owner over the body of the black woman/slave she does not do it in a more postcolonial context. Anzaldúa calls it 'the colonial rape against native and Black women.' Anzaldúa, in my opinion, broadens her own idea, standpoint if you will, in relation to Collins, because even if Anzaldúa is talking more to the Chicana, she's addressing every single body that has been under colonization. It did not happen just in the U.S. And this fact becomes even more important, not only when one looks at the 'level' of this colonial rape in the construction of racial relations in different countries but also in how people from these countries in America and from other colonies from other continents never have stopped coming to the U.S.

"Collins talks about, and only in the second edition of her book, the necessity of entering in a dialogue with other black women in other countries and continents, between women of African descent, First and Third World. She says that this dialogue remains difficult. C'ammon, these people live here in the USA, doing all kinds of work in this society. These people, men and women with different races, ethnicities, gender, backgrounds, few are even in the academia. It is not more about a establishing of identity and a home place as suggest by colonization, but displacement, diasporas, or as Trinh T. Minh-ha points out the question, it's not who am I? But how am I?"

"See? The body again. The hybrid embodiment of theoretical discussions of personal identities!" Marcelo says.

"How do Latinos fit in there? Are we white, black, brown or what? Anzaldúa uses her ethnic and sexual identity to theorize postcolonial hybridity that is a product of the relationship between colonizer/colonized, challenging the physical borders (Texas-U.S. Southwest/Mexican border), 'the heart' of this relationship in all aspects of life. It created a flux of identities and possibilities. I learned from her that I could invent my own roots, that I was neither crazy nor dumb. Not only that, she addresses oppression outside but also inside, within, her own culture.

"There is a space for Collins and her work in the postcolonial (among other things) framework of women of color or Third World feminism. However, for many of those women (even the black ones) the space 'reserved' for them, their bodies, in Collins's framework, is not quite there."

"I get it. But I still want to make sure I understand what you mean by 'between.' Between what?" Marcelo asks.

"The spaces between two cultures, races, ethnicities, and so forth. Anzaldúa shows that it is the Anglo who wants everybody tied up in notions of a racial/ethnic purity. . . ."

"Why would Anglos want that?" Marcelo says, interrupting Cláudio mid-sentence.

"That's easy. They need the categories to control, and the studies to justify the colonization project."

"There you go. Binary thinking. 'They' are not all the same, or a monolith. Do you really think all Anglos want control of the Other? Or that all Anglos are even aware of controlling mechanisms?" Marcelo asks.

"Course, not . . . you sound like Dan Cook," Cláudio says laughing. "All white men are bad. But you are white. Norman Denzin is white,"

Cláudio says impersonating Dan Cook. "It's a category . . . that's how Anzaldúa uses it. That is how I use the figure of the white man in my work. That is part of the linguistic trap. Things that are 'in' are not only 'in' something. They are also 'out' of other things at the same time. The white man is also a moving category. What I try to do is to make the category static and move the other possible identities around this specific category. Not only to fight the oppression that comes from the category itself but also to illustrate the messiness within the category and the multiple identities or possibilities between them. That's why I assume the position of a privileged white man."

"You mean off-white, right?" Marcelo says with a smile.

"That is exactly the point! When I am writing, I use the static white man to expose the privilege and use all the other possibilities of my body to criticize and undermine that whiteness. In that way, I can't fit in the static black and white racial construction still present in most American scholarship. Again, the betweenness!"

"Okay. One more thing about your notion of betweenness and Anzaldúa. What does being a threat had to do with Anzaldúa's theory of the flesh?" Marcelo wants to know.

"I am answering this in the words of Cherrie Moraga, Anzaldúa's writing partner in the 'Bridge.' I know it by heart:

> 'A theory in the flesh means one where the physical realities of our lives—our skin color, the land or concrete we grew up on, our sexual longings—all fuse to create a politic born out of necessity. Here, we attempt to bridge the contradictions in our experience.
> We are the colored in a white feminist movement.
> We are the feminists among the people of our culture.
> We are often the lesbians among the straight.
> We do this bridging by naming our selves and by telling our stories in our own words.'

"Even the bridge metaphor, I believe, is exactly what we want our book to be. Borrowing from her and Moraga, the bridge called *our backs*," Cláudio says laughing.

It's the first time Marcelo hears of this. "What is the bridge metaphor? We have talked about Anzaldúa's work a thousand times and this bridge metaphor has never come up."

"Sorry, I took it for granted. Both of Anzaldúa's collections of essays use the word 'bridge.' She positions herself as bridge of these in-between spaces, of different people. That's how she envisions *El mundo zurdo* (the left-handed world), a new tribalism that envisions embodied bridges between and among people whose differences are celebrated and who come together to resist and transform reality through their collective experience born out of these differences. In our book, we are bridges, too."

"Do you know where Anzaldúa got the term *betweenness* from?" Marcelo asks.

"*Nepantla* is the term where 'between' comes from. It is a Nahuatl word that means a state of in-betweenness and changing possibilities. Nepantla is a *place* where the fixed binary thinking and taken-for-granted hegemonic ways of knowing and producing knowledge are challenged, and where resistance and transformative change can be organized and taken into action. Those who can achieve these states of in-betweenness, *nepantleras*, the betweeners, can manage multiple worlds at the same time and be facilitators of such transformation."

"Lovely! I particularly appreciate the constructive notions of resistance that this concept of betweeners evokes. I think it allows for the re-creation of memories about silenced struggles that carry the hope of evoking compassion in *nos/otros*—as opposed to the more pervasive blaming/defensiveness dance. It is the possibility for compassion that attracts me to the notion of betweenness. As I see it, we are all betweeners in some aspects of our identity. I think betweenness is a rare space where all humans can find communality. More obvious betweeners, I believe, can help bring awareness about the similarities buried under the more conspicuous veil of the Other, of 'them.' I believe we can use the common human experience of betweenness as an emotional connection with the different, the Other, even if many of our differences seem insurmountable. To be sure, much of social injustice can be traced to such differences. Highlighting our connection through betweenness is not an attempt to deny the existence of brutal differences in physical and intellectual being but an attempt to propose a common ground from which imaginations and policies of inclusiveness can continue to grow," Marcelo says winding down.

ON OPPRESSION

What does oppression mean to us? We contest static notions of oppression/oppressor/oppressed as enforcers of exclusiveness in concepts of the Other. We still live in the betweenness of the postcolonial world: we are privileged in our positions of Third World scholars working in First World institutions yet do battle every day against the colonizing paradigms informing education, academic scholarship, and production of knowledge about the Other.

"Norman asked me how I can be oppressed when I live under the privileges of middle-class America," Cláudio says, exasperated.

"What did you say to him?" Marcelo asks, already chuckling.

"Nothing. I was shocked," says Cláudio. "Mad, too, but mostly shocked. What do you think? I mean, why did Norman ask this?"

"Perhaps he thinks you are also privileged, in addition to have been oppressed?" Marcelo asks.

"Can one erase the oppression on the marked body? We are the first to acknowledge our privilege. Of course, there are many layers and forms of oppression that come from the intersections of race, class, gender, religion, sexual orientation, and so forth. We've been around misery, violence, and poverty for so long. . . . And we don't dare to compare the good deck of cards that life gave to us with many of the lives present in this book.

"It's funny though, or maybe a coincidence, that when this question is asked, it usually comes from someone who has never been there. There, you know? The same can be said with questions on racism, illiteracy, sexism, homophobia, etc.

"Again, we acknowledge our privilege. Does Norman, when asking this question, acknowledge his?"

"I imagine he does. But perhaps it's hard to see your marked body through the layers of present privilege. I know it's something that didn't come to my mind until you pointed it out just now," Marcelo says.

"You know, Marcelo, for me just asking this question demonstrates a position of power. Is this person reflecting his or her own position, when asking this? I always go back to the example of Anzaldúa not being accepted as a Ph.D. student at Santa Cruz, even though they were using her book in their graduate seminars. Can we erase the oppression in the marked body?

"Another example," continues Cláudio, "I have a family, a Ph.D., a temporary faculty job at a research-I institution. . . . However, I remember every violent act I did, suffered, or witnessed. Remember is not the word I want, it's too soft. Me, my body, and my English. . . .

"Can we pass as white in this country? If yes, under what circumstances? Are we totally white in Brazil? See, here we go, the betweenness over and over again. Let me invoke bell hooks: Do not forget the pain. I ain't forgetting it. I can't.

"I remember eating dinner not sure about tomorrow's meal. Does the fact I am able to eat now erase that? Didn't I know back then, that just having today's dinner I was much better off than many of my childhood friends? You bet I did!

"You know, this question does not make sense at all. Sorry, it is a white middle-class question. It is the question I would ask, if I decided to forget. . . . If I decided to be the next white stuff. And here is another similar question I've faced often . . . 'So because you had a hard life, should we go easy on you?' I heard that at a national communications conference. Like, we do not produce 'good scholarship' and are asking for their lenience? It's insane. . . . It's the other way around, can't you see? Where is this person standing?

"Last time I faced this question, I told the person. 'I'm here, I need no help. I survived. I'm playing your game at your home turf. I know that if I face adversity I will find a way out. I know I will survive. But let me ask you: what is so threatening about me and the critique about the way even self-proclaimed postcolonial academics have kept visceral knowledge of oppression under the theoretical weight of theoretical sophistication?

"Let me paraphrase Paula Gum Allen: I did more than survive. . . . I loved, had children, nurtured, and went to class. I read, wrote, got published, and taught. I hang in there no matter what."

"I haven't gone hungry like you," Marcelo says. "My idea of oppression is informed by my observation of dehumanizing treatment of others. And Paulo Freire gave language to my feelings of despair and need for resistance when I read his Pedagogy of the Oppressed. But I don't know the feeling of hunger and the uncertainty of food."

"Hey pal, it's time for the performance. Let's do it together," Cláudio demands.

"You start, Thuggy!"

Who Gives the Authority to Ask Questions?

Who gives the authority to ask questions? Who gives the authority to invade people's lives to do research? We offer an alternative model. It's all over our work.

Like Anzaldúa, we ask to be met halfway.
Then, we can talk.
There, in the halfway place, we can have a dialogue.

We beat and got beat
I've been peed on
But never peed on nobody
Roni was our friend
Andre was five years old and was raped
In front of the silent Cláudio
The privileged say, you
Are oppressed no more

Can we erase the oppression in the marked body?
Listen to our thick accented tongue
Correct our improper writing

We are thugs with a Ph.D.
We ain't nobody's subject
Do the talk
Sing the song
We cannot erase the oppression in the marked body
But we can allow the wounds to speak up
In their own bodies

ON WHY WE WROTE TOGETHER

This book is also about our dialogic collaboration in trying to write more situated social sciences. Instead of writing alone, each with his own book, we decided early on to bring our research and writings together in an attempt to instantiate our call for collaborative production of knowledge. We do not know how this will work for you. But we think this writing joint-venture exemplifies the very connectedness and co-construction of meaning that we advocate in any type of social science preoccupied with empowering praxis. We have been friends since our late teens, long before either of us knew what career to pursue, and have been closely connected ever since. Writing this book together seems, to both of us, like another important completion of the many intersecting experiences in our lives: friendship, migration, profession, scholarship, and a keen attraction to a vision of inclusiveness.

NURTURING NEW BATTLEGROUNDS

The decolonizing classroom—the territory for struggle moves from memory to the classroom in the endless making of renewed narratives of resistance, transformation, and inclusiveness.

The public performance stage—moving from decolonizing discourse toward decolonizing praxis, toward the dream in which people come to academia to do the talking not just the answering, marking the invasion of the institutional space by the oppressed and marked body, not as object of research but as expert of own struggle. Our text itself is a battleground, where we speak of possibilities in how to do decolonizing scholarship, and where we show it.

OUTLINE OF THE REST OF THE BOOK

In Chapter 2, we make a brief statement about our ontological and epistemological standpoints as a background canvas on which our performative texts rely. Part II, Stories from the Margins, the book's centerpiece, is divided into six chapters, each underscoring a particular theme of betweenness that we find relevant in our work. Our dialogue, in this case, is carried out by our idiosyncratic angles to the six themes: betweenness in identity, class, race, sexuality, indigenousness, and knowledge production. It is a textual collage of Marcelo's short stories and Cláudio's autoethnographic texts offered as instantiations of representations that attempt to be authorially self-reflexive and situated while also bringing visceral knowledge of oppression from the periphery to the center of decolonizing knowledge production. It is a juxtaposition of Marcelo's fourteen short stories based on his ethnographic fieldwork with street kids in Campinas, Brazil, and Cláudio's performance self-reflexive acts based on his marginal life in Uberlandia, Campinas, and the United States. Cláudio's stories also include his ethnographic work with Torcida Jóvem, an underclass organized soccer fan club in Campinas, Brazil.

The final section, Part III, comprises two chapters: Chapter 9, Methodological Acts and Detours, where we discuss the theoretical and methodological framework informing our (auto)ethnographic studies and forms of representation, and Chapter 10, Words to End With, where we discuss our vision of possibilities for future decolonizing scholarship, the in-between space where we see Anzaldúa's *El Mundo Zurdo* intersecting and dialoguing with Paulo Freire's Pedagogy of Hope to break the binary ideology of us-versus-them and to offer possibilities of common ground through the awareness of our betweenness. We conclude with a return to the conversation about the battlegrounds (the classroom and our respective disciplines) where we live by and practice our ideas of decolonizing everyday scholarship in the hope of more inclusive notions of social justice.

Chapter 2

ONTO-EPISTEMOLOGICAL STANCE

This chapter outlines our onto-epistemological journeys so far. The indivisibleness of being is our starting ontological standpoint. We both approach the examination of lives with the assumption that human experience, including its study, happens in a holistic manner. We see the apparent dichotomies of mind and body, physical and metaphysical, object and subject, theory and method, as differentiations of one, all-encompassing, system: Being. We align ourselves with Maurice Merleau-Ponty's (1969) late ontological notion that the only path to the understanding of reality and being is an indirect one, through "the flesh," through our physical presence in and perception of the world. The mind and its interpretations of reality and being are not separate from the flesh but part of it—one perceives the world before any reflection can take place. We align ourselves with Gloria Anzaldúa's (1981) notion of humans as beings that cannot escape visceral, bodily knowledge of the world.

    We embrace the knowledge that comes from the streets and sugar cane fields and reject the much-denied yet prevailing academic ideology of "scholar knows best." We are trying to become scholars who truly engage in dialogue with "the different" by calling attention to "the others" within each of us. Thus, we start from the position of our bodies in relation to others in our world. Marcelo writes about street kids from the perspective of someone who arrived at notions of social justice through theoretical reflection. Cláudio writes about class, race, and gender from his own experiences growing up at the margins of Brazil, between the instability and vulnerability of a child in poverty and the mitigating privilege of being male and light-skinned.

We refuse to erase the flesh from the study of being human. The so-called disenfranchised humans in our collection of stories, self-reflections, and other positivistically incorrect narratives of being experience the world through a very specific physical location: their bodies. We, the writers of this collection, do the same. Bodies are physical, psychological, social, cultural, and political, all at once, always. Thus, the study of reality and being cannot be neutral, under any circumstance, regardless of intent, despite paradigmatic efforts and promises.

We know we are not neutral. We also know that, despite our self-reflexive efforts, we are unable to know or represent a complete outline of our ontological stances here. But we want to declare the ethics of our ontological stances as clearly as we are able so that you can understand our epistemological approaches (that is, our way of knowing about reality and being). Subverting P. F. Strawson's (1959) own positivistic attitude toward ontology, we choose to examine reality and being by embracing an ethic of revisionary metaphysics (that is, concerned with the construction of a better structure of reality and being), as opposed to embracing the ethic of descriptive metaphysics (that is, description of the structure of our thoughts about reality and being) that continues to dominate scholarship in the English-speaking world.

We want to use education, in the broadest sense of the word, to promote a form of conscientization that moves others to think of social justice in ways more inclusive than its perennially parochial conceptualizations. Here is what we mean by inclusive social justice: all humans, not all white rich males, are created equal. Civil rights must be a duty, not a privilege, of the upper crust. Democracy can be more empowering if based on social equality, not economic power. An ideological system that makes it possible for a nation to be among the wealthiest in the world while allowing thousands of its children to go hungry and unprotected wouldn't exist in a world of inclusive social justice. Under inclusive social justice, immigration would not be framed as national security or Labor Department problems but as a human rights challenge not to be skirted. How on earth could the citizens of the self-proclaimed free world support a pre-emptive attack on a sovereign nation knowing that thousands of innocent lives would inevitably become collateral damage were it not for minds that think of social justice in exclusive, not inclusive, ways? More specific to education, postcolonial inquiry wouldn't be so populated by intellectuals who think their literary knowledge of oppression is superior to first-hand struggle with the colonizer.

This is our way of looking, examining, reflecting, interpreting, and representing life at the margins of society. We are not claiming that this is the only or the best way of writing social sciences about and against the ideologies of domination that underlie the stories of "us-versus-them" that we bring together in this book. We are claiming, however, that visceral knowledge has been kept at bay (when not completely denied) in the social sciences in the English-speaking world. We are claiming that the dominant discourse in academia is still colonized by the ontological dualism of logical-positivism (that is, idealism versus materialism, mind versus body, fact versus fiction, science versus arts). In both our experiences as young scholars, we have witnessed an endless string of self-proclaimed resistance scholars declaring to value lived experience while in the same breath continuing to privilege theory over practice, Foucaultian analysis of power over pedestrian narratives of blood and profanity. We are here to spread our wings and add to the visceral knowledge on oppression that we see as scarce in the social sciences in general and the critical postcolonial inquiry in particular.

As you can tell by now, each of us has a particular visceral knowledge of the world. Thus, our individual ways of examining human experience within ideologies of oppression have their respective idiosyncrasies. We hope that these analytical idiosyncrasies add needed interpretive tools that you can take to the larger stories we are trying to tell: the stories of our situated encounter with the visceral experience of oppression. We think our universal singularity makes these stories common to all of us—because how many people haven't felt, at some point in their lives, that they were born on the wrong side of the tracks?

We came of age in the same country. We also shared a number of early-life cultural experiences, such as generational cohort and the unearned privileges from being light-skinned, male, and heterosexual. But one sociocultural difference was very significant in the way each of us grew up: *social class*. We share the core of our ontological and ethical approaches to decolonizing scholarship, but the significant difference of our authorial situatedness (that is, opposite social class status) has led us to differentiated epistemological and methodological stances. We hope that you will experience the same vitality of epistemological situatedness that we experienced in the making these pages. In Chapter 10, we return, in greater detail, to the attempt to ground the epistemological and methodological standpoints informing our stories in the chapters of Part II by weaving the juxtapositions and uniqueness of each of our theoretical frameworks.

Part II

STORIES FROM THE MARGINS

Cláudão e Marcelo botam a boca no mundo juntos . . .

Chapter 3

BETWEENNESS IN IDENTITY

STORY 1

STREET LIFE

I saw Dalva crossing the street as I got off the bus. She was carrying a brown bag in one hand and a can of Coke in the other. Dalva, 16 or 17 years old, was one of the first kids living on the streets that I met and I'd become really fond of her. She was walking toward Rosario Plaza, and I rushed through the crowd to catch up with her. "Hey Dalva, wait up!"

"*Tio*! You are lucky . . . I just got some food . . . are you hungry?" she said between gulps of Coke.

Kids say *tio*, which means "uncle," to anyone visibly older than them, and I was already getting used to it.

"No, thanks Dalva, I just ate lunch." We walked together until she found some shade under the trees on the quiet side of the Plaza. She sat down and took a plate of commercial food out of the brown bag. "It looks good . . . where did you get it?" I asked looking at the small mountain of rice and beans on her plate.

"You know that new self-service restaurant they just opened next to that big bookstore?" she pointed.

I followed her finger, imagining a line shooting from it through the busy-looking passersby, through the luxurious bank building on the corner, through all the shops on that block, until I saw in my mind the "big bookstore." I had been there the day before trying to find an illustrated book about pregnancy and birth. I had spent almost an hour in the bookstore but didn't find any book with more illustrations than text. Katia couldn't read much and Marga, a female street educator, thought that a book with illustrations showing how a baby develops inside the womb would catch her interest. Katia, who had just turned 15, was well advanced in her pregnancy but hadn't seen a doctor yet. She had moved in with her boyfriend's parents when she found out she was pregnant. Her boyfriend had been taken to a juvenile reformatory, and she didn't feel safe on the streets of downtown. But she was now back on the streets, and last time I'd seen her, after dark in front of Orly Bakery, she was sweet-talking another girl, Kleo, into giving her 50 cents.

"Come on Kleo, you selfish girl, just 50 cents. I already have 4.50 and I know where to buy a *stone* for 5 bucks." Stone is slang for a small portion of crack. "I'll let you smoke some with me . . . ," Katia said getting closer, trying to grab the coins in Kleo's hands.

"No way, Katia!" said Kleo putting the coins in her pocket. "I'm gonna buy myself some bread with this money . . . all I ate today was an ice cream. . . . I'm hungry!"

"One more reason why you should take a few hits, girl," Katia said smiling and putting her arm around Kleo's shoulders. "No! And you shouldn't be smoking with this!" Kleo said poking Katia's belly and pushing her away.

"Wow! You sure sound just like some of them street educators," Katia said laughing and walking away.

Later that night I'd see the two of them from a distance, walking together, teasing and laughing at some taxi drivers standing next to a hot dog stand.

"Yes," I said looking at Dalva again.

"Well . . . I was sitting by the door asking the people coming in and out of the restaurant for money . . . then the manager came and said he would give me a plate of food if I went away, so I did. . . ." Dalva paused to stuff her mouth with food again, "but I guess I'm going back there again soon!" We looked at each other and laughed.

"You know, many restaurants now have security guards to keep us away," Dalva said, still eating. "Some security guys are nice, they let us stay near the door for a while, but some are real mean. Did you hear what happened to Tate?"

I shook my head no, feeling from the tone of her voice that something bad had happened to him, imagining what it could be while she finished chewing. Tate was a very good-natured boy of about 16, always smiling and ready to tell some story about his "other life," as he used to refer to his life before coming to the streets of Campinas from a small town in a neighboring state. I never understood whether he left home because of an abusive step-father, or because he got a girl pregnant, or because of other stories he only half told me. But I learned a great deal about farm animals, birds, and plants from his detailed and rich narratives. His travel adventures were told with gaiety and wit, and he had a special talent for making himself look foolish without losing his dignity. People in downtown seemed to be especially fond of him, perhaps because of that. He was so peaceful that I had a hard time imagining that someone had harmed him.

"He got beat up real bad by that security guard working in front of the computer school, you know, near the restaurant where he is always watching customers' cars. He didn't do anything. This lady had just parked her car in front of the restaurant and he went up to her, asking if he could watch the car for her. You know, that's how he makes money. He doesn't steal or anything. But she must have thought he was gonna rob her and started screaming. You know how these rich people is . . . they see a dirty kid coming to talk to them and they already think we are gonna rob 'em. So the security guy started pushing and punching Tate before he could say anything. Celi and I were the only kids around and we were too afraid of getting beat up too. People started coming out of the shops to see what was going on. Some men started laughing at Tate. Nobody did nothing to stop the beating. Poor Tate . . . he was all bloody and crying by the time the guy let go of him, and nobody did nothing. Then this man who was talking to the lady started coming toward us shouting that we should be in jail, that we should be . . . hmmm . . . how do you say . . . terminated?"

"Exterminated?"

"Yes, like those kids who were shot dead while sleeping by that church in Rio de Janeiro."

"What happened to Tate, then? Did he go to the hospital? You said he was bleeding. . . ."

"No, he said they would treat him bad at the hospital too because he was all dirty and smelly. Celi and I walked around to find a street educator to take him to the hospital but didn't find no one. When we came back Tate had disappeared. I haven't seen him since then . . . nobody knows where he's hiding. Do you know that security guy?"

I shook my head no.

Dalva started eating again. I felt that she wanted me to go talk to him. But I didn't know what to do. We were in silence for a while. Then she wrapped the food left in the plate, some rice and beans and a chicken leg, with a napkin and put it inside the brown bag.

"I'm gonna take this food to Kleo and Grace. They are sleeping behind the post office and will wake up hungry," she said getting up.

The post office is a large old building in one of the busiest areas of downtown; the wide sidewalks surrounding it are crowded with food and cheap merchandise stands, and there is a bus stop connecting downtown with the working class neighborhoods right in front of its main entrance. It's a noisy place in the middle of the afternoon. "How can they get any sleep there?" I thought out loud.

"We didn't get much sleep last night," Dalva said helping me up on my feet.

The post office was only a few blocks from where we were, and as we walked Dalva began telling me how they had been on the lookout for this woman dealer who was after them. "She said she's gonna kill us if we don't pay our crack debts, and we don't have no money. It's in the night that things happen, you know. So last night we kept on going from place to place, trying to stay awake."

Dalva told me they lay down at the doorstep of a pediatric clinic, but that after a few minutes a police car stopped by, some policemen came out and got them up, saying they couldn't stay there. I had seen this clinic before. It had caught my attention one afternoon when I was looking for some of the kids. I remembered thinking that it was in an odd place, squeezed between small clothing shops on one side and a crumbling hotel where some young women and men took their clients on the other side. I had stopped in front of it and read the sign with big yellow letters: WHERE WE CARE FOR THE CHILDREN OF CAMPINAS.

Dalva said they then walked to the church, lay down again, and the same cops came and kicked them out of there. The sun was already rising when they fell asleep in front of a vegetarian restaurant on a tiny street a little hidden from the busy streets of downtown. But at 10 A.M. the manager came to open it and woke them up.

"We then went to the post office and lay down by the back entrance, you know, where nobody goes. But the sun was cooking us and we couldn't fall asleep. Kleo and Grace rolled under a parked car and fell asleep in no time. I was too scared to fall asleep under the car . . . imagine if they didn't see us and just drove away! So I left and started looking for something to eat."

I shook my head, imagining. Dalva started to sing a rap tune:

We're 30 million street kids
But you pretend you don't see us
We're tugging at your Armani suit, begging
Still you pretend you don't see us
You drive expensive cars
We knock on your window, begging
But you pretend you don't see us
You see us getting beat up by the police
Still you walk by, you pretend you don't see us
Is a blade on your throat the only way
The only way to get your attention?

Dalva told me the rap is by a new band formed by ex-street kids from Sao Paulo. She said she'd give me their tape. "Two bucks for a pirate tape at the bus terminal market," she said winking.

We got to the post office, walked past food stands, lines of people waiting for buses, and men trying to sell lottery tickets. Going around the building to the back entrance, we saw Kleo and Grace under an old blue van. The blue van's chassis was really close to the ground, and I had to bend down to see the girls. I hadn't known many people who looked under their cars before driving, so I understood exactly why Dalva was too afraid to join her friends. She put the brown bag next to Kleo, under the van, without waking them up, and sat down leaning against the post office wall. I sat next to her and we watched the van till the kids woke up.

The church bell had just struck 2 P.M. when first Kleo then Grace came out from under their urban tent carrying the brown bag with them. They sat down in front of us and, stretching and yawning, unwrapped the food.

"My hair is a mess, *tio*," Grace said pulling her black curly hair back with both hands. "Give me your cap, *tio*, I don't want you to see me like this."

I took my cap off my head and gave it to her, saying that she looked fine. "Don't bullshit me, *tio*, I know I look horrible, I'm all dirty and smelly and haven't washed my hair in days." She put my cap on and grabbed the cold chicken leg from the plate.

"They don't let us shower at Casa Aberta anymore, *tio*," said Kleo with her mouth full of rice and beans.

"Yeah, but sometimes *tio* Marcio lets us use the shower to clean up and wash our clothes," Dalva said.

"But only when the other staff members aren't there, those sonuvabitch don't want us there no more," Grace almost shouted between bites, just as a middle-aged couple walked out of the post office through the back entrance. They first looked at the three girls, their faces sulking, and said something I could not make out. But as they kept on walking away, the woman looked at me and asked, "What are *you* doing among these *moleques de rua*?" *Moleques de rua* is a pejorative term for street kids, so I knew she wasn't really asking a question, and I just watched as the couple disappeared in the crowd . . . and hoped they couldn't hear Dalva and Grace show off their own repertoire of pejorative names for women.

A few weeks before, I had seen Lucio, a 15-year-old boy, almost get into trouble for a similar thing. Another street educator and I were hanging out with several kids near the newspaper stand in Rosario Plaza that day. It was near lunchtime, and the Plaza was packed with passersby. Celi was standing alone a few yards from where we were, gnawing on an ice cream she'd been given (though not very willingly) by a young girl walking to or from school. Lucio got up and, sneaking behind Celi, took the ice cream from her hand and ran away with a mischievous smile. As Celi started chasing after him, Lucio bumped into a well-dressed man in his late 30s who was walking by, spilling ice cream over his suit. Celi and the other kids began laughing at Lucio, who stepped back from where the man was standing, looking at his spotted suit. The man took a handkerchief out of his pocket to clean the mess, and cursed at Lucio as he began to walk away. Lucio stood there staring at the man for a while, then used the same name-calling to offend the man's mom. The man stopped, turned around, took something we couldn't see out of his briefcase, and started trailing after Lucio. Lucio darted across the jammed street, the man after him, and we didn't see him till later that afternoon, when he bragged about knowing his way around downtown like no one else.

"Can you take us to Casa Aberta, *tio*? Maybe they will let us take a shower and wash our clothes if you talk to them," Kleo said after a while.

"Okay," I said to Kleo. But I knew it'd be difficult to convince the people at Casa Aberta to let the girls use their facilities. I had taken Lara there the week before and heard the whole spiel about Casa Aberta's new policies. Casa Aberta, which means "open house," used to be a place where street kids could always go for a meal, a shower, and sometimes for a session of occupational therapy. But, as I was told by an administrator, feeling that Casa Aberta was serving as a crutch for kids who didn't want to commit to recovery, they decided to change it into a half-way house for adult recovering addicts.

"Kids came here just for the food and shower, not wanting to stick to the hardships of recovery and salvation. We realized we were not helping them get out of the streets but were instead keeping them dependent and unmotivated by being so lenient. We have now adopted the philosophy of tough love, so the kids have to prove they are really willing to stick to the program before they can go to the shelter," the same administrator told me. Then looking at Lara, who was standing next to me, "These kids need to know that everything has a price in life." Lara didn't smile back.

"And how can they prove their willingness if they are no longer allowed to come in here?" I wanted to ask. "Lara has a doctor's appointment today and wants to clean up before going," I said instead.

Lara'd told another street educator, a woman, that she thought she might be pregnant, or have some venereal disease.

"So we were wondering if you could let her use your shower, just today, as a favor . . .," I said, being interrupted by Lara.

"I don't have any other place to go, *tia*! And I can't go to the doctor like this," she said pointing to her dirty bare feet.

The administrator, an older woman with short gray hair and a large wooden cross resting on her breasts, looked at Lara, touched her chin softly, and said that she was sorry but couldn't make an exception, that it wouldn't be fair to the other kids who were coming by for the same reason.

"I won't tell anybody, I promise!" Lara said.

"Sorry honey, but I can't do that...."

Lara's eyes watered. She turned around and started to walk away. I asked her not to leave, saying that we would find another place.

"Where?! In your house?!" she said to me crying. "All I want is to take a damn shower," she shouted at the woman with a cross standing next to me and then bolted out of our sight. Lara was gone.

As the administrator talked about the problem of street children and the lack of love in their families, I tuned out and began wondering how I was going to tell the doctor that she wasn't going to make the appointment, because we couldn't find a place for Lara to bathe.

Lara had just turned 17 and had lived in foster homes since she was 3 years old, when her mother was sent to jail. She had just come to the streets again, after a quarrel with the young woman coordinating the Baptist female shelter where she had been living. After a night on the streets of downtown, Lara tried to go back to the Baptist shelter and apologize for having left in anger. But the Baptist shelter was also following the "tough love" philosophy, and Lara was told she'd have to wait a week before being allowed to return. Her punishment was to spend a week on the streets so that she'd learn to appreciate what she had at the shelter.

"And they said I can't hang out with Dalva or Katia or Celi, or any other kids they think are bad, if I want to go back at all!" Lara said to me on the first night I saw her on the streets, with Dalva and Celi in front of a pizza place. "But I'm too afraid of being by myself here ... I'm not used to making money on the streets, you know, I don't know how to steal and am too embarrassed to beg. I'm afraid someone I know will see me sleeping out here or dressed in rags." Here Lara was interrupted by Dalva.

"But somehow you always have new and clean clothes, nice shoes ... I wonder how you get the money for these things," Dalva said, affecting an innocent air.

Lara gave a mean look to Dalva, who then made a gesture of ironic apology. "It's not fair what they did, *tio*. I apologized, on my knees, and they didn't believe me. I know I was wrong when I called her names and left the shelter.... I was angry ... all I wanted to do was watch the soap opera, you know, that one that everybody's talking about. It was my birthday, so I thought I deserved to watch what I wanted and not that boring religious channel.... I know I have a bad temper ... but I apologized...." Lara started to cry softly.

"It's true, *tio*, she doesn't know how to live on the streets," Dalva told me, "she can't even ask people for food, she gets too embarrassed, so I have to take care of her, right Lara?"

"Yeah, Dalva got me some food tonight.... I was starving."

"She started to cry, *tio*" Dalva said, smiling a little.

"My stomach was hurting!" Lara replied.

"I know, I'm just teasing you, Lara. It's not right what they did to Lara, *tio*!" Dalva told me, her face turning somber. "It's dangerous to be here alone, especially after dark, and I can't take her with me when I go buy crack, you see, the dealers don't like when people that don't smoke come with us, they think you are spying for the police, and that's bad business. So I have to leave her alone sometimes, or she'll have to come along and pretend she smokes too."

"I'm afraid to do that, Dalva."

"I know . . . it's unfair what they did, you know? They say they want to help us, but they don't even know how! I'd like to see one of them rich goody-goody kids staying in that shelter, see how long they would last there . . . and I bet that their parents don't send them to the streets for a week when they act like brats," Dalva burst out.

Celi, who had been standing by the pizza place's door the whole time while we talked, came over where Dalva, Lara, and I were and, laughing and talking at the same time, told us that a couple had just given her a bill worth 5 bucks. It was a lot of money for spare change. "I think they were too drunk to see the bill they were giving me," Celi said pointing to the couple. We looked at them and, from the way they were walking, wondered whether they were seeing two sidewalks where there was one.

"We have enough money for a *stone* now," Celi said looking at Dalva.

"Sorry, *tio* . . . we gotta go," Dalva said with an impish smile.

"See you later," I said, wondering where they were going to sleep that night. I watched as they disappeared into the night, Lara going with them.

Grace and Kleo were finishing eating when Dalva pointed to a man opening the blue van's door. He threw a large mail bag in the passenger seat, started the engine, and drove away in a hurry. Kleo and Grace looked at each other and started laughing, stopping only when Dalva began a graphic description of what their smashed bodies would look like had they still been sleeping under the van. "You are sick, girl," Grace said to Dalva and they all began to laugh again. "That's a good way to die anyway, in your sleep, you don't feel anything, just like going to sleep, but you'll never wake up," Grace said.

"I think so too! It's better than getting shot and left on a ditch to die slowly, like Pedro," Dalva said.

"And Marcy too . . .," Grace recalled.

"You are so gloomy! I don't wanna die young . . .," Kleo was beginning to say.

"Get real, girl!" whispered Grace. "How many street kids do you know live much beyond our age?! Huh?!"

"I'm gonna get out of the streets . . .," murmured Kleo gazing past us.

"Yeah right! Only if *tio* Marcelo here marries you," Grace said and we all chuckled. Only I blushed.

"Let's go, guys, it's getting late, and I want to shower today!" Dalva got up and we followed her lead.

We were two blocks from Casa Aberta, walking through a street market, inebriated by the smells coming from the third-class steaks barbecuing on dozens of grills all around us and from the countless fruit stands stacked with ripe tangerines and guavas, when Dalva abruptly stopped. I stopped too and looked at where Dalva was looking. I saw a woman with black straight hair in a ponytail, wearing jeans and a loose white shirt, only a few steps ahead, staring right back at us.

"It's Regina! Come on Kleo, hurry up, time to split," Dalva said pulling Kleo by the hand and running back toward the way we had come. I didn't even see which way Grace had gone, and just stood there. I figured the woman was the dealer Dalva had told me about. She came up to me and asked for a lighter. I lit up her cigarette trying not to shake too much.

"Do you know those little sluts?" the dealer said looking fiercely into my eyes. I was glad that Dalva had seen her in time to escape, and that I was in a place with lots of people around.

"I was trying to help them find a place to shower . . ."

Act 1

Fragments

Valdecir Paiva de Lima, 37 years old, started to feel sick early in the afternoon of September 12th. Valdecir fainted and died a few hours later at the San Francisco Hospital in Ribeirão Preto. According to colleagues, Valdecir had already felt badly sick in previous occasions, but the doctor at the sugar cane plant Engenho Moreno, where Valdecir cut sugar cane, said that Valdecir did not suffer of anything beyond "laziness for working hard" (*Brasil de Fato*, 2005).

I: A Paper inside a Paper or Some Crazy Poetry

Because
I am a
Smart ass Ph.D. student
Streetwise lost in a doctoral program

In a fight with my trained mind and in love with my body

I am
Full of hope and shit
And I care and believe

Life is unfair in an unphilosophical sense
Andrezinho was raped
And so was Celita
And Knowledge is power
And Knowledge is legit, and experience is not

After working all day long, Domício Diniz, age 55, fainted when he tried to get on the bus. He died before help arrived. It seems that the cause was excessive work. It may have been. Domicio cut an average of 12 tons of cane per day. (*Folha de São Paulo*, 2005)

I am trapped in a Foulcaltian power system
That disciplines and punishes
Whose name is Higher Education.

Every time I understand hook's words better: Do not forget the pain

Rosaldo started to question his scholarship when he lost his wife.
I never talked to Rosaldo, but I can picture him questioning himself while writing about the other's pain when feeling that he could not represent his own.
Is this the truth? Does it matter?
And I am not denying the importance of theory. I just do not want this power over my head.
And I am trying to find ways to resist.
In the good moments, I believe I am going to find my own way/voice/body or theory/method.
I just do not know when. However, it is going to be written differently.

Not long ago, Justino told me in bad Portuguese that before he went to a meeting in the City Hall, he looked up the meaning of the word *democracy* in a dictionary. Then, he told the city councilors that he did not understand well what he had read in the big book called dictionary. But he said he was sure that what the City was doing to him, to his family, and to the community that he represented could not be, in any way, democratic or democracy.

Some people say that our mission as scholars is to analyze experiences and that we need to use theory as a tool in order to do it well. There has been little or no effort to compare knowledge and experience. I say no. When I look at the system of higher education, I realize that one needs to question what is considered knowledge. What I do not need is a "theoretical body of knowledge" that lacks experience or views experience as less legitimate—a knowledge that just acts or takes a concrete form in academic discussions.

What I am talking about is the lived experience of the oppressed in any circumstance. The lived experience that is needed for an academic action that is committed to social justice. The lived experience that each one of us has and whose freedom is limited by academic walls.

I am writing this sentence at home, and my Dani is sad.
We hugged each other in front of my smiling son.
And I love her.

When a professor from the Department of Advertising asked my friend Aisha S. Durham what the difference was between the stories that she told and real research, she answered that all research is storytelling. What I am trying to say here is that both theory and experience are forms of knowledge. However, one is more appropriate/legitimate than the other in the academic setting. I am pretty aware of being repetitive. I mean it!

One of the problems with this educational system is that it serves as a filter, a barrier. An example would be the fact that the system sees the education of a doctoral student as a linear process with an end point. A process that is more adequate to a specific kind of student. The discussion I am trying to launch is similar to the one Freire had launched with adult education. I would mention perseverance as the most important quality for a Ph.D. student that is in a situation similar to mine. If the objective of the system is to have a student who perseveres, it is doing a hell of a job. The system works just fine.

I had a friend named Roni

The end of a doctoral program does not mean the end of the learning process. The way things are set up, one kind of student with one kind of background and one kind of scholarship has been privileged. These are the same privileges that permeate the existence of the white male.

This system is based on a utilitarian-rationalism ethic model.

I cannot write under a system that tries to divide me. I am whole: father, husband, graduate student, white, male, Latino, and so on.

I was walking with Justino in the streets of his neighborhood. Parque Oziel is Justino's neighborhood. He usually says it aloud: "It's my hood, my *favela*, my shit!" Justino is a former sugar cane worker and one of the community's leaders. The "streets," if we can call them that, do not have any kind of pavement, and I was paying attention to the kids who were playing close to the open sewers that line the streets. Then, I saw a white little boy who reminded me of my son. He was on a dark woman's lap. Tears started to come down from my eyes. His whiteness was a loud contrast to the brown *favela*. The lady had the kid in her arms with her feet almost *tocando o esgoto a ceu aberto*.[1] I was staring so intensely at that boy that I was not paying attention to my steps. Suddenly I felt the water touching my toes. I did not have to look; it was the sewage lines, the water full of shit and piss going through my toes. Still, I could not take my eyes off of that kid.

That kid reminds me of my own . . .

I have a daughter, Analua
And I have a son, Francisco

I cannot accept a system/institution for which this experience does not have the same value as a theory . . .
I looked at the kid, I was reminded of my son, and I felt the shit on my toes . . .
The sadness, the rage, the indignation . . .
The wish of never stopping . . .
This system that fucks me more than it helps me . . .
There has to be a place HERE for the fear I felt and the risks I took!
Next day, I went alone to Parque Oziel
There has to be a place HERE for my fragmented/ing voice and whole body
There has to be a place HERE for those oppressed people whose lives have helped to build many academic careers
There has to be a place HERE for you. Only, and only if you wish to . . .

In those moments I do not care about Focault, Gramsci, Marx, Freire, Hall, hooks . . . you pick a name. . . . It is all a lie. I do not give a damn about the kind of tests of knowledge that the system throws at me in order to succeed and being able to do what I want, where I want, and the way I want.

I cannot keep going apologizing for being a recovering alcoholic or for having a wife and two children.
I cannot tell Dani to find way to take care of the kids alone because I have "important" work to do at the university.

I cannot take another four years of living with a $1,000 monthly budget.
I do not want to do interviews in a safe white middle-class suburb.
I do not want to analyze articles in magazines either.
I do not want to conform.
I will not tolerate the disregard that is in the faces of the powerful when lives such as the one of that kid I saw are on the line.
I do not know what was worse: The sad look in that kid's face or the faith stamped in Justino's expression.

When I look in some libertatory academic movements, such as British Cultural Studies, Black Feminist Thought, Indigenous Theories, Chicana Studies, and Queer theory, to name a few, I see movements whose origins were based on people with different backgrounds in race, gender, social class, acting as both teachers and/or students.

My friend Ted once said that I need to master theory if I want to speak with people in academia. However, academic people do not need to know the experience I have to talk to me. PRIVILEGE, MORE OFTEN THAN NOT, IS TAKEN FOR GRANTED.

I am trying to save my fancy ass. I am fighting for survival. I am trying to "discover" my own roots/ body/self, fighting for a different way through which my work can be measured and judged.

Last year, some other students and I presented our work at the UICC conference in Chicago. My presentation was the last in my panel. In the end, another ICR student named Andrew came to talk to me: "Cláudio, your words touched me. I always have been skeptical towards authoethnographic work, but you show me its importance. Nice work."

Andrew had changed. The reason I'm telling you this is that other works presented there did not have to go through the "filters" I have. Some of these students are "well read," and their work fit nicely in academia. They are walking fast to a great academic life, and yes, they work hard. They are good students, no question about that. However, the way it stands now, I think my work is much more engaged with social changes than others I saw in that conference. I can reach people, or at least I care! I have to adjust to those other students; they do not have to adjust to me. I do not want to exclude other students; I just want to include myself and others. Otherwise, academia will still have much more "well-read" students (which per se is not all bad) than Cláudios.

Why?
Why did I write all of this?

Because
I am a
Smart ass Ph.D. student
Streetwise lost in a doctoral program
In a fight with my trained mind and in love with my body

II: *First Words*

Lately, I have opened my performances with the same two statements:
"I have not chosen performance autoethnography as a method, it has chosen me."
and
"Do not expect this performance to make sense to you. My life does not make sense. Other lives I have loved and interacted with do not make sense either. Why in hell does life have to make sense so it can fit academia?
Remember, life is fragments . . .
Survival skills as a form of resistance and intervention . . .
Hence, I started to look for a scholarship that would allow me to write my body . . .
Then, I heard about Norman Denzin . . .
Then, my love affair with performance autoethnography started. . . .
Here again I look for help from Holman Jones. How can I write about performance autoethnography without performing one? She says I cannot. Hence, where is the performance?

III: *Being a Kid, Sugar Cane*

> Being a kid, Sugar Cane
> Pau de arara, Cabeção
> Arataca, Paraiba
> Baiano, Cabeça chata
> Comedô de farinha
> All new pejorative nicknames for kids
> Whose parents are from Northeast.
>
> Being a kid, Sugar Cane
> Migration, Labor force
> Moving south, Better life
> Permanent residents in a new city
> Seasonal workers, Better life
> Hunger
> Bullshit.

Being a kid, Sugar Cane
Cutting cane, working knives
Playing with them
Cutting bellies
Big belly
Full of worms
Going to dance, faith in God.

Being a kid, Sugar Cane
Being two kids that are not the same
Same life, same parents
Not some states, but why?
Born in different states
Sao Paulo and Paraíba
Fighting over a soccer game
You're stupid Paraíba, Cabeça chata! I ain't like you. I am Paulista!

Being a kid, Sugar Cane
Pau de arara, Cabeção
Arataca, Paraíba
Baiano, Cabeça chata
Comedô de farinha
But wait, I am not
I am no Pau de arara, Cabeção
I am no Arataca, Paraíba
I am no Baiano, Cabeça chata
I am no Comedô de farinha
I am a White Male

"When we rest, we're carrying rocks." (Justino, resident of the Favela Parque Oziel/Campinas, about his former job as sugar cane worker, July, 2005)

Every year, about 200 thousand workers coming from the poor regions of the country—such as Valley of the Jequitinhonha, in Minas Gerais, and the northeast hinterland—migrate to the State of São Paulo to work in the cutting of sugar cane. To have an idea of this market in Brazil, the area of the country used to cultivate sugar cane is about 5 million hectares, the equivalent to the region of the entire Espirito Santo State. Just the macro region of Ribeirão Preto in the interior of Sao Paulo State, which encloses 85 cities, is responsible for 30% of the Brazilian production and occupies an area of 1.125 thousand hectares. (*Brasil de Fato*, 2005)

The year is 1996. It does not matter which month. I am drinking a beer at the cafeteria in my university. Yes, one can have a beer in Brazilian universities. I am sitting outside at a table, staring at the sun. Without me noticing, the professor I am working for approaches and sits by my side. His name is Ademir Gebara, former department head, and the chief of the division of Leisure Science. The Department of Physical Education has three divisions: Leisure Sciences, Sciences of Sport, and Human Movement Sciences. Anyway, Gebara is an important man.

Gebara does not waste any time and goes straight to the point:

"I got a job for you," he tells me.

"Let's hear it."

"I know you have relatives in Leme. The mayor contacted me yesterday, offering a job. For years Leme has received many workers from the northeastern part of the country during the harvest months of sugar cane. Those people come, work for four months, and then go back to their cities. Are you following me?"

"Yes. I am familiar with this situation."

"Good. It makes things easy. Anyway, for the last five years or so, with the advancements in the sugar cane industry, there is no harvest period anymore. It now happens all year long. Hence, these workers and their families moved from their home states (in the northeast) to Leme. The dorms that the sugar cane farms used for those people were emptied. The *Nordestinos* have been living in the city."

A pause to ask for another beer and Gebara keeps going.

"Those people, the *Nordestinos*, were the ones that elected the mayor. During his campaign, he and his party worked hard on those people. First, he had to convince them to transfer their voting rights to Leme. Later, he had to convince the *Nordestinos* to vote for him. The whole thing is a nasty situation. Local people hate the *Nordestinos*. In their opinion, the *Nordestinos* are impoverishing the city. Locals say that Leme used to be a nice and safe city. . . ."

Interrupting Gebara, I said.

"Yeah. I know all of this. I spend most of my weekends in Leme, remember. The *Nordestinos* are guilty of bringing crime, drugs, *favela*s, bla, bla, bla. It's like everywhere else. People in the whole São Paulo State hate them. We hate them! They are good for cheap labor, but we do not like the consequences of it. Plus, the perception is that they continue leaving their cities up there and keeping coming down here. According to my father, these *Nordestinos* do not know when to stop. I do not want to be rude, but what is the job?" I have to cut him off. Why do professors have to contextualize everything? Tell me about the job for God's sake. If I like it, I take it.

"Okay. When the mayor started talking to me I thought that he had big plans. He told me about federal money he got to build housing projects for those people. The big *favela* is gone. The *Nordestinos* now live in this neighborhood away from downtown Leme. So he told me that he needs a leisure project that can integrate this relatively new population into the city. He, the mayor, threw all the right words on me: education, citizenship, etc. B.S. All he wants is someone who can organize a 'happy Sunday in the hood' so the *Nordestinos* can be happy in their projects and, more importantly, stay away from downtown. This way the locals will be even happier. Plain and simple. I was really offended, and said no. However, I saw it as an opportunity, for you. The guy is a son of a bitch, but he'll pay $300 a month for the person who organizes the leisure activities. Plus, $8 an hour for everybody working in the event. He wants one event every other Sunday. If you want the job, you go to meet him this coming Monday at Leme's city hall. It's up to you."

IV: Fleshing Out My Embodied Bleeding Epistemological/Theoretical Position

It's an exercise.
Close your eyes.
Imagine me tearing out, with my bare hands, my racialized, gendered white
    body. My entrails jumping out . . . my guts being vomited from inside
    out . . . all of it in the middle of a torrential rain of decomposing food,
    shit, and blood. This is my feeling right now, while I am performing
    myself, my guts, to myself and others, inside my office—210 Armory—
    in the great University of Illinois.
My epistemological/theoretical position is not outside . . . It's inside my being! It's my being!

V: Life In-Betweenness

"Hey Gringo."
Yes, this is how my people call me in Brazil. Do you want to know why I call them my people? You might have to wait a little longer.
I am a gringo in Brazil and an alien here in America.
I am a betweener! I live life in-betweenness (Anzaldúa, 1999).
Right here I am standing . . .
As a white male
As a poor child
As a father
As Latino
As a husband
As a grad student
As all and none
As many and few

As a shifting some
As an In and Out
As a betweener

VI: City Hall

Leme's City Hall: I am talking to Renato in his office at the city hall. Renato is the second in command at the Leme Secretariat of Sports, Tourism, and Leisure. He is explaining my job.

"So, Cláudio, during the next two or three weeks you need to contact the neighborhood association of São José. Remember the name: São José. We do not use the word *favela* around here. São José is a neighborhood. Senhor Celestino is the president of the association. You are going to meet him tomorrow, here at the city hall. Once, you know him you two schedule the meetings between the two of you. Any questions?"

"No. So far so good."

"Remember, we want to have recreational activities for all ages. The residents can include some of the activities. For the first event, the mayor himself is going to show up around 11:30 A.M., so make sure that the activities will stop for his arrival."

"Okay"

"Once you have defined a plan for the day, bring it here, or fax it to me. It needs my approval. After I sign it, you are free to move."

"Renato, for the first event I will hire 20 physical education students. We need a big impact in the first event if we want keep people asking for more. I cannot risk a shortage in personal. After that, we can have a better idea of how many we'll need."

"That's okay. Other questions?"

"No"

"So, let's see the mayor."

We walk to a kind of conference room, and Geraldo Makarenko is waiting for us. We shake hands, exchanges a few words. Makarenko starts to talk to Renato.

"Is everything okay? Good. Make sure you are here at least 15 minutes before our meeting with Celestino. That *Nordestino* is always early. So you can entertain him, and I will not waste much of my time."

Turning to me: "Cláudio, now we take the pictures for tomorrow's newspaper. Did you bring your notes?"

I was supposed to write a few paragraphs describing the importance of leisure activities for children and, in the community in general, linking it to education, citizenship, blah, blah, blah. These notes are to be used by the reporter who is going to write for the newspaper. I feel guilty for using all the right words.

We posed for pictures. The mayor and I.

My aunt Lidia, the one who lives in Leme, still has that newspaper. Any times she wants to annoy me she says: Okay let's see the picture of you and your best pal.

VII: *Bleeding Embodied Epistemology*

I am not a poor kid in Brasil anymore.

Poor Brazilian kids don't read Denzin and don't go to classes and don't reflect upon their situation supported by the knowledge of history, theory, method, and philosophy.

I consider what I am doing as an ontoepistemological endeavor—as a being-in-knowing, and a being-in-doing (Barad, 2003).

It is about commitment.

It is about a commitment to a Bleeding Embodied Epistemology.[2]

How this is theory revealed in this performance?

The body

Living . . . Performing . . . disrupting . . . resisting

Performance theory disestablishes/subverts the supremacy/division of mind and body often acknowledged in academic settings. Performance is theory that lives in the body—"It need not be written about" (Jones, 1997, p. 55). My own theoretical framework is not a piece of clothing that one wears to work. It is located even deeper than the tattoos that mark my body. It is visceral.

The embodiment, the physicality, and the energy are the flashing "flaws" of[3] performance.

The flaws are the beauty.

Autoethnography though, in this sense, performs self and other, and self as other.[4]

Do you have to trust me?

Yes, you must.

Maybe.

Not at all.

What I ask you—the audience/reader—is to critically engage in the questioning what you accept as truth and how your truth is shaped by my perspective of truth in the performance, in the action of seeing my body—self and other, and self as other—resisting, challenging the master narrative.

VIII: *Gender Class?!*

It's the day of the first event. It's Sunday morning. We have five stations in the morning. All of them for kids. Later in the afternoon we will have adult activities.

Station four is a gym class. Not the formal one. Just to teach the kids some moves on the floor: back flips, things like that. Usually, kids like it a lot.

Suddenly, a fight erupts. Two kids, 12 or 13 years old—who knows their ages?—are going at each other pretty badly.

After my friends and I are able to separate them, the accusations start to pop up.

"You, know *tio*, it's his fault. He called me names."

"What names?"

"Faggot."

"Why did you do that?"

"Cause, he is. He is such a fag."

"Stop it. You cannot play here if you behave like this. You need to apologize."

"No way *tio*. I ain't never apologize. He is a fag. A big one." Looking away from me. "You are a silly fag and . . ."

"Get lost, kid!" I say interrupting him.

The kid did not blink:

"I won't. Let's see if you are man enough to make me go."

I want to beat that kid up. I am losing it. My friend Spon, who knows me better, is already grabbing my arm.

Fortunately, Celestino shows up.

"Valdir—this is the kid's name—go home and stay there, or I am going to take you to your father."

And like that, the kid is gone.

I turn my attention to the other kid now. He is crying hard. I get him by the arm. I start to walk with him way from the confusion. We walk for 15 minutes or so. He was calming down. Then, he starts talking . . . .

"That bastard. It's his entire fault."

"Hey, that kid is gone, calm down."

"It's not the kid. It's my father. Mother died few years ago. It's my father, my sister, and me. When we get home from work, we're all tired. But my sister has to clean the house, cook dinner. . . . It's a lot of cooking. There has to be enough food for supper and lunch. Afterward, we eat, and she prepares our lunch boxes, so we can have something to eat in the job. She washes the dishes, the clothes. She does everything. I feel sorry for her, so I help her when my father is out. One day he saw me helping her. He beat the shit out of me. While beating me, he said that he was raising no faggot. That I need to be a man. Then he went to a bar, and he told everybody what happened. That I was an embarrassment to him. He beat me a lot in the next days."

The kid is talking fast. It seems that he cannot stop. We do not make eye contact.

"I am no fag. I was just helping my sister. She works as hard as everybody else. She gets no help. . ." and then he runs away.

The next moment in qualitative inquiry will be one at which the practices of qualitative research finally move, without hesitation or encumbrance from the personal to the political. (Norman Denzin, 2000, p. 261)

Born in Brazil. The famous *mestiço* country of samba and soccer and injustice. The same Brazil where the minority white dominate the colored other.

I grow up and live life as a white man, as a poor child from a middle-class family who "went down," having to move to the poor neighborhood in town. A border child, living in between two cultures, at least: the Brazilian colonized poor and the Anglo, as a member of a family identified in my own country with the colonizer. There are so many Brasils. So many Brazilian borders. These permeable borders are marked by the intersection of race, class, gender, religion, and so on.

XIX: Rebelling . . .

"Mother, Francisco is white like me, and Analua is brown like you," I say.
Son (with anger): "I'm not brown!"

Even though my border-crossing from Brasil to the U.S.A. and then back to Brazil gives me my accented speech and my oppositional gringo/Latino identities, it does not "darken" my skin.

I cannot, and I repeat it, *cannot* pretend to ignore the privileges and guilt that I have because of the color of my skin and the penis between my legs. But I can question old definitions and create new meanings.[5]

What I can and want to do is to place my body as an allied other, as a member of the third world, as a colonizer/colonized, as a journey man fighting oppression, as a product of the colonial rape, looking for and creating my own roots. I position myself in this anticolonial space, possessing the negated brownness of my mother and the darkness/native looks of her father. I situate myself as border man, having in one arm my brunette brown-eyed daughter and in the other my blond blue-eyed son.

Celestino

It is my second meeting with Celestino. The meeting is in his house. The neighborhood association does not have its own place, so meetings take place in Celestino's house or in the bar close to it. In fact, the meetings usually start in the house, and then move to the bar.

"Celestino, it's already 45 minutes after 8, and it's just the two of us."

"Yes, I know. But people are tired after a long day. That's why you need to do well in the first event. Then, people will come. Before, when we lived in the tents, before we got these houses, it was easy to mobilize people. We want the houses. We couldn't continue to live like that. So, no matter how tired you were, you would come. But now, they got a little conformed. We got a roof above our heads. My work here has been hard."

"Yes, I can see . . . but hey, let's use this. I mean, the park they built is crappy. There is nothing there. Use this event to bring your people together. We need restrooms and drinking fountains. A club house would be nice. Make a list, and on the Sunday of the event, ask people to sign it. Then, we can register it in the city hall."

"I don't know . . . the mayor has been good to us. We got the houses. People like him here. He is going to put asphalt in the streets. It'll start next week. . . ."

"Hey, this asphalt thing . . . you are paying for it. I already showed you that. Your house payment is around $110.00. Almost $20 is for the asphalt."

"Still, I need to be careful. But I like the list idea. Let's do it."

A month later, back in the city hall: "Cláudio, you're fired." Says Renato. "You were supposed to make these people "happy" and not go making any lists."

X-Body

Hence, if I cannot represent my body,[6] how can I represent others?
If you are looking for a complete story, you are not going to find it here. If your "trained mind" is
looking for the whole thing, that is not here either.

"You know, Gringo . . ."
I am the Gringo. I am the Brazilian Gringo.
". . . sorry, I forget your name again . . ."
"That's Okay Justino. Cláudio, my name's Cláudio. But Gringo is fine too."

"It's not just the long hours. It's everything. The weather, the fucking sun that gets in your face, making it look like a lizard. Not much money, not much at all. You keep cutting the cane, cutting the cane. Swinging the knife as a crazy man. There is not a day that goes by without one being badly cut. When we rest, we carry rocks. Hunger, oh my . . tiredness, exhaustion, fatigue . . . Look at my arms: look at the scars . . . look at it?! Hands . . . each joint in my finger looked like an 8 snooker ball. Then, the wife gets pregnant, and I leave. Don't want my kid in that life. Come to the big city and . . . look at me now. I am no better . . . fuck, same shit, different places."

This is a fragment. Not a thick description. Tell your Western-trained mind to stop looking for details or categories. You do not need them. Nor does Justino, in his black body.[7]

X: Final Words

Yes, I am an angry man. And I have the right to feel a "just ire . . . founded in my revulsion before the negation of the right to be 'more' . . ." (Freire, 2004b, p. 58).

Yes, like Freire . . .

"I have the right to be angry and to express that anger, to hold it as my motivation to fight, as just I have the right to love and to express my love for the world, to hold it as my motivation to fight . . ." (pp. 58–59).
And yet
What am I doing?
For my performance autoethnography to succeed, I/we need more.
As Denzin has been saying, rage is not enough. It is necessary to move, to create a safe, non-naïve utopic space.

It is necessary to hope.
To dream.
My dream?
In the "summer time"
It is to be able to BE with a community of the oppressed in Brazil or elsewhere
To talk to, and with, "this people"
Together, to invent our roots
Shared roots that unify different, economically racialized, gendered bodies
And then
They and I become a different us
And then
The different we
Identify and define our needs and desires
And then

We
Start to explore possibilities (Madison, 1998)
The possibility
Of us
Together
Create performances
For
Us
The possibility
Of us
Together
Create performances
For the colonizer other
For us
Together
Improve our lives
And then, consequently
Improve
Yes
Together
The lives of the Colonizer OTHER
Remember Freire
Only the oppressed can liberate the oppressor
Meanwhile
In the no "summer time"
I move/come back?
To academia
Using the performances created by my people and me
To hold their places here
While they hold mine for me over there
Wherever over there may be
And then
Have the same process of liberation here
Wherever this academic here may be
For me and my bunch
And For everyone else who want to share our invented roots
Opening the academic doors
For my bunch
For other bunches
Who come in peace
Who have hope, love and dreams
And also
For you and me

I position myself here—now—visiting my past, doing field work, performative living my life as whole. I position myself here—in the academic public space—as an indigenous ethnographer; as a member whose membership is not mine . . . yet. I position myself here to decolonize inquiry, to decolonize academia. In the hope that some time from now, when I or one of my people, ask "where are the poor?" And by poor I mean

> No money in the pocket
> Eating lunch not knowing about dinner
> "Where are the poor?"[8]
> I will see more bodies standing in the academic setting.
> I am tired, so I ask Bryant Keith Alexander to end it for me
> ". . . issues of personal survival motivate scholarship production . . . I am exploring and sometimes exposing my own vulnerability to racial, gender, and cultural critique as a method of both understanding self and other, self as other, while engaging in performances (written and embodied) that seek to transform the social and cultural conditions under which I live and labor." (Alexander, 2005, p. 433)

Thank you Bryant, but on a second thought, it would be better if I do it myself.

I am possessed by my anger now. Can you feel it? This section is ending and my anger is in a kind of crescendo. I angrily want to have my own room in the Masters' house. My room, full of hope and love—for me and for my bunch who share the same (invented?) roots; for me now, and for the other bunch who will come—yes, they will—in the house of the Masters.
We have different tools.

Story 2

Back on the Streets

The streets were empty as I walked toward Rosario Square on that Saturday, late in the afternoon. The narrow streets and alleys that usually roar with open markets and people were quiet and deserted, which made me understand a little better why most kids I know living downtown don't like weekends.

I had just arrived in town after taking Celi to a recovery center in a rural area some 50 miles west of Rio de Janeiro. I was exhausted from the 8-hour trip each way but, excited about Celi's more promising future, I decided to check on some of the other kids. The streets had been really rough those days, and I'd spent the last two days working around the clock to get Celi out of the streets. I mostly wanted to know how Dalva was doing. She'd had some close calls that week, getting attacked, along with Celi, by two men two nights before I took Celi to Rio. They'd been on their way to Old Town to buy crack when two men on a motorcycle coming from behind stopped abruptly. They told the girls to stand against a wall, pointing a big gun at Celi's head, and started to feel and press their bodies against the wall. The men threatened to kill the girls if they didn't have sex with them, but somehow Dalva managed to escape their grip and create a confusion that attracted people and led the men away. That's how they told the story to Marga.

Then within a few days Dalva, along with Kleo, was almost lynched by a mob of angry men and women accusing them of stealing a purse or wallet near one of the bus terminals. They got away only because they'd had time to reach the fire station across the street before the mob could grab them. The girls swore they didn't steal anything that afternoon. Later, when we were coming back from Rio and I was telling Celi about this incident, she laughed wildly at me. "I'm sure Dalva and Kleo stole something and were caught, I'm sure, they always lie to you, to all street educators, about this stuff; you know, so you don't get mad at them. They are full of shit, I'll tell you that!" she said wiping the tears off her cheeks. I'd never asked Dalva and Kleo whether they'd stolen something anyway. I'd been too frightened by the idea of lynching to worry about petty thefts, and so had Dalva.

I didn't see anybody hanging out in Rosario Square until I looked behind the Spiritist newsstand. Sitting there were Dalva and Marta.

"Hey *tio*! Did Celi stay at the farm?" Dalva said getting up and giving me a kiss on the cheek.

"Yeah, she did. It's a beautiful place. I would like to spend a few months there myself," I said to Dalva then looking at Marta. I told Dalva all the details of the trip she asked me. She said she was happy for Celi, that she was going to miss her on the streets, but that she knew this was the best thing for Celi.

"You spent some time there too, right Marta?" I said sitting down next to her.

"Yeah, I was there for more than four months. I wanted to stay more but they told me my time was up, that I was clean enough to return to a normal life," Marta said playing with her dark curly hair.

I had never seen Marta before that day but recognized her face from pictures Marga'd shown me. Marga had helped Marta go to the SN recovery center, and they had written each other during those four months. I knew from Marga that Marta had gone to São Paulo City with one of the women she met at the farm. But in the past weeks Marga had gotten several phone calls from Marta, who was unhappy with the way she was being treated by the woman's daughter. She wanted to go back to Campinas and wanted Marta to help her find a place to stay and, if possible, also a job. Marga couldn't find either and grew worried that Marta might come to Campinas anyway, which would mean going back to the streets. And that's exactly what happened.

"I'm surprised to see you here, what happened?" I asked Marta.

"My friend helped me get a job, as a maid, and I was going to meetings every day, you know, NA meetings, to help me stay away from drugs. I was doing fine, but my friend's daughter was always on my case, always saying that I'm a drug addict, that I'm black, that I smell, she called me *trombadinha*."

"Bitch! Sorry, *tio* Marcelo," Dalva said touching my hand, "but that's not right, I'd have beaten her up."

I nodded. I was mad too. *Trombadinha* is one of the most pejorative names for street kid; it comes from the Portuguese word *trombada*, which means "crash" and refers to the way some street kids crash into people to take their purses and wallets. It is taken as a serious insult even when coming from one street kid to another.

"What did your friend do about it?" I asked Marta.

"Her daughter never said anything in front of my friend. I didn't say anything to my friend either. I tried to stay cool and hoped *tia* Marga was going to find something for me here. But I couldn't take it anymore. I got into a fight with her yesterday, and when her mom came back from work the bitch raised hell, saying that she was afraid of me and all those lies." Marta paused and looked at the ground.

"And then . . .," I probed.

She looked up at me, her eyes watering, angry. "She asked me to leave."

Dalva shook her head.

"I left without packing," Marta said.

"What are you going to do now?" I asked.

Marta looked at me, surprised, then smiled. "I think I'm gonna check myself into a nice hotel, then get a good job. . . . I think I'm gonna buy myself some nice shoes too. I don't think nobody will give me a job looking like this," she said pointing to her dirty feet.

Dalva and I tried to laugh, but then were quiet. I tried to imagine what the daughter's version would be.

We made small talk for a while. I was feeling really tired but was too embarrassed to tell them I was going home to take a shower, eat, and rest. So I told them I had an appointment and had to go.

"Can you help me go back to the SN farm? Dalva says you have been helping kids to get out of the streets," asked Marta as I was getting up.

"Yes. Let's meet here on Monday, and we'll go together to the SN office."

"Can we go today? Or tomorrow?" she asked.

"The office doesn't open till Monday, Marta, sorry," I said not wanting to look her in the eyes. I said goodbye and left without looking back.

When I saw Marta again, Monday afternoon, next to the same newsstand in Rosario Square, I had already called the SN office. They had told me they could see her for an interview in a week. Roger, the manager, seemed supportive, and I wanted to tell Marta the good news.

Marta was sitting around with a bunch of other kids. I greeted them and sat down next to Dalva and Lucio. As they were telling me their weekend adventures, I kept glancing at Marta. She looked much dirtier than the last time I'd seen her, her hair full of pieces of small dead leaves and dust. She was rocking back and forth and seemed to be talking to herself, her head constantly turning backward. Lucio must have seen my eyes on Marta.

"She's just in the *noia* stage, *tio*," he said smiling, or laughing, at me. *Noia*, slang for "paranoid," is a common stage after the crack high, when one thinks she is being chased.

"I think she's afraid someone will come from the Pizza Hut to beat her up," Dalva said, pointing in the direction that Marta was turning to look after every other word she said to herself.

I looked over Dalva's shoulder at the Pizza Hut just across the street from the Square.

"The security guard from Pizza Hut hit her in the back with a bat last night," Dalva said.

I looked at Dalva, then at Lucio, who was laughing.

"She was asking for money from a lady who was leaving the place, and the security guard came and grabbed her by the arm and pushed her away," Dalva said mimicking a push.

"Yeah, then Marta got a stone and threw it reaaaally hard at him," Lucio said, "but it missed him and hit a table inside where some rich people were eating.

"Then the security guard started chasing Marta. But he didn't get her. She went back and threw another stone inside. They had to close the place for a while. People were screaming inside, and we were all laughing outside," Lucio concluded.

"A few minutes later, the security guard came quietly from behind and hit Marta really hard. She was down for a while. Then the police came and we split," Dalva said.

"I wanted to give her some news," I said looking at Marta, who was still doing her thing.

"If you smoked crack you'd know it's a waste of time now," Lucio said laughing.

A week later, the day I was supposed to take Marta for an interview at the SN office, I ran into Kleo and Grace in the bus terminal market. They told me that she'd been taken by the Juvenile officers the night before. I went straight to the Juvenile Court and Peres, one of the officers I knew best, told me that Marta had caused a lot of trouble that night. They were taking her to her grandmother's house in a nearby city when she broke the back window of their van with her fist and tried to jump from the moving car. They stopped the van to control her, but she fought one of the officers, biting him on the hand, and ran away.

"She really pissed us off this time, but now she's screwed," Peres said grinning. "We found out, talking to her grandmother last night, that she just turned 18. Next time we get her she'll go to jail. For a long time. And it'll be one less punk to give us a headache." His face was beaming with excitement.

Less than two days later, Marta was caught by the police with a stolen golden necklace and sent straight to jail. It took me more than a month to find out which jail she was sent to. A year later she was still there, still waiting for the trial, and sharing a small cell with twelve other women.

Story 3

The Streets or Not the Streets

I saw Kleo sitting on the sidewalk in front of one of the several banks surrounding Rosario Square. She was alone, which was unusual for any of the kids in downtown. I approached her slowly and asked if I could sit down with her. She looked at me, and I saw she'd been crying. She nodded yes and put her head back between her legs flexed against her chest.

"Where're you going pretty like this?" I said noticing her clean clothes and somewhat worn-out sandals. She also had a bright red lipstick on her full mulatto lips.

"Nowhere," she answered curtly, still in the same position.

"Do you want to be alone?" I asked starting to get up.

"No. I'm just tired of this life," she said straightening her back against the bank wall, and then wiping the tears off her cheeks. "We can't walk around here without those damned officers harassing us. We can't ask for money in front of the shops without the owners sending their security guards to shoo us away. We can't sleep here or there. We can't go to the shelters, because they don't want us. We have no place to go! We can't do anything!" Her eyes started to water again.

"I can try to help you find a place if you want," I said mildly.

"I'm tired of this life. I know there is no way out for me. It's too late . . .," she was saying without being dramatic in her tone.

"What about going to the Mission for girls. I heard it's a nice place, more like a house, not as big as the other shelters," I said interrupting her.

"Perhaps if I'd left the streets when I was younger. I could have had a chance then. But I'd go to the Mission if they took me in," she said looking me in the eyes.

I saw she had some blue make-up around her eyes. "I'll talk to Berta, the woman who is running the house. I'll talk to her today. Where can I find you later?"

"I don't know!" she said, as if I'd asked an absurd question. "What time is it? I'm gonna be late." We both looked at the Marlboro clock in the middle of Rosario Square.

"I'll look for you around downtown," I said getting up.

"Try the market next to the bus terminal," she said also getting up and starting to walk toward the south end of the Square.

We parted, and I turned to watch her from a distance. She stopped on the corner for a few minutes. Then a red imported car stopped where she was, the driver rolled down the window and they started talking. As Kleo walked around the front of the car, I caught a glimpse of the driver, an older man with a white mustache who seemed to be nervously looking around. Kleo got in the passenger's seat and the car left in a hurry.

That afternoon I went to the Mission for girls and talked to Berta about Kleo. She seemed positive that Kleo would be able to stay there if she really wanted to. I went straight back downtown but didn't find Kleo until late in the night, in the market area near the bus terminal, now closed and quiet. She was with Celi and Dalva, eating some unsold barbecued meat left next to a large garbage bin. I approached the girls and immediately saw the purple bruise on Kleo's left cheekbone but pretended I hadn't. Before I could sit down next to them, Kleo got up, took me by the arm, and said she wanted to show me something.

"I don't want Celi to know that I'm trying to get out of the streets," she said when we were at a safe distance from the other girls. "She'll come after me and will get me out of there if she finds out where I am," she said pointing to a building as if she were showing me something. "She always does that. I like her, she's a good friend, but she can't see us leave the streets. She comes crying saying that we abandoned her, that she's alone and afraid, and I always leave the shelters with her."

"Are you afraid of her?" I asked trying not to sound challenging.

"No, but I can't say no to her. I don't know why, but I always leave with her for the streets. I don't want to leave this time."

"Well, I talked to Berta, and she said you could stay there," I said trying not to look directly at her bruise. "We can go now. I'm sure Berta wouldn't mind if we woke her up."

"No, I can't go now. . .," she paused and looked at Celi already coming toward us. "I need to meet you alone. Celi won't let me go. I need to go. . . ."

"What are you talking about?" Celi almost shouted at us.

"Nothing," Kleo said quickly and grabbed Celi's hand. "We have to go, *tio*."

The next day I walked around downtown for several hours trying to find Kleo, without success. I had lost hope, thinking that she'd changed her mind, when I ran into Dalva, Celi, and Lucio under a tree in Rosario Square. They told me that Kleo was probably at the Juvenile Court. They had been all together that afternoon when two juvenile officers came in a van and started to chase them near the cathedral.

"We ran away from them, *tio*, but Kleo, that traitor, just walked to the van and got in," Lucio said.

"Even the officers looked surprised!" Dalva said.

I looked at Celi, and she was staring at me.

"Why would she do that?" I said avoiding Celi's eyes, beginning to understand what Kleo had done thanks to her.

"She's a snitch, that's all!" said Lucio under his breath.

"Don't be an asshole! Maybe she just needs some help," Dalva said.

"She needs a good beating, that's what she needs!" Lucio said making a fist.

I didn't look at Celi again, but I could feel her eyes on me as we wondered about Kleo's motives. I said goodbye and headed for the Mission, making sure I wasn't being followed.

Kleo came to greet me at the door. "I knew you were here," I said smiling as she let me inside.

"Do you think they suspect I'm here?" Kleo said.

"I don't think so. They seemed a little upset that you went with the officers without putting up a fight, though."

"I know that. But when I saw them coming I realized that was my chance to lose Celi. It took me a while to convince the officers I really wanted to get out of the streets, but they finally brought me here. They looked so surprised when I got in the van by myself," she said beaming.

I said I was proud of her and promised to visit her several times a week. She wanted some clothes, and I promised her that too.

On the afternoon of March 13th, I went to the Mission to visit Kleo and talk to Berta. Celi had been looking for Kleo, asking the street educators where Kleo was, saying she just wanted to know if Kleo was safe. There were not many shelters in town, and I knew Celi would eventually find Kleo. I was hoping to talk Kleo into saying no to Celi when she came to get her back on the streets.

Kleo had been there for two weeks and looked healthy, her bruise gone, her clothes clean, and well-rested. But Berta told me that Kleo had talked about leaving the Mission twice in the last few days, so I asked to talk to Kleo in private. She told me that she was feeling fine but that she missed the fun of the streets, the lack of rules, her friends, and drugs. We talked for a while, and she ended up promising me that she would stay, even if Celi showed up. I told her I would buy the new pair of shoes she wanted and left the Mission. The same night Celi showed up, raised hell in front of the small house that served as shelter for six girls in a quiet neighborhood several miles from downtown, threw rocks at the windows, and finally left with Kleo at her side.

A few days later I saw Celi and Kleo in front of a bakery shop one block west of Rosario Square, so high they could barely talk. They saw me and asked for money before I could say hi. I didn't even stop to talk to them that night. Then I didn't see Kleo for almost a month, and nobody seemed to know where she was.

The next time I saw her, in front of the same bakery, Kleo was all dressed up and in high spirits. She told me she had spent several weeks in a new shelter for girls, managed by Adventists, located on a farm just outside of town.

"You didn't like the place," I asked, trying hard to sound impartial.

"I did! The food was good, and they didn't make us pray all the time. We could even watch the 8 o'clock soap opera!" she said smiling and fixing her skirt.

I smiled too.

"But I became friends with this one girl, from another state, I forget the name of the place now, and she said she'd never seen Campinas. So I told her I'd show her downtown. We were just gonna spend the day here and go back before dark . . . but then . . . then you know, I met the girls and they were going to the Old Quarter, to get high, you know. I couldn't resist and went with them. My friend took a bus back to the shelter."

"You didn't feel like going back the next day?" I asked.

"Oh yes, I did! But I was too embarrassed to go back. I was too embarrassed to tell them I'd smoked and all that. I knew they were gonna give me shit, because I fled the place and took that girl with me." She looked at me and shrugged.

I said I thought they would welcome her back.

"I don't know . . . what time is it? I need to go. I'm gonna be late," Kleo said turning around and fixing her top, then her hair.

Story 4

Off the Streets

"I'm doing well," said Roberto untying his soccer shoes.

"Me too, *tio*," Gilberto said opening a large smile. "I like it here. We have classes in the morning, then we play soccer in the afternoon. I like it. It's better than the streets."

"Yeah, we're happy here. We sleep well, and the food is okay. I wish my brother Drigo was here, you know? He says he's having fun living on the streets and all. It's fun, I know, but it gets really tough after a while," Roberto, the older of the brothers, said.

Drigo is the oldest of the three brothers, 13 or 14 years old.

"He's smoking too much crack. That's why he can't leave the streets. He's too hooked, man." For a 10-year-old boy, Gilberto looked unnaturally concerned.

"I'm glad we came here before crack hit the streets," said Roberto looking at his brother.

"Yeah, Drigo is so high all the time he can't think straight. He keeps saying that he's gonna join us here but then never does," Gilberto said.

"I see him once in a while," I said.

"Is he still thin like a toothpick? Last time I saw him he looked like a strong gust of wind would break him in two. Last time he came here to visit us he was really thin. He said he was gonna stay. Father Lelo said he could stay. But he left after he ate. He said he was gonna smoke a cigarette outside and be right back . . . but he never came back. I don't know what to do. I wish he'd come and stay here with us." Roberto stroked the grass as he talked.

"It's time to clean up," Gilberto said getting up.

"We need to go, *tio*. We have to get ready for the 6 o'clock mass," Roberto said putting his hand out.

I shook hands with Roberto. Gilberto gave me a hug, like he used to do every day when I left the street corner where he and his brothers hung out until a year and a half ago.

"See if you can talk Drigo into joining us here," Roberto said as he began to walk toward the big building that had once been a hotel and now served as the catholic home for boys.

The same day, I found Drigo on the very corner where I used to hang out with him and his brothers. He saw me from the other side of the busy avenue.

"H-hey *t-tio* Ma-marcelo!" he said opening his huge smile, his teeth brown from crack. "Lo-look at th-this!" He didn't used to stutter before, I thought.

Then he walked to the middle of the avenue and lay down on the asphalt, playing dead. I tried to scream, but all I heard was a car screeching. The car stopped less than a foot from the body lying down. The driver looked as white as a ghost. Drigo sat up and smiled at me.

Notes

1. "Touching the open sewers."

2. "Performance may be theorized about, but theory of the performance is imbedded in the performance itself, "flaws" and all. The provocative question is not "What theory created this performance?" but "What theory is revealed through this performance?" (Jones, 1997, p. 55)
3. "The performance that interests me is not a literal 'illustration' of a theoretical proposition, but I find that much performance theory and criticism suggests it is or ought to be, and often the degree to which the performance disrupts the elegance of the theory is the degree to which it is said to be 'flawed'" (Phelan, 1995, p.186, quoted from Jones, 1997, p. 55).
4. "...an act of seeing the self see the self through and as other" (Alexander, 2005, p. 423).
5. "*Soy un amasamiento*, I am an act of kneading, of uniting and joining that . . . has produced [not only]. . . a creature of darkness and a creature of light but also a creature that question the definitions of light and dark and give them new meanings" (1999, p. 103).
6. I can represent only glimpses, vignettes, fragments. My fragments. And through my fragments, I can show others' too. Just fragments, because it is by them that I lived in my surreal postmodern "reality." This has been one of my struggles in academia. My fragmented surreal postmodern life is not neat enough to fit in a more traditional or complete understandable theory/method. If my own life is not neat enough, how can I assume that the others are? I cannot and do not. I do not have this imperialistic arrogance. That's why I was easy prey for performance autoethnography.
7. When my white male body performs my relationship with Justino's black body, it not only disrupts abstract notions of race/class/gender, but it also physically breaks them. The white body, which is unsuccessfully trying to negate its own whiteness and exposing the racial construction in a western patriarchal society, fights for social justice.
8. This question was inspired by Jones (1997), "Sista docta: Performance as critique of the academy," and also by Paulo Freire's question, during his visit to the University of Illinois: "where are the workers?"

Chapter 4

BETWEENNESS IN CLASS

STORY 5

WITH GRACE

"What do you think should be done about the street kids hanging around the downtown area?"

"I don't know," said a man in his late 30s, in a low voice, without slowing down.

"Do you have any suggestions on how to help the street kids living in the downtown area?"

But the elderly couple didn't answer her, looking more concerned with changing pace and trajectory.

"We are not getting much cooperation with this important matter," she shouted looking for another passerby. "Here, a nice looking man, let's hear what he has to say about the situation of street kids in downtown," she said approaching a business-looking man who was walking fast across the Cathedral Square.

He gave her a coin without saying anything or slowing down.

"Oh, money! Maybe that's the solution to the problem," she shouted again as she turned swiftly on her heels, fixed the video camera made of cardboard on her shoulder, and started to walk toward two women walking past and carrying shopping bags.

"Good evening!" she said, sounding like the 7 o'clock news anchor, standing in the path of the two ladies, who discreetly grabbed each other's free hands and changed direction slightly, as if to avoid the camera-girl without being obvious about it.

"Why do you fine ladies think that people won't talk to street kids here in downtown?" she said standing in their path again.

The two women then made a 90-degree turn and began walking faster.

"Oh look, they are holding their purses," she said out loud and turned to look in our direction. "Do not worry, fine ladies! I'm working now . . . but I sure hope to see you again when I'm not!" she said, stressing the word *not*, to the two ladies already a few yards away.

She then continued to walk around the Square in front of the cathedral, video camera on her left shoulder, interviewing passersby. Regi, one of her friends who had been watching everything from a distance with Tate and me, got a cardboard mic from a table dressed with signs announcing AIDS AWARENESS DAY, and joined Grace. Before leaving us, Regi said she was going to find a cute guy to interview.

"How should the mayor help the street kids of our beloved downtown?" Regi asked a young man who stopped to talk to them.

"I think he should buy them ice creams," the young man said smiling.

They laughed, and then Grace asked for his phone number. They laughed some more, and the young man walked away waving them goodbye.

Then Grace spotted two young women walking together a few yards away and began to approach them. The two young women saw her and started to run. Grace, looking through the fake lenses all the way, started to run after them shouting, "Why are you running away from us? Are you scared of us? Do we smell that bad?"

Tate, a 16- or 19-year-old boy, and I continued to be entertained by the girls until a woman who seemed to be one of the coordinators of the AIDS AWARENESS gathering asked Grace and Regi for the camera and mic.

"You would be a good reporter," the woman told Grace.

"I'd like to do that with a real camera."

"I'll bring you a real one someday, and we'll get some real interviews," the woman said.

"When?" Grace asked before the woman finished her sentence.

"Uh, I don't know, one of these days."

"But when?"

"I'll come here to find you when I arrange things."

"Where are you gonna find me?"

"Here?"

"Can I keep the camera till you come back?" asked Grace.

"Sure," said the woman smiling and walking away.

Grace and Regi came over to where Tate and I were, and I asked her, Grace, what the best way of handling the street kids' situation in downtown was.

"Well, running away and holding your purse tight seems to be the most popular choice," she said grinning. "But I personally prefer the ice cream solution." We all cracked up, and getting the hint, I took them to an ice cream place a few blocks from the Cathedral Square.

"What do you call a person who interviews people on the streets?" Grace asked me with her mouth full of chocolate chip ice cream.

"A journalist?"

"I wanna be a journalist."

"You'll get a chance to taste it when that woman comes with a real camera and mic," I said.

Grace looked at me gravely, her face revealing her thoughts, and went back to licking her ice cream cone.

Act 2

My Bad English: A Letter to Norman Denzin

Before everything else, there are some things I need to say. I wrote this piece in a stressful moment of my life. I was in the middle of answering my prelim question for Professor Dan Cook. Those were days with long hours, not seeing enough of my family. Life can be tough sometimes. I was mad.

However, what I really want to say here is that in the following pages I criticize one statement made by Professor D. Soyini Madison, trying to engage in a dialogue with her. My intent was not, back then, and it still is not now, to dismiss, or to attack Professor Madison. Professor Madison's work is beautiful and powerful. It has heavily influenced me, not only as scholar but also as human being.

Madison's (1998) "Performance, Personal Narratives, and the Politics of Possibility" is one of the most powerful pieces I ever read. It touched me deeply. Madison's influence is presented in my whole work. Even the idea to write a letter to Norman Denzin came from Madison's letter to Fanon.

I am also aware now, not back then, of Madison's (2006) "The Dialogical Performative in Critical Ethnography."

With that being said, I would like to apologize in advance to Professors D. Soyini Madison and Norman Denzin and reader 679. No offense was/is intended.

I was mad then
I am not mad now
Cláudio.

I: Dear Norman Denzin,

I learned from you that "writing creates the worlds we inhabit" (Denzin, 2003, p. xii), and these performative written pages started as a letter for you, and then they transformed themselves in many other things, such as a kind of manifest or a rupture in my answers to my prelim questions. You were out of town, and I was pretty mad at some of the comments from your letter (and the ones made by Reader 679) about my paper, "Fragments." What I need to make clear to you is that I love you, but I was mad.

II: Rupture

I need to make a rupture in my answer right now. I am mad, really angry. Norm is out of town and I have just this space to express my feelings. I've been trying to avoid it but if I don't say what I want to say, I will not be able to finish my question. Instead of working I am thinking all the time about this letter. It is Wednesday afternoon. This morning I went to the ICR office to tell Andrea and Bonnie that I am going to take one of my exams tomorrow. Andrea, the secretary, wasn't there so I went to check my mailbox. There was only one letter sitting there. It was from QI signed by you, Norman Denzin. The letter says that my paper "Fragments" went under another revision and is conditionally accepted by the journal. This paper went under review before, and Stacey Holman Jones asked to include, fleshed out, my theoretical/epistemological position. Being in conversation with you, I developed the "New Section." She also asked me to move my poem to the beginning of the text, so I did. This new reviewer, "Reader 679," however, asked me to take out all the theory I wrote and have it as footnotes and move the paragraph about "theoretical body of knowledge" to the beginning of the text. But that is not what I am mad about. It is frustrating, but that is it.

What I am fuming about are two comments in the first page, signed by you, that according to you "are not in any way intended to be critical":

4—Sage does not publish profanity
5—I don't think your written English needs to be impeccable—but it should not call attention to itself.

Sage is saying that it does not publish profanity. Thus, it does not publish the spoken word of the uneducated Other. I do not swear in my everyday life as today ... and yes, I understand the big picture ... I do not want my daughter Analua saying "bad" words. However, the questions that stay are these: Whose voices are not going to be published by Sage? How is the Other going to be represented? Is the Other wearing Fanon's "white mask"?

Concerning the second comment, Reader 679 adds:

"Remove grammatical errors. Consider a peer review before sending a formal journal submission. For example, change *Foulcaltian'* to *Foulcaltian*

(p. 2)." The emphasis is mine, and, yes, Reader 679 wrote the same word twice. My guess is that the apostrophe is what is wrong.

Where does my bad English come from? I wrote a paper that I liked and am proud of. I've been reading a lot of published written performances, and my piece is good. I performed this piece as an effort to decolonize inquiry/academy. I ask for inclusion and . . .

I got in this country in August of 1999 without any English, not written or spoken. In my first day at the Intensive English Institute here at the U of I, having a friend as translator, I told my teachers about my plans. All of them said to me that my plans were impossible. One, named Dan, came forward and said that I have no chance of getting the scores I need to be accepted as a grad student in the university. I'm glad I didn't believe them.

It is all about gatekeepers.

Again, where does my bad English come from?

I have two friends I've been asking to look over my papers, Desiree and Aaron. Both of them are grad students, extremely kind and loving persons, and busy. Does Reader 679 know how hard is to get to ask someone to read your papers? I also have been writing a lot. I am embarrassed to ask my friends for help. However, both of them looked over "Fragments."

It is all about positioning the "Other."

Again, from where does my bad English come from?

It is no coincidence that my written (and spoken) English is probably the worst among other Brazilians grad students here at the University of Illinois. From the other Brazilians students I personally met, I know this for sure.

It is no coincidence that I probably have the poorest socio-economic background among other Brazilians grad students here in Champaign-Urbana. From the other Brazilians students I personally met, I know this for sure.

It is no coincidence that I have very few Brazilian friends here in town. There is not much to talk about. Plus, I am known in the Brazilian community here as the "one who trashes the country."

It is also no coincidence that the few Brazilians I call friends are, for the most part, neither grad students nor professors.

It is also no coincidence the Brazilian who used to frequent my house is a woman who is barely formally educated and was extremely poor in Brazil. My friend is from the Northeast. Dani, my wife, and I met this friend here in Champaign five years ago, in a barbecue to celebrate Brazilian Independence Day. Nobody in the party went to talk to her.

All the Brazilians
Who have good English
And were at the party
Tried very hard to ignore her presence   *she is not one of us"*
All of them, but Dani

Again, where does my bad English come from?

My former two officemates had a proofreader. They paid $14/hour for the guy. Just yesterday, my friend Aaron told me at my home that he was proofreading a paper for a Brazilian Professor in Engineering. He charged $30/hour. He helps me for free.

Mary Weems (2003) in her beautiful book, *I Speak from the Wound in My Mouth*, tells me that

Racism is so personal

I am telling you that

Classism, illiteracy, is also so personal

For the most part I do not assume I fit/belong in the system. Can I?

Another example would be how my work is relegated or how I can position my self in the academic world.

D. Soyini Madison is a famous name in the field of performance studies. I read many of her pieces. She graduated from NWU and is a professor at the University of North Carolina. I am going to use her work with audience as an example of her positioning of the Other, and in doing so, of how she dismisses my work.

Madison's work in question is a book called *Critical Ethnography: Method, Ethics, and Performance* (2005). It is a very good book. However, in the 245 pages of the book, she talks about autoethnography once, and only to belittle it:

> "We understand that our subjectivity is an inherent part of research, but in critical ethnography it is not my *exclusive* experience—that is autobiography, travel writing, or memoir (or what some people call autoethnography)." (2005, p. 9)

Madison does not even mention who "some people" refers to. She goes on, saying:

> "I contend that critical ethnography is always a meeting of multiple sides in a encounter with and among the Other(s). . . . A more detailed explication of the relationship and dialogue with the Other is further elaborated in the corpus of work by Dwight Conquergood . . . (1991, 1998)." (2005, p. 9)

In "Rethinking Ethnography" (1991) Conquergood comments on/critiques some aspects of the "old" more traditional approach in ethnography:

> "the obligatory rite-of-passage for all ethnographers—doing fieldwork— . . . participatory nature of fieldwork is celebrated by ethnographers. . . . Ethnographic rigor, disciplinary authority, and

professional reputation are established by the length of time, depth of commitment, and risks(bodily, physical, emotional) . . . letters of recommendation often refer approvingly to bodily hardships by the dedicated ethnographer-malarial fevers, scarcity of food, long periods of isolation, material discomforts, and so forth, endured in the field." (pp. 352–353)

Are those ethnographers trying to be the Other? A black friend and former student, and also a football player, once told me: "These white kids wanna be like us but not us."

In the introduction to her book, Madison tells us how angry she was after watching a documentary related to women's right in Ghana, West Africa:

"My blood was boiling. It was a gross and dangerous misrepresentation of Ghana and her people."(2005, p. 3)

Madison knows what she is talking about because she:

". . . lived there for almost three years conducting field research with local activists on human rights violations against women and girls." (2005, p. 2)

I read some of Madison's work about people in Ghana. It is beautiful, important, and powerful.

However, let's come back to "what some people call autoethnography" and the question who is the Other?
Who are the Others?
Where are the Others?
The different
Using Madison's own words
The subaltern and subversive body

III: Fictionary Tale

Let's suppose that Madison's next topic of studies is children's labor, and yes, it is going to take place in Brazil. As a good professor she gets grants and goes to that country, not only as a black woman, but as an American professor from a famous university. Let's also imagine that she is going to conduct her research in a fast-growing town named Uberlandia in 1979/1980. In Uberlandia, she gets access to a factory that sells, among other thing, Walmet's tractors and parts, named Trimag.

In the factory, Madison[1] sees this white kid whose hands are hurt. Next time, she comes back and notices that the kid's hands have newer wounds over the old ones. Madison approaches the kid. She is quickly able to establish rapport with the kid. The professor knows what she is doing. "To think of ethnography as critical theory in action is an interesting and productive description" (2005, p. 13). In teaching how to do ethnography in her methods class/book she calls the first step "Who Am I? Starting Where You Are" (p. 19). She talks to the kid. She goes to his hood. She does her fieldwork.

Back in the U.S., she works on the data. She is careful. She "learned from Stuart Hall . . . that how people are represented is how they are treated" (2005, p. 4). She re-presents the kid's voice and by voice, she does

". . . not simply mean the representation of an utterance, but the presentation of a historical self, a full presence that is in and of a particular world." (2005, p. 173)

The professor goes on. She takes the stage carrying plough blades that cut the kid's hands. There is blood in the "kid's hands" or in her performance of those hands. Her goal is

". . . to present and represent subjects as made by and makers of meaning, symbol, and history in their full sensory and social dimensions." (2005, p. 173)

She goes on with the performance. Presenting and re-presenting whatever she thinks is appropriate about what she saw, about what the kid told her, and, more important, about what she and kid constructed together in a dialogical relationship.

Is the professor going to perform the fact that the kid could have only a tiny sandwich for the whole day? That after he eats it, all he can do is just to think about food? I do not know. Ask her.

The performance goes on. The professor believes or creates an audience that

"Whether one (her audience) likes or not the performance, one cannot completely undo or un-know the image and imprint of that voice—inside history—upon their own consciousness once they have been exposed to it through performance. Performing subversive and subaltern voices proclaim existence, within particular locales and discourses, that are being witnessed-entered into one's own experience—and this witnessing cannot be denied." (2005, p. 172)

The professor also believes/imagines that the subject, the Other, in this fictional case, the kid, can benefit by her performance, because the creation of this space—in the moment—of the performance

"... gives evidence not only that 'I am here in the world among you,' but more importantly that 'I am in the world under particular conditions that are constructed and thereby open to greater possibility.'" (2005, p. 173)

And I am not questioning the fact that the professor's performance benefits the subject, the kid. I, too, believe in it.

My questions Who are the Others?
Where are the Others?
The different
The subaltern and subversive body
The professor can re-present the kid because she did the field work. And, it is not her *exclusive* experience.
The professor did the field work and I . . . just lived my life?
The professor has field notes and I have memories,
Can I re-present, perform that kid's hands?
Sure. But it would be what some people call autoethnography.
Whose hands were wounded?
Was my experience as a laboring child alone in the world?
Wasn't I interacting with others?
Wasn't I interacting with other people who touched my life?
Who, besides me, has more right to interpret my experiences in a specific historical moment in relationship to the others who touch my life?
Professor, can't I perform my experience as a 10-year-old white boy illegally working for Trimag?
Yes, but then I would see my work being minimized to what "some people call autoethnography," in a book titled *Critical Ethnography: Method, Ethics, and Performance.*
Where are the Others?
The kid grew up
He is living the "experience-of-becoming" (Conquergood, 1986)
A scholar
It is all about audience
For the most part I do not assume I fit/belong in the system. Can I?
I am an angry man
And my hands are hurting

It is very difficult for me to use this metaphor, because I remember my own pain. I remember the blood in my hands.

As an ethnographer, I more easily use the metaphor "My hands are hurting now." For a poor child, the same metaphor is impossible, because there is no metaphor. When re-presenting the hands, the author/writer/

performer have the luxury, the privilege, the power to use a metaphor. How may I use this metaphor? I am not the poor kid in the factory, or am I?

Professor, can't I say that

"whether one (MY AUDIENCE) likes or not the (AUTOETHNOGRAPHY) performance, one cannot completely undo or un-know the image and imprint of that voice—inside history (MY VOICE, MY BODY)— upon their own consciousness once they have been exposed to it through performance. Performing (MY) subversive and subaltern voices (VOICE) proclaim existence, within particular locales (AND TIME) and discourse, that are being witnessed—entered into one's own experience—and this witnessing cannot be denied." (Madison, 2005, p. 172)

Who is performing the kid?
The black woman/colonized or the American professor/colonizer?
Both?
Neither?

In *Performance, Personal Narratives, and the Politics of Possibility* (1998), Madison quotes Anzaldúa. But she does not quote "La Prieta" (1981). In "La Prieta," Anzaldúa shows how it is impossible to separate the private and the public; the personal and the political; the writing and the body who does it. She shows us that in changing ourselves we do change the world. I have been reading a lot of Anzaldúa's writings. Anzaldúa does not name her work "autoethnography." However, she always goes from her personal life story/experience in a borderland to address her political agenda.

"I can't discount the fact of the thousands that go to bed hungry every night. The thousands that get beaten and killed everyday. The millions of women who have been burned at the stake, the millions who have been raped. Where is justice to this?" (1991, p. 208)

Always positioning and re-positioning herself and Other and self as Other. And not ashamed to say that she is not sure, that she does not know.

"I cannot reconcile the sight of a battered child with the belief that we choose what happens to us, that we create our own word. I *cannot resolve* this in myself. I don't know. I can only speculate, try to integrate the experiences that I've had or have been witness to and try to make sense of why we do violence to each other. In short, I'm trying to create a religion not out there somewhere, but in my gut. I am trying to make peace between what had happened to me, what the world is, and what it should be." (1981, p. 209)

Always performing for her concrete/imaginary/co-performers/community.

"Third world women, lesbians, feminists, and feminist-oriented men of all colors are banding and bonding together . . . only together can we be a force. I see us as a network of kindred spirits, a kind of family." (1981, p. 209)

It is never about Anzaldúa's *exclusive* experience. It is "the pull between what is and what should be," that changing ourselves we change the world.
That

"traveling El Mundo Zurdo path is the path of a two-way movement—a going deep into the self and expanding out into the world, a simultaneous recreation of the self and a reconstruction of society" and more, "I am confused as to how to accomplish this." (1981, p. 208)

That is

"The new mestiza consciousness" (1999, p. 103).
Who are the Others?
Where are the Others?
The different
The subaltern and subversive body

"*Soy un amasamiento*, I am an act of kneading, of uniting and joining that . . . has produced . . . [not only] a creature of darkness and a creature of light but also a creature that questions the definitions of light and dark and give them new meanings." (1999, p. 103)

Positioning and re-positioning her body as self and other as self as other (Alexander, 2005).

"The mixture of bloods and affinities, rather than confusing or unbalancing me, has forced me to achieve a kind of equilibrium. Both cultures deny me a place in *their* universe. *Between them and among others,* I built my own universe, El Mundo Zurdo. I belong to myself and not to one people." (Anzaldúa, 1999, p. 209)

Hers, mine oppositional/differential consciousness (Sandoval, 2000) that can be possible only under Anzaldúa's idea of "between and among" that unifies women/people who do not share the same culture, race, sexual orientation, religion, or even the same ideology. In Anzaldúa's concept "differences do not become opposed to each other" (1981, p. 209).

> "We are the queer groups, the people that don't belong anywhere, not in dominant world nor completely within our own respective cultures. Combined we cover so many oppressions. But the overwhelming oppression is the collective fact we do not fit, and because we do not fit *we are a threat*. Not all of us have the same oppressions, but we emphasize and identify with each other's oppressions. We do not have the same ideology, nor do we derive similar solutions. Some of us are leftists, some of us practitioners of magic. Some of us are both. But these different affinities are not opposed to each other. In El Mundo Zurdo I with my own affinities and my people with theirs can live together and transform the planet." (p. 209)

This is how I see my person in the world, embodied written performing community. This is how I live life as human being, father, and husband. This is how I play scholar. This is how I share, negotiate, and disrupt the power dynamics between my co-performers and me.

I am an angry man   and a loving one
But I'm feeling better now
Not really . . .

When I am doing my embodied/written performance autoethnography from the borders, I cross to the places I live and labor, I am performing community. I/We speak the truth "to the people about the reality of my/our lives" (Collins, 1998, p.198), equip me/us "with the tools I/we need to resist oppression, and move me/us to struggle, to search for justice" (pp. 198–199).

My piece, "Fragments," is not published. However, I already performed it four times. My brown woman Puerto Rican friend, Mariolga, a former U of I grad student and now a professor, was a co-performer in one of my presentations. She brought "Fragments" with her to the International Conference of Community Psychology. There, she gave it to a black male from South Africa, who is a grad student in Australia.

"Fragments" has been re-performed. I have been re-performed.
Performed through them.

"Fragments" is out there in the world, being performed, re-performed, and co-performed.

My bad English is out there, with its improper grammar, spelling, and refusal to hide experience behind euphemisms that protect the oppression imposed by the status quo!

My agency—sharing, creating, shifting, negotiating power in the same and different ways that it does with "Reader 679." I addressed his comments and re-submitted "Fragments." However, as you see, I am writing this performance.

My moving fingers
As a gentle knife

Similar to Denzin (2003), I see performance as sensuous and contingent, where there is a tension between performativity—doing—and performance—done. Where the

> "'I' neither express an interior truth nor am 'I' constructed in discourse. 'I' am 'I' insofar as I speak [my bad English], but insofar as I speak [my bad English] I engage multiple others in the negotiation of [co]performed meanings." (Pollock, 1998, 43)

I try to create embodied/written performances that are evocative, powerful, and vulnerable.

I expose my body.

I take risks

Audre Lorde's words speak into my heart,

> "Those of us who stand outside the circle of this society's definition of acceptable women; those of us who have been forged in the cubicles of difference; those of us who are poor, who are lesbians, who are black, who are older, know that survival is not an academic skill." (1984 p. 112)

My performance autoethnography inhabits the between space of what Foucault coined as

> "'subjugated knowledges' to include all the local, regional vernacular, naïve knowledges at the bottom of the hierarchy—the low Other science." . . . "These are nonserious ways of knowing that the dominant culture *neglects, excludes, represses, or simply fails to recognize.*" (Conquergood, 2002, italics added)

My betweenness is physically expressed, among other things, in my written and spoken English
Between and among
Others
I take risks. I am not protected by a codename—Reader 679.
When I am writing/doing/presenting my work I imagine . . .

"Setting a scene, telling a story, carefully constructing the connections between life and art, experience and theory, evocation and explanation . . . and then letting go, hoping for readers who will bring the same careful attention to your words in the context of their own lives." (Holman Jones, 2005a, p. 765)

> With my bad English
> "I Speak from the Wound in My Mouth,"[2]
> And sometimes
> From the other hole . . .
> Now, I feel much better
>   Cláudio

End of the Letter

ACT 3

BATHROOM

The year is 2001. It is around midnight. I am on the first floor bathroom in Gregory Hall. The bathroom is a mess. School papers are all over the floor. The smell of urine, as always, is strong. But the worst comes from the third toilet on my left. I open the door:

"Shit." I say aloud.

Yes, this is what it is. Shit. Someone did not flush.

"Shit."

It probably has been sitting in there for the whole day. This is a bathroom rule. One opens the door, sees the shit in the bowl. She/He then, closes the door very fast, and looks for another toilet if she/he can. One never flushes . . .

I look around. I want a cigarette. Cannot close the door and run. Have to clean this shit. Why?

I am the janitor. I already cleaned the bathrooms on the third and second floors.

Wait a minute. I am a grad student. I am writing a master thesis.

Got news from you my boy: You might be whatever you want or think you are, but you are, for real, a janitor first!

Yes, this is from where the money comes.

I think about Dani, probably sleeping at home.

I look again at the toilet bowl. Somehow, a front page of *Daily Illini* got stuck in there.

I put my gloves on and throw my hands in there . . .

In the shit.

The smell kicks strong in my nostrils.

But, it is not so bad. I am used to it. I've been smelling shit since I was a kid.

And,

I hang in there no matter what!

I take the paper out of the shit and then . . .

I flush.

"We survive war and conquest; we survive colonization, acculturation, assimilation; we survive beating, rape, starvation, mutilation, sterilization, abandonment, neglect, death of our children, our loved ones, destruction of our land, our homes, our past and future. We survive, and we do more than just survive. We bond, we care, we fight, we teach, we nurse, we bear, we feed, we earn, we laugh, we love, we hang in there, no matter what." (Paula Gunn Allen, 2001)

The year is 2004. I am standing in front of a professor's desk in Gregory Hall waiting. My thoughts are not really here. I am thinking about Dani and her big belly. She's seven months pregnant with our second child. Our first, Analua is 14 months old. I am thinking about my son living in Dani's womb. He's been diagnosed with Down Syndrome.[3]

The professor comes in.

"Sorry I am late."

"That's okay." I replied.

"I asked you here because I cannot accept your final paper."

"But you told me that I could do whatever is important to my project. Autoethnography is what I do. "

"You probably misunderstood my words. What I meant was that you could do an initial interview, analyze it, and then do a follow-up. Or you could choose an event, place and observe and describe it or even a research paper on the theoretical/methodological topics we studied in our class. I gave you and the other students many options. We did not cover autoethnography in our qualitative methods class."

"But I thought . . . I mean autoethnography is part of qualitative research . . . are you negating it?"

"That is not what I'm saying, and I'm not negating it . . ."

At this moment I stop listening. I just don't care anymore.

Whatever . . .

I leave the professor's office.

I am sad and mad . . .

I stop at the bathroom in Gregory Hall. As always, I walk over and flush all toilets and stuff. Then I choose one to pee in.

A whisper:

You know what, professor; I cleaned after your shit and piss. I cleaned after all people who shit and piss in Gregory Hall, my supposedly academic house, and other buildings at U of I.

And,

I'm not going anywhere.

I hang there no matter what!

And then

I flush and go on to wash my hands.

A conversation

"Cláudio, in the last half hour or so, you've been talking about your work in a much more articulated way . . . you even used Foucault! Bring this to your project. Do a more traditional ethnography. Be marketable."

"You don't get it . . . that's not me. This is not who I politically choose to be. Not what I wannabe either. Here, in ICR, there are other students that not only are more qualified than me, but also more willing to do this kind of work. Me? I want to write about bathroom and shit."

Story 6

Newspaper Picture

I heard Tate calling out my name from far away, his country-boy accent rising above the comfortable murmur typical of afternoons in the Square. I lifted my eyes from the newspaper without finishing the sentence. I could see every corner of the Square from where I was sitting but couldn't see Tate. I heard Tate's voice again. I saw people walking in all directions, people gathered around benches and food stands, a bunch of young school kids surrounding the popcorn man, an old woman calmly throwing grains to pigeons in the middle of the Square.

"Here, *tio* Marcelo, here by the newsstand," Tate shouted from the other side of the Square.

I followed the sound of his voice and saw his hands waving in the air.

"Come here, I want to show you somethin'," he shouted again.

His large smile greeted me as I got closer, his finger pointing to a picture in the front page of a local newspaper.

"Look, look! My picture is in the paper! In the front page! Ain't I lookin' good?" he said holding the paper with both hands in front of him.

I saw the newsstand clerk coming toward us. I reached into my pocket and gave the clerk a coin for the paper. He took the coin without looking at me, and staring at Tate he mumbled something I couldn't make out.

"I saw some photographers here yesterday and thought I had left before they could take any pictures of me. But I guess this one was too fast for me!" Tate said laughing and looking at his picture.

"How do you know it's you?" I asked looking at the grey, low-definition picture.

"Are you that blind, *tio*? Look, it's my hair, I'm the only kid aroun' here with this haircut. And this is my nose, look at my nose, can't you recognize it? This is my mouth, see it? I wish they hadn't covered my eyes with this black strip, though. My eyes is what makes me good-lookin', and they covered them!"

"You know they have to cover the eyes of kids under 18, to prevent people from recognizing you."

"Yeah, right! Like this black strip will do that! Everybody knows it's me. It was the popcorn man who told me my picture was in the paper!"

"It's the law. Newspapers are required to do that," I said.

"Sometimes I wonder about you, *tio*! That's not true. Look at these pictures," Tate said opening the paper on page 6. "See? These kids are much younger than me, and they have no black strips coverin' their eyes."

The pictures Tate was showing were at the top of an article about Mother's Day, and they showed young kids laughing in a new playground the city had just built near a high-class neighborhood.

"That's because they're talking about these kids in a nice way," I said unconvinced of my own explanation.

"What are they sayin' about me then?" Tate said looking at me.

I read the headline: CRACK STILL A PROBLEM IN DOWNTOWN.

"It's not really about you, Tate. It's about the crack situation in downtown."

"But I was not smokin' crack yesterday! I haven't smoked in more than a week!" he said turning to his picture again. "I'm just walkin'. Look, anyone can see I'm smokin' no crack!"

"I know..."

"Maybe that's why the street educators keep tellin' us to stay away from photographers and reporters," Tate said in my pause.

"I think you're right, Tate."

He looked at his picture again and shook his head.

"I was not even smokin'..."

I read a few lines of the article over his shoulders. It said that the street kids were keeping the demand of crack high in downtown and that...

"But I'll keep this picture anyways!" Tate said grinning. "It's not every day I appear in the front page of a paper. I'll give it to my mom next time I visit her up north."

"You'd better cut off the article," I said smiling at him.

"I wish they'd taken a profile shot... that's my best angle," Tate said looking at the picture with examining eyes.

Notes

1. I do not know exactly why, but I will avoid using Madison's name. I really like her and it just doesn't sound right.
2. Mary E. Weems's book and dissertation title.
3. Although our son was born without Down Syndrome, we kept receiving informational mail from the doctor's office for several months after his birth.

Chapter 5

BETWEENNESS IN RACE

ACT 4
───────────────────────────────────────

WORDS

Ah! Homens de pensamento,
Não sabereis nunca o quanto
Aquele humilde operário (*menino*)
soube naquele momento! (Vinicius De Moraes, "O Operário em
   Construção")

Racism,
Black, white, red, yellow,
Is it about color?
Smoking another cigarette,
Is racism about skin color?
Roni didn't know
Neither did I.

Remembrances of things that I try to understand
In a world full of deaths . . .
Coffee, cigarettes, and memories
"Ah! Men of knowledge
You will never know
As much as that operário (*kid*)
Knew at that moment."[1]

Roni and I didn't know
We never heard the word
Racism, racism, racism!
But we wanted chocolate
We desired it,
We stole it.
The brown kid wearing just a pair of shorts went first
The white boy went after
Security was following the black? Brown? kid
Hell, the white one stole the candies!!!!

Drinking coffee, smoking . . .
I cannot remember being told about the big word
Racism, racism, racism!!!
But, the boys knew . . .
That they were different
They were in the same shit
But the black? Brown child stinks more.
But, the weekend before last I have in MY HOUSE, in my own home
A Brazilian man of knowledge
A white Brazilian man who is going to be a professor next fall
A Brazilian man who owns a gorgeous apartment in one of the most beautiful beaches . . .
In Brazil
Saying that Brazil is a country free of racism!!!
What the fuck is that?
I don't need this shit! Not in my own home.
But you know what
It is natural
Whites are better than Blacks, Yellows, Reds, or Browns
And that is not racism, it is life
But deep in my soul I looked inside that white Brazilian man and
We do not come from the same country (there are so many Brazils)
We cannot be made of the same stuff
He is not one of my own
He did not have a friend called Roni!

"Ah! Men of knowledge
You will never know
As much as that operário (*kid*)
Knew at that moment."
Poetry is knowledge
Is salvation

And for god's sake
Is revolutionary.
It goes with dreams
It goes with desire
It not just about needs
And needs are all that the oppressed people dare to ask for
It is a tool for liberation, freedom, and democracy
But the boys (Roni and I), we didn't know it either.

Marx somewhere explained
The alienation of the workers
And how they would discover the power that they have,
Or at least, it seems to be
Roni and I didn't know the words
But fuck, we knew a lot!
We had dreams
He wants to be a truck driver!
Later, we were stealing pieces of cars
Three cops came in our way
Roni was brown or ebony
It really didn't matter, or it probably did
Two cops went after him
Just one after the white kid
Roni got caught by the cops, by the system,
Trapped in the world of men
And I tell you now, he was done for life!!!

"Ah! Men of knowledge
You will never know
As much as that operário (*kid*)
Knew at that moment."
And they were men!
Men who made the knowledge!
White men!
Men of power!
White men in a poor country!
White men somewhere!
Even those kids were the oppressors
In their own small world!
Please, please, please hooks:
Never let me forget the pain.
Please, please, please June Jordan:
Never let me forget your words:

"I am struggling to make absolutely manifest
A principled commitment
To the principles of freedom
And equality" (1998, p. 179)

Next time I saw Roni
Rape, abuse, and beating were all over his face
There was no need for words . . .
We still did not know them . . .
But fuck, we did not cry
And I am not going to cry again, not now, not for those fucking men of knowledge and power!!!
Cultural studies, hegemony, post colonialism, interpretative research, feminism,
Help me now! Do let me cry!
Let me fight!
Let me be revolutionary!
Let me be poetry!

Story 7

Too Blond, Too White

"I know who you are," said a soft young voice.

"Hi," I said looking up from my notepad.

"You're *tio* Marcelo, and you take care of the street kids," she said sitting down in front of me.

I looked at her for a moment, trying to imagine how this well-dressed, Nike-shoes-wearing blonde girl, who spoke like an educated person, knew the same kids I knew.

"How do you know my name?" I asked her.

"The kids told me. The *tio* with blue eyes and long hair," she said smiling.

"Who do you know?" I asked, growing more and more curious about how this middle-class-looking girl knew the kids and me.

"She's my sister!" Celi said, showing up from nowhere and sitting down next to Tara with a plate of rice, beans, and grilled chicken in her hands. "Isn't it true, Tara?"

"Of course it's true," Tara told Celi and then, looking at me, shook her head no as soon as Celi turned her attention to the plate of food.

They talked for a while. Tara wanted to know what Celi had been doing, if she needed anything, acting like an older sister. Celi didn't say much and kept her eyes down at the plate on her lap the whole time. But there was something different in the way Celi was responding to Tara, a sweetness, a respect that I'd never seen come from Celi before.

Tara asked if Celi would like to go home with her. And Celi said yes! It was the first time I heard Celi respond so kindly to a person offering her a place to stay—but then I'd never heard anyone offer their own place.

"But you'd have to promise not to take anything from home. Do you think you can do that? I know how hard it is when you're in a craving mood," Tara said gently.

I frowned as I waited for Celi to explode and get mad at Tara.

"I promise," Celi said without looking up, just as gently.

"You can't stay on the streets anymore, Celi. Look at you, so pretty but so dirty. Look at your feet, Celi, all black and scarred. You definitely need a shower! We are going to do something about that, right?" Tara said, lifting Celi's chin softly with the tip of her fingers.

"Right," Celi replied, lowering her head again.

"And finish your food!" Tara said smiling at Celi.

Tara got to her feet and, excusing herself, crossed the Square to talk to two young men, who were drug dealers according to Celi. I was baffled at how docile Celi had been with Tara. Celi left shortly after that, but I stuck around the Square a little longer hoping to get a chance to talk more to Tara.

"So, how do you know Celi?" I asked Tara when she came back to where I was sitting.

"From here. The streets. I lived here for a couple of months last year." She paused. "I was adopted by a couple when I was 10, five years ago. They are nice. They live in a nice house in a nice neighborhood. But they are older and didn't let me do anything. I wanted to go out after school, or at night, but they wouldn't let me go. But then I started to come here, to downtown, and started to hang out with Celi and the other kids. One day we had a fight and I left home. I hung out with Celi and the others for almost three months. It was fun, but also hard, you know? The street has good things: you are free to do whatever you want, you don't have to go to school, you can sleep whenever you want, you smoke drugs and have lots of fun with the guys and girls, you can date whoever you want," she said suddenly laughing.

"But there are also many bad things: you get beat up by the police, security guards, and other adults, you get harassed by drug dealers because you don't have the money to pay the debts. Sometimes you don't even want to be in a situation where you owe money to the dealers, but they come all friendly, give you the drug and say it's a gift, it's free. Then next time they see you, they say you owe them money for it. They say they don't remember giving it to you for free, that you are trying to rip them off, and blah blah blah. It's screwed up!

"Then you are always dirty and sick, and there are no places for a shower anymore, to wash your clothes, or to see a nurse. There is no real freedom on the streets, you just think you are free but you are not! How can you get into places like a nightclub when you are so dirty. When my adoptive parents found out I was here, they came and asked me to go back home. I did. I was ready to leave the streets. I wanted to be able to pee in peace, without worrying someone was seeing me."

"Did things get better at home after that?" I asked, already impressed with her.

"It did get better! They are letting me go out and date this boy, who is black. They didn't want me to date him before, and that was one of the reasons I left home in the first place. I like him. I really do!

"Now I just got a part-time job, in the afternoons, here in downtown. I want to do well at school, too. I want to be responsible now so I can have a good future."

"Good for you," I said with a large smile.

"Are you going to help Celi?" she asked after a while.

"We're trying to get a place for her in that recovery place in Rio, you know?"

"Yeah. She says she's my sister, but it's not true. I let her say that because it's a sign of friendship and I like it. I've tried to get her out of the streets, too, but she's so difficult and restless. I bring her clothes sometimes, but she always exchanges them for crack! I gave her a brand new Nike pair for Christmas and a few days later she was shoeless again," she said shaking her head.

"I even thought about bringing her home with me, but my parents think it's dangerous. They are afraid she will get crazy without crack and will steal things from the house. It's possible, you know? I've seen her get desperate, because she doesn't have a stone with her. She'll do anything!"

"You two still talking?" Celi said coming over licking a popsicle.

"Tara is telling me how she got out of the streets," I said quickly.

"She's lucky to have rich parents," Celi said, perhaps figuring out I already knew they were not blood-related sisters.

Right then we all spotted Dalva on the other side of the Square, walking toward us. Tara seemed very nervous all of a sudden and said she had to go.

"No worries, Tara, you with me. Dalva won't do anything to you," Celi said and Tara moved a little closer to her.

I didn't know why Tara was afraid of Dalva. I'm still not sure, though I got a clue after I saw many of the girls interacting with Tara during my time in downtown Campinas.

"That one just lost her watch," Celi said cracking up, pointing to a woman who was being shadowed by Dalva.

Dalva came to where we were sitting with a watch in her hand. She showed it to us and put it in her pocket. I looked away. She said hi.

"You look like a rich bitch, Tara," Dalva said showing her disgust in seeing Tara.

Tara winced and didn't say anything. Dalva stared at Tara then started to talk to Celi and Lucio, who had just arrived. Tara left after a few minutes, when Dalva was distracted making plans with Lucio to go and buy crack with the money she'd get from the watch.

I saw Tara again three days later near the Spiritist news stand, on a corner of Rosario Square. I'd been talking to Grace and another street educator. Grace'd broken up with her boyfriend—gigolo?—and was on the streets again. She'd been beat up by a security guard and her left ear was full of pus, and Marga, the other street educator, was trying to convince Grace that she needed to see a doctor.

"Sorry I didn't say hi to you earlier, Grace, but I was busy running errands for the Spiritist stand," Tara said approaching us timidly.

"Get lost Tara, I don't wanna see your white ass here," Grace snapped.

"I'm really sorry, Grace! I was running late and didn't greet anybody. . . ."

"Sorry my ass! You think you can go around snubbing the rest of us just because now you wear clean clothes and smell good?" Grace said measuring Tara from head to toe with her eyes.

"Hey, be nice Grace, she's apologizing," Marga said.

"Bitch," Grace said looking at Tara with contempt.

"Grace!" Marga said like a mother scolding a disobedient child.

"I didn't mean to snub you . . .," Tara began to say.

"Get the fuck outta here 'fore I kick your ass!" Grace yelled.

"Sorry . . .," Tara said walking away with a sad face.

"Why were you so mean to her?" Marga asked.

"She thinks she's better than us . . . next time I see her I'll steal her Nikes and beat the shit out of her."

I didn't say anything the whole time, but I felt bad for Tara. It was her first day at work.

A week passed without things getting any better for Tara. Indeed, they got worse.

"I'm very worried about Tara," Nancy, the woman who took care of the Spiritist newsstand, told me.

"Are the other girls still giving her a hard time?" I asked.

"To put it mildly," she said shaking her head yes. "Tara's job is to carry things from here to the banks and our main office. She has to walk all around downtown. And she's always running into one of her old friends, if you can call them that, and they invariably harass her, calling her names that make my eyes want to pop out. Then sometimes, when Tara is helping me here, Grace or Dalva will come by and call her names. I don't know what to do. . . . But the worst thing happened today!" Nancy said, sitting down next to a man who owns the newspaper stand next to Nancy's and who was visiting her.

"A woman carrying a baby came here today looking for Tara. She looked like a drug dealer, if you ask me. She threatened Tara, saying something I didn't quite understand, and hit her really hard in the head. All of this right here inside my business! The woman then said she won't let Tara work here and left without even looking at me. I'm very scared . . .," Nancy said looking at nothing.

"The only way out of this mess is to kill all these kids," the man said without betraying any emotion.

I stared down at him.

"You see, they don't want to be helped. There are a bunch of institutions and shelters in town trying to help them, but they are here on the streets, terrorizing old ladies and scaring our clients away," he said calmly, rubbing his beard.

"And how is killing the kids going to help?" I asked trying to keep my cool.

"Look at Tara's case, for example. She's a good girl who wants to make her life better, but she will have to quit this job 'cause those little rascals keep pestering her. The old folks will be able to come to the Square in peace and read the paper without having to worry nonstop about their watches and wallets. The corners of the Square wouldn't smell like pee and the ground wouldn't be covered with crumbs of food they throw everywhere."

"Killing is not right," Nancy said.

"It's the only solution though . . . these kids were born bad and there is nothing you can do to help them. Look at all the shelters that close down, because they don't have enough kids. In the meantime downtown is full of them. I grew up very poor and knew a lot of kids like that. I worked hard and got out of the slums. But kids like them don't want to work, don't want to change their lives . . . they like to be bad!" The man's voice was calm throughout.

"I wonder if Tara owes that woman money," I said to Nancy trying to change the conversation.

"I don't know . . . the woman said something about Tara being a bad example for the other kids," Nancy said.

"I wonder what we can do to protect Tara," I said.

"Killing all the kids is the only solution, I tell you," the man said looking at me, smiling.

"People like *you* are the ones who should be killed!" I said completely losing it.

"No, no, my friend, not me . . . them!" he said emphasizing the word *them*, still smiling.

I said goodbye to Nancy and left, my legs weak with anger, already feeling bad for having lost my temper with someone I knew nothing about.

More than a month later, I heard from another street educator that Tara was at the city's homeless shelter, a place where only adults are allowed to stay. She had been scared away from downtown by the drug dealer after a few days on her job and had to quit. She'd left home again shortly after that. I had to take Lara to the homeless shelter that night, and knew I was going to see Tara there.

"Hi *tio* Marcelo!" Tara said hugging me tight.

"I heard you were here," I said pulling her gently away.

"Yeah, things didn't work out well," she said unsmiling. "But I'll be taken to another family. She was my teacher a few years ago. She likes me very much. I think my mom, my adoptive mother, somehow got in touch with my teacher and told her about me leaving home again. My teacher called the Juvenile Court and asked if she could take me home with her. I'm gonna see her tomorrow, then she's gonna take me with her. I think I'm gonna get along better with her than with my adoptive parents, you know. They are old and don't know how to handle an adolescent these days. They're too strict. My teacher is young, and she's used to being around kids. I hope she'll let me go out," she said smiling again.

I told her I was happy that she was not going to the streets again.

"No kidding! The kids were being really mean to me. I don't know why . . . I never did anything to them," she said biting her nails.

"Maybe they were jealous 'cause you had a job and you're going straight," I risked.

"Maybe . . . but they never said anything about my job . . . all of a sudden they started to say things about my white skin and blond hair . . . they called me albino and other worse things."

"It's good that you will soon have a place to live."

"Yeah, I'm afraid of staying here," she said looking around us. "There are a bunch of men here and they keep looking at me in a funny way, sometimes whistling when I walk by them."

"I brought Lara here tonight, so you will be safe hanging out with her," I said.

"I'm worried about that too, *tio*," she said looking at me with anxious eyes.

"Why? Was she calling you names too?" I asked, not very surprised.

"No, but I heard that she wanted to beat me up. She thinks I was telling the kids that she's hustling to get money. But I never said anything! Even if I knew anything I wouldn't say that to anybody. I think they were just saying it to make me look bad. They know Lara would want to beat me up for that. It's a lie! But I'm afraid Lara will not believe me," Tara said.

"I'll talk to her before I leave," I said.

I said goodbye to Tara and started looking for Lara around the old building. I found her sitting in the dining room. I told her that Tara was in the shelter and I was counting on her, Lara, to take care of Tara.

"Don't worry, *tio*, I won't beat her up. I was mad at her because Grace and Dalva said Tara was saying I was going out with men for money. But I know they were lying just to get me mad at Tara. I'll take care of her, *tio*. I'm afraid of being alone here too," Lara said smiling.

It turned out that the teacher's family gave up on adopting Tara, because they were afraid the drug dealers were going to find her there and do something bad to the family. I asked Tara one more time why the dealers were so angry with her, to the point that the family was afraid of retaliation. She was evasive in her answer, and I learned nothing new. She said that at least Lara was treating her well and they were helping each other.

Lara told me, separately, that Tara was hitting on all the men in the shelter, teasing them, and was afraid they were going to get Tara by force. Lara also told me that Tara was getting drunk and high almost every night. I asked Lara to keep taking care of her.

The next time I saw Tara, a few days later in the homeless shelter, she was so affectionate that I felt embarrassed. She kept on hugging and kissing me, talking non-stop and seeming not to listen to a word I said.

"Why don't you adopt me, *tio*. I will be really good to you," she said in a mischievous way.

I told her I couldn't adopt her, trying to free myself politely from her embrace. Leaving the shelter was quite a task that day.

I contacted her adoptive mother. I asked her if she would take Tara back, saying that I would look for psychiatric treatment for Tara. She agreed to receive Tara back in her home, and I got an appointment with a psychiatrist friend of mine, for free. But Tara left home again before she could ever see the psychiatrist. She moved in with a young man, who was a drug-dealer-pimp according to Grace.

"The whitey will get in some trouble soon if she doesn't stop hitting on other people's boyfriends," Grace said.

I just looked at Grace, waiting for her to tell me more about Tara.

"She hit on my boyfriend," she said looking at me. "Why do you think that woman, the dealer, wanted to get a piece of her?"

Act 5

The Tales of Conde, Zezao, Master Cláudio, and Cláudio

"'There was no confrontation, as had been said by the media. What happened was a massacre. Conde was walking from his house and then he was surrounded by fifteen Sao Paulo's fans. They fractured

Conde's head in seven different places,' said Marcio Rosa, member of soccer fan club *Torcida Jovem Amor Maior*." (10/17/05, *Agencia Futebol Interior*, www.futebolinterior.com.br)

I feel empowered by this "new writing," this new method. Therefore, I am rejecting my old—not so old—formal academic training. I dare to write/perform in a different manner. I am performing my entire body, which is fragmented/ing represented, in my surreal postmodern "reality," to uncover the apparatus of culture and power that operate as structures of oppression. And yes, I am inviting you to dare, too. "If you are looking for a complete story, you are not going to find it here. If your 'trained mind' is looking for the whole thing, that is not here either." (Moreira, 2008a, p. 677)

Characters/Voices

ZEZAO: This is how I named Conde in my master's thesis, when I was concerned about keeping Conde's anonymity.
CONDE: For my doctoral dissertation, I returned to his real nickname, Conde. Conde's official name is Anderson Tomas Ferreira, and he was a Ponte Preta Soccer fan who had helped me in my fieldwork in Brazil.
MASTER CLÁUDIO: This is a representation of me when I was a Master's student in the Department of Leisure Studies at the University of Illinois.
CLÁUDIO: This representation reflects where I was later on—a doctoral student at the Institute of Communications Research at the University of Illinois.

I: First Words

Conde is dead.
Conde was beaten to death.
He was 26 years old.
He was a soccer fan.
Conde is dead, but Zezao is alive.
When I first wrote about Conde, I named him Zezao.
Yes,
I changed his name.
I was/am the powerful researcher.
And Conde?
He was just the subject.

It is the end of year.
I am at my office at the U of I.

Looking at my computer screen
With my moving fingers
Why write about Conde?
Why write about this soccer fan?
He is dead . . .
Conde is fucking dead, and I want to yell it across my locked window!
And I am struggling to get the window open.

ZEZAO I

Sunday at noon. It is an important time for Brazilian soccer. Millions of Brazilians are in front of their TVs. They are cooking out in their houses with their families and friends or in the bar with their buddies or in the swimming pool of their clubs. Even those who are working have small radios near their ears to listen to the sports shows. There is only one topic of conversation: their beloved soccer teams. It seems like everyone knows about the history of his/her team or players. They know the standings of the team, the problems with the stars or managers, the scandals, how much money the players make, and so on. Discussions or arguments about which is the best team or if a player deserves all the money that he makes never end. The atmosphere is different from other days. Soccer is in the air. If the national team were playing that day you could walk naked in the streets and no one would notice.

The whole country stops to watch the games. But the poor working-class people go and *live* the game. The word "watch" cannot describe their actions. They really "live" it, become part of it. Soccer is in their "blood," one might say. Many say that it is the reason for their lives, that through soccer they can feel alive. They breathe soccer.

Jose, or better Zezao, is one of these people. This Sunday, he is going to meet his pals at the bar; he woke up a couple of hours earlier with a huge hangover. "Better start drinking again, so this fucking headache goes away," he thought. Walking to the bar, he gets excited about the game. His beloved Ponte Preta is going to play this afternoon. Walking in the streets of his neighborhood, he keeps thinking about the game. The streets do not have any kind of pavement, and Zezao is not paying attention to the kids who are playing close to the sewer lines that run free in the landscape.

In the bar, which is just a room with some tables, his friends are waiting for him. All of them belong to the fan club of the Ponte Preta soccer team *Torcida Jovem—Amor Maior*, which means "Youth Fans—The Biggest Love."[2] There, in the bar, they drink *pinga* (a popular Brazilian cheap liquor made with sugar cane) and a few beers. "Just warming up for the game," one of them says.

From the bar they go to the bus stop. They are dressed with the team's T-shirt, and Zezao has his fan club T-shirt under this. Only a few fan clubs are considered outlaws, but none of them are allowed to have their members wearing their clothes and flags in the stadium. Zezao's plan is to go unnoticed by the cops and, once in the stadium, show off his shirt (and, of course, his courage).

Conde I

> "The next moment in qualitative inquiry will be one at which the practices of qualitative research finally move, without hesitation or encumbrance, from the personal to the political." (Denzin, 2000, p. 261)

I am lying down, having my left arm tattooed by Drigo. Conde introduced him to me few days ago. Drigo plays the drum during the games. His sister used to be Conde's girlfriend. Conde is sitting near us, very excited by yesterday's fight. Early, we have been recollecting the last day's adventure. Now he is bringing back other stories:

"Remember that day Drigo? Your sister and I had that big fight. I got stoned really bad. Then, you came to pick me up for the game. Man, I was bad that day. *Virado na encrenca*.[3] At halftime we went to piss. Remember Drigo?"

"Yep, I do. We were peeing when that sonofabitch got in to the bathroom saying shit about Ponte Preta. You jumped on him so fast that he had no fucking idea of what was happening." Drigo starts laughing.

"I beat him gooooooood."

Looking at me, Drigo says: "Gringo," then pointing to Conde. "This guy was so high, that he didn't even put his dick back in his pants. One minute he was peeing. The next, he was beating the shit out of the motherfucker," laughing even harder. "Conde was beating the guy with his dick swinging all over."

"Hey, I forgot, okay?" said Conde, also laughing. "You know, Gringo, I was just looking for something and then, that guy show up. I just realize that my dick was of my pants after the guy passed out in the floor. Then I saw his Santos hat with blood all over and took it. The hat was my prize. Later, when I walked to Drigo's crib, I left the hat over the fence for his sister Tania. She would know that I've been thinking about her. . . . One day we're gonna get together again."

Zezao II

When Zezao and his friends enter the bus, it is already full of fans singing and dancing. Regular people, or *povao* (how the fans call them), do not take the buses that go to the stadium. They know better. After three stops, the bus is so full that the driver skips the next stop even after seeing that there is a group of four or five fans waiting. The fans in the bus get irate.

"Go back and pick them up, you asshole," screams one.

Others begin to break some seats. Zezao goes straight to the driver.

"Look here, motherfucker. You gonna stop the bus and wait for my bros. And you gonna stop for every Ponte Preta's fan till we arrived in the stadium. Do that! Otherwise, I gonna beat you so bad, that even your slut mom will not recognized your sorry ass!"

After that, things get "squared way." The fans "own" the bus. At the traffic light a "careless" woman stops her car near the bus. The fans go to the windows screaming all kinds of things to her, from "you are the daughter-in-law of my mom's dreams" to "hot girl I wanna your pussy." She quickly closes the window and moves the car, even if the light is still red.

Master Cláudio I

Soccer has a strong role in Brazilian society. In the 1970s, while the military Brazilian government was killing the "communist enemies of the country," the fans were in the streets celebrating the victory of the national soccer team. The fans were proud of being Brazilian; "We are the only country in the world that has won three world championship trophies," they would boast.

Soccer is an important thing to large majority of Brazilians, but it is much more important for the working-class. As Piracicaba (a Ponte Preta fan that you are going to meet) says:

> "Gringo, July is the worst month of the year, and you know why? There is no soccer. Every July, I get lost. Soccer is everything to us. Tell this to your boss. I've seen people sell their shoes in order to get tickets for a Ponte Preta game. I have a girlfriend. Do you know why we're still together? She knows better. She never would question my love for my team and for my fan club? If you don't believe me ask around...." This passion for soccer has race, social class, and gender aspects. It is black or mixed of race; it is poor; it is male, where the female supports her partner.

Zezao III

Zezao is having a good time. He can barely remember the headache. He is looking into the streets, seeing the regular fans get excited. He gets off the bus and together with his buddies walks in the direction of the fan clubhouse. The house is in front of the stadium, less than a block from its main entrance. More than one hundred people are singing, dancing, drinking, whatever. This is a *festa* ("party"). There are fireworks, announcing that the fan club is ready. Zezao has two wishes: first, that Ponte Preta wins; second, that he finds some fans from the other team or better, that he finds a fan from Guarani[4] and beats the shit out of him.

As they enter in the stadium, Zezao puts his fan Club shirt inside his pants, under his underwear. The police are watching everything carefully. Some cops are on horseback, controlling the streets. Thousands of people are doing what they like most: attending their team's game. The fans get in line, and the cops pat them down. There is a lot of pushing, and Zezao passes through the inspection without a problem.

In a part of the stadium that is informally reserved for the fan club, Zezao shows off his trophy (his fan club uniform) and the fans go crazy. Another fan, Cobra (snake) takes a shirt from the rival Guarani and sets it on fire causing another ovation from the fans. Cobra was a street kid and has spent some time in jail, and the other fans respect him a lot. They respect his wisdom, since he had survived in jail. But fan club members respect Cobra more for his role in the games. Cobra does not watch the game. During the game, he faces the fan club crowd so people can see what song he is singing and follow it. His job is not easy. The goal here is not only to get the fan club involved but also to get everybody else to cheer for Ponte Preta. Cobra does it. Usually all the fans sing the song that he chooses.

Master Cláudio II

Brazilian fans show these *festa* characteristics everywhere, turning any event in a carnival. As Robert E. Rinehart observed at the Olympic Games:

> "Brazilian fans bring their own creation of carnival atmosphere. They fill the metro cars, chanting and singing, laughing and dancing into the night while the train runs. One 6-feet-4-inch woman jokingly banters at the Coca-Cola Pin Trading Center with a pin trader about having the AIDS virus; otherwise she would gladly have Sex with him. During the first day's swimming prelims, a large group of uniformed Brazilians (wearing bright yellow shirts with 'Brasilia' imprinted on the back in green) play music, sing, and cheer for their (and some other Latin American) competitors. At the spectacle, they are themselves a spectacle. In a sense, they provide role reversal: swimmers (now tennis players too—a Brazilian named Gustavo Kuerten is the number one—so Brazilians have invaded the tennis courts), unused to anything but applause and an occasional plastic horn, look up to find a seven-piece orchestra playing *merengue* (samba) music during the most important meet of their lives. The Brazilians seem to take the whole areas; they have no qualms about bringing a Mardi Gras atmosphere to the Olympics." (1998, p. 132)

Brazilian fans bring this carnival atmosphere everywhere they go; it is part of being Brazilian. To watch a soccer game with around 100,000 people dancing and singing for their team is not only beautiful, it is also spectacle.

Zezao IV

During the game, the fan club does not sit or stop singing. Often a fan club member gets beaten, because he stops cheering. For the fan club members there are always two competitions. What is the best team, and who has the best fan club? Provocative songs are being sung on both sides as each fan club tries to out do the other in demonstrating loyalty. The fans love it.

Ponte Preta wins this game. Fans are really proud of their team. Then the inevitable happens. Outside the stadium the fan clubs from Ponte Preta and Guarani meet each other.[5] Both teams have won, both fans are happy, and, ironically, both are looking for a fight. Zezao and his friends run straight into the Guarani fans. The fight begins. Regular fans are running away trying to find a safe place. The police take action using horses and throwing tear gas bombs. Fans throw rocks, bricks, and so on. Cobra received a rock in his face. Bleeding through his nose and mouth, he continues to fight.

Suddenly, someone starts shooting. The confusion is immense. People are screaming like they are in hell. The police are beating everybody. Zezao finds his way out. Members of both fan clubs know that it's time to run. If they stay they will go to jail. However, it does not end the fights. The fans are going to fight all the way back home. They are going to break everything that they find in their way: buses, cars, and a park bench.

"Let's go the bus station. Those motherfuckers need to go home. We still can kick more asses," says Zezao.

"Who did the shooting?" asked someone.

"João was the one who shot.[6] The cops caught him. Let's go, baby. We are still in business now!" says Zezao to his pals. Then they move toward the bus station.

II: Master Cláudio and Conde—The Scholar and the Fan

> Campinas: "Conde's burial, carried through in the cemetery of Amarais, in Campinas, was followed by approximately 400 people, the majority belonging to the soccer Fan Club named *Torcida Jovem Amor Maior*. The Fans had not wanted to speak of the subject, but they leave in the air the possibility of revenge." (10/18/05, *Journal Estado de São Paulo*, www.estadao.com.br)
>
> São Paulo, 10/20/05: "It is not possible to coexist with human beings (they for sure do not act as one) that instead of lamenting a death, cry out that they go to kill and to avenge. That was the case in the burial of Anderson Tomas Ferreira, a.k.a. Conde. . . . The

laws are very weak, the legislators do not disclose their opinion or actions, and when they do, they make it in a demagogic form, the police civil, but we know of its limitations. . . . The Ministry of Sport created a group of studies aiming to evaluate and to present suggestions for the violence that surrounds soccer. But the work is very slow and we have the necessity of acting with urgency. The Organized Soccer Fan Clubs are the great villains of the problem. By the way, it has been some time that they have been forbidden to act officially. However, in stadiums these fans were in the same places and sang the same hymns of war . . . and the authorities saw to that and they did not do anything." (Márcio Bernardes is anchor of the *Net Transamérica de Rádio*, commentator of the TV Culture and university professor—www.marciobernardes.com.br)

Master Cláudio III

As I said before, my argument in this study is that the stories of the fans who belong to organized soccer fan clubs are not part of the dominant discourse in Brazilian society. Then, what people know about these fans (received knowledge) is a part of an over-simplified, hegemonic, and oppressive representation.

You, dear reader, might have thought after reading the introduction that these fans are really bloodthirsty. You might still think that it is right. We hope that you might change your opinion when you finish reading this work.

The fans often are seen by the tales of their lived experiences expressed in the dominant narratives such as fights, drug consumption, criminal infractions, sexual promiscuity, and so on. This is also how they perceive themselves, how they try to make sense of their lives.

Conde II

You know Gringo, the thing that I hate most is people's faces. That look you know. That look that an old lady used to give to me when I was a kid. Like she feels sorry for me . . . "Oh, look this poor cute little robber!". . . That's what the look says. Or the look that a well dressed men used to give, like I was a piece of shit, that I was ready to rob him, that I have a very contagious illness and I am not allowed to get close to "the good people." There were times that I robbed people just because of the look in their faces. But it doesn't happen anymore. Not anymore. Now people are scared. I can see the fear in their faces, and to tell the truth Gringo, it is much better! I mean, much better. Other day, I took the bus wearing my fan club uniform. I sat in front of an old lady and kept looking at her. It was funny. It seemed that she had ants in her pants. She couldn't stop moving. Less than 5 minutes later she moved to another seat.

Master Cláudio IV

Conde does not see the hegemony in Brazilian society. He also does not see the dominant discourses and narratives. What he sees and interacts with are everyday values and beliefs. Since these values and beliefs are hegemonic, they are perceived as natural, as "God's will." Conde also constructs his social identities through the looks that he receives by the "good people." Conde knows that he is "bad," because he is not able to fit in the available stories. School, jobs, good life, and family are things that are not for him. Not only is Conde not able to get them, but also he thinks (to a certain extent) that he does not *deserve* them. Conde knows that he is "bad," because he does "bad" things. Let's take sexual behavior as an example. Once he told me that after he was expelled from the Brazilian Army, he had not been able to find a decent job. When someone is expelled from the Brazilian army, he has a code number in his ID saying it, so it is hard to find a regular job. Conde's captain in the army found out that he was having sex with a man. That man was giving money to him. Then, Conde spent some time in a military jail and afterward was expelled from the Brazilian Army. In Brazilian homophobic society, especially in the Army, Conde's actions are unacceptable. Paradoxically, Conde shows the same hatred toward homosexuality when he tells me his story. Let's hear the Brazilian macho.

Conde III

Gringo, when my little brother and sisters were sick, it was that money that I used for buying medicine, you know. I like women. I am "macho." I am not a fucking faggot! I don't know how many times during sex, I had to imagine the happy face of my mom, brothers, and sisters when I bring some meat to them. I had to think about it otherwise my dick wouldn't do the job. Me and my family had some good Sunday lunches thanks to that fucking money, you know? My captain gave me a big lecture, full of bullshit. At the end I asked him if he would give some money if one of my brothers gets sick. I asked him, if he would give some cheap meat so my family could have a decent meal. His answer was about school, jobs opportunities, and shit like that. That's BULLSHIT, YOU KNOW GRINGO! BULLSHIT! What can school do for a guy like me? No one cares, no one ever did!

Master Cláudio V

Since Conde feels that he does not fit in society, he resists it. He fights. He sells his body. He sells drugs. He struggles for survival. He looks for other ways to achieve respect and a better life. He "gives the finger" to values, beliefs, and looks that he receives. But he knows that he is "bad." And "knowing that he is bad," he (even without noticing it) supports all the hegemonic values and beliefs in our society. Conde has Freire's notion of "being" or "nothingness." Since Conde cannot be "something human" he must be "nothing." For changes to take place, we must all realize that there is more than just "being" or "nothingness," that there is the possibility of "being more human" negating the "nothingness." Hopefully, my stories might help to transform this scenario.

Cláudio I

Can you tell? Conde sold his body! And I? Why am I still telling instead of showing!

III: Master Cláudio—Discovered by Autoethnography

Lately, I have opened my performances with the same two statements: "I have not chosen performance autoethnography as a method, it has chosen me" and "Do not expect this performance to make sense to you. My life does not make sense. Other lives I have loved and interacted with do not make sense either. Why in hell does life have to make sense so it can fit in academia?

Remember, life is fragments . . .

I was "discovered" by autoethnography while writing my Master's thesis. Suddenly, memories that were supposed to be buried came to life, haunting me in my everyday existence. Without noticing, those memories, represented in my thesis, provoked comments such as: "There is too much of your own narratives in this thesis. I do not want to know about your life, I want to know about the other lives that you studied. This is not a good social science."

However, those comments did not make sense at all; the only way I could write about "the Other" was through my own lived experience.

> "Hence, I started to look for a scholarship that would allow me to write about myself . . .
> Then, I heard about Norman Denzin . . .
> Then, my love affair with performance autoethnography started . . .
> Here again I look to Holman Jones for help. How can I write about performance autoethnography, without performing one? She says I cannot. Hence, where is the performance?" (Moreira, 2008a, p. 668 Except from "Fragments")

Master Cláudio VI

As you may have noticed, there is a lot of my own story in this project. I have been criticized for it. Hearing such things as, "Okay, I know about you but how about the fans?" has happened very often. The point is that I do not see myself as only the researcher in this project. I am also a "subject" of it. Through my own lived experience I make sense of my life and then make sense of the fans' lived experiences that I am interacting with. The result of this interaction is this work, especially the stories that I am telling. Even in the stories, I am a character in them. I am in action. I am not just telling facts.

Planning this study, I was looking for a form of writing my research that could allow me to go beyond the constraints of traditional research. As I said before, I was trying to decrease the distance between the "real" and "academic" worlds. I was looking for a more personal relationship with the people that I study. I wanted my work to contain life, emotions, and smells. I was looking for a work that contained "humanity." Also, during all my life, I have been concerned with the stories that we can tell and the ones that we cannot, and furthermore, how we can tell a story and how we cannot tell one.

I found out that many stories from my childhood were not good enough to be told. It seems that there is a pact—if someone does "well" in life, he/she is supposed to forget his/her personal stories. However, if he/she really wants to tell them, it must be done in an appropriate way. Then, I was not surprised by the fact that I could not find stories similar to mine. I remember telling someone at a party, that when I was a kid and wanted a candy, I just went to a grocery store and stole it. No big deal, right? Wrong. I could tell from people's reactions that I was not supposed to say that. I embarrassed people. It would be all right if I had said that I was poor, so I needed to work, and if I wanted to eat a candy, I would buy it using my own money. I worked when I was a kid. I received half of the Brazilian minimum wage. It was not enough money for buying candy. I stole candy.

My life's story, lived experience, background, is part of my motivation to starting looking for forms of writing, for ways of telling my stories, and also some kind of scholarly support. I am fond of the work of Carolyn Ellis and Arthur Bochner, because I could match my desires regarding writing style with their detours through theory. I am impressed by their statement:

> "In personal narrative texts, authors become 'I,' readers become 'you,' subjects become 'us.' [. . .] Readers, too, take a more active role as they are invited to the author's world, evoked to a feeling level about the events being described, and stimulated to use what they learn there to reflect on, understand, and cope with their own lives. The goal is to write meaningfully and evocatively about topics that matter and may make a difference, to include sensory and emotional experience . . . , and to write from an ethic of care and concern. . . ." (Ellis and Bochner, 2000, p. 742)

Consequently, one must take a look at what they call narrative inquiry, or a "story that creates an effect of reality, showing characters embedded in the complexities of lived moments of struggle, resisting the intrusions of chaos, disconnection, fragmentation, marginalization, and incoherence, trying to preserve or restore the continuity and coherence of life's unity in the face of unexpected blows of fate that call one's meanings and values into question." (p. 744). My stories of the fans' lived experience—interwoven with of my own—reflect this concept. I believe that my stories create reality that exposes hegemonies, conflicts, struggles for survival, and so on. These stories carry life and show the dynamism of society. They are not static.

I hope that my stories might help the fans make better sense of their lives. However, I know for sure that my stories (about myself and the fans) are helping me to make sense of *my own life*, both as a person and as a graduate student.[7] The stories are helping me to justify my presence here in the U.S.A., so far away from home; because through them I am trying to improve people's lives in Brazil. They help me to say to myself that I am not here just for my own sake. That I am giving—or at least trying to give—more justice to more people. My own personal stories constantly remind me of my origins, and about my goals in life. In this way, I can understand my own struggle for survival, my own dreams, and my own work. Thus, making better sense of my own life supports me to have a better understanding of someone else's life.

Returning to Ellis and Bochner (2000):

"Why should we be ashamed if our work has therapeutic or personal value? Besides, haven't our personal stories always been embedded in our research monographs? The question is whether we should express our vulnerability and subjectivity openly in the text or hide them behind 'social analysis'?" (p. 747)

I am neither ashamed nor hidden behind "social analysis." I am trying to show the importance of my own personal stories in this project. I am letting you know who I am. I am showing to you my vulnerabilities as a person and as a scholar. I am exposing others and myself, and this is not an easy task. While writing this project, there have been days that I get so depressed that I could not talk even with my wife. Forgotten memories from my childhood that should have been buried in my past suddenly become part of my life again. And it is not just about my life. I expose the fans, hoping that this work might be a small step in order to improve their lives. In exposing myself, I also expose the ones who love me such as my wife, Dani, and my children, Analua and Francisco. By saying that I was a poor kid, I expose the economic failure of my parents and relatives. Some Brazilians do not like my work, because by exposing myself, I am also exposing my country. Doing and negotiating these things are not easy.

I state here that through my personal stories the reader can understand better the stories of the fans. I feel the need to explicitly explain how it occurs. What is this strong connection between my own personal stories and the stories of the fans? The connection of my stories with the fans' resides in the fact that both groups have been silenced. Both types of stories are not included in the dominant discourse of the Brazilian upper-middle-class. Both discourses—the fans' and mine—are being told through my fieldwork and my life history, discourses that help to deepen the understanding of the reality of gendered, racial, and social class oppression in Brazil. That is how my own experience becomes "data," a word I cannot stand.

I am exposing all these lives because I struggle for a more democratic world. Because I believe that in order for this project to achieve its goals, it must reveal/embodied lives. Nothing is more frustrating for me than a social text in which I cannot see the people's faces. Therefore, in this project there are a lot of lives—including mine—inviting you, the reader, to glimpse "our" stories.

IV: Purple Conde

> "This is a personal social science, a moral ethnography that reads repression and pain biographically, existentially. It knows that behind every act of institutional repression lurks a flesh-and-blood human being who can be held accountable, at a deep level, for his or her actions. The new writing asks only that we all conduct our own ground-level criticism aimed at the repressive structures in our everyday lives." (Denzin, 2003, p. 142)

Purple Leisur[8]
Purple Conde
Soccer and Leisure are good
Soccer as Leisure is also good
Watching soccer games is Leisure time
A good time
Is fighting over a soccer game good?
Nope.
I learned the name in one of my leisure classes
It's purple leisure!
Purple Leisure, Purple Conde,
Did Conde's body become purple?
Thrashed, bruised body.
Beaten purple dead body.
Just a lifeless soccer fan

A reflexive man
A fighting one who had been beaten before
A tooth lost in an ugly fight
A touching tongue looking for the missing tooth
A body full of guilt

I lost a tooth
Conde lost his life
Do I dare to compare?
Not in a lifetime that I do have and he don't.
Yes, he don't. Put the grammar away.
A white grad student in the U.S.
A black poor soccer fan in Brazil
I got a Master's thesis
Conde got beaten to death
I got a degree
Conde got a place in heaven?

See, I'm not so sure
And
And
As a matter of fact
I'm
I'm still using purple Conde
Fuck!

For God's sake I wanna help Conde
Got some news for you
Too fucking late, white boy
White boy
Fairy tale ending
Just the white boy standing

V: Cláudio

> "... a kind of writing where the body and the spoken word, performance practice and theory, the personal and the scholarly, come together." (Miller and Pelias, 2001, p. xii)

> "Writing about the loss of my father really helped. I did not think I was going to make it. But no, I will not start to write autoethnography. I mean, I might do a little bit on the side, but this is not my thing. I have my research and all that." (A professor, in a

conversation with me at the 2nd International Congress of Qualitative Inquiry, May 2005)

I have heard that autoethnography is self-indulgent, easy, and so on. I am writing this paper, right here in my office, and it is not easy. Not easy at all. Writing this performance is anything but easy. Words do not come easy; they are ripped from my soul, kicking and screaming. I am writing from the heart. I am searching for a methodology of the heart:

> "I feel the lack in those critical arguments tied tighter than a syllogism, those pronouncements given with such assurance, those judgments that name everything but what matters. I know there is more than making a case, more than establishing criteria and authority, more than what is typically offered up. That more has to do with the heart, the body, the spirit." (Pelias, 2004, p. 1)

After looking at Pelias's words, how can this writing be easy? I cannot give you that. If a person uses performance autoethnography as a one-time deal after a loss or for a class, it might be easy. Or if someone uses this writing as a "side dish from time to time," I would say, well, maybe. However, my experience with this method/theory as a "full time job" says it's not easy, but rather extremely complex. I do performance autoethnography. That's it. This is my thing. I am continuously doing it—interrogating methodology, theories, and experiences from the intersection of apparatus of oppression, trying to promote social justice.

When I am writing, I am trying to represent my body—not only my mind, ideas or thoughts, with all my feelings, emotions, lived experiences, beliefs, values (in that moment or shifting moments) in the paper. I am not daring to represent Conde. I am not *giving* him voice. He has his own. I am performing my own experience of my relationship with him grounded in my commitment with social justice—rounded in my own progressive political agenda then and now. My agenda, not Conde's.

Adding to this, my writing is not who I am—it is not my feelings, nor my body. My own representation of my own body is incomplete. Hence, while rereading my performance, I am not looking for my whole body, but for fragments of it, for pieces that I can be at least satisfied with. But also, and more important, a writing piece that not does not just express my fragmented, surreal reality but something that is open enough for the audience to take over and transform into whatever they like (but only if they want to). In the moment it is performed, my piece is not mine anymore. Ownership is gone. I let it go. It belongs, as fragments, to whoever wants it.

Fragments, Anzaldúa (2000) reminds us, come from "betweenness":

"It's actually the white Anglo dominant culture that privileges the white in us, that tries to erase, to hide the fact that we have African blood the fact that we have Indian blood, and only a very small percentage of Spanish blood." (p. 181)

I am a betweener! I live life in-betweenness (Anzaldúa, 1999).
I grow up and live life as "white." As a poor child . . . a border child from a fucked up family identified with the colonizers in my own country. The border man—a "gringo" among my people and an alien here in America.
There are so many Brasils.
So many Brasilian borders.
My body is both: the poor kid in Brasil and the grad student in the U.S. It is also the better way for me to have a dialogue with my people. And Conde is one of my bunch.
Yes, I am claiming Conde as one of may own. And he is claiming me as one of his. Conde holds my place there for me, while I hold his here. He and I invented our shared roots . . . becoming a different "we."
It is also the main reason of why I am writing: this way is the only way that I accept to live and labor in academia

Ambiguity?
Or
How this feeling of fragments (living and seeing life as such) comes from people born in this "in between space"
Having to deal with the "diasporic" body, losses of home (land)
Internal/external colonization
Slavery-past/present
Race/gender/religion
You name it . . . no wait, I named it
Provoking destabilization
De-center identities
Oppositional . . .
Like people born out of multiple and violent fragmentations.

When I write performance autoethnography, I write from an interior space at the center of the self. It takes courage to stay there; to perform from that space; to perform from this space right now. And, this space constantly changes. I am never done writing from this space. I can only write from there. Myself/Experiences as a vehicle, commenting, speaking from and to, on/in the historical universal singularity, in which my body is immersed.

I am We are
A moral agent carrying messages
Speaking truth of power
Accountable self
Accountable others
Truth speaks to power
Agents for transformation
Agents for power
Writing from memory
Re constructed
Moving
Ongoing experience
Truth of memory?
Memory as moral discourse
Bringing the bite!

All sciences—social, hard, and otherwise—are always already political and moral. The difference is that performance autoethnographers place themselves in their texts. In this way, I am damn explicitly clear in my commitments to live by a feminist communitarian ethic[9] that craves to empower people in an ideology of love, hope, care, and commitment to justice.

VI: *Final Words*

Decolonizing Inquiry
Decolonizing Academia
Resisting the colonizing impulse
Resisting the straight white male
Being critical and political
Transformation
Moments and forms
Movements
Global movements
Free in a post colonial space
Free in a non naïve utopia
Take control and erase the apparatus of oppression
No! No! No! Not a hierarchical shift
Afro Centric Feminist Ethic site
Performance
Love
Hope and care

Story 8

No More Soccer

Paradise hadn't changed much since the last time I was there, in the winter of 1994. The landscape was still dominated by shacks made of cardboard and pieces of wood, unfinished unpainted brick houses, and dirt streets running parallel to open sewage ditches. The only apparent differences now in 1996 were the surprisingly high number of imported cars on the streets and the few fancy houses towering over their neighbors—a sign of prosperity?

Paradise is as poor as many other neighborhoods surrounding Campinas, and besides the fact that it's the closest to downtown, I never understood why most of the kids I knew came from there. Some of the kids living in downtown still maintained some contact with their families in Paradise. I'd gone there that Wednesday afternoon looking for T's mom, to tell her that he'd been taken to a juvenile reformatory in Sao Paulo. I didn't find T's mom, but ran into Pelé.

"Say, fella, you want to play some soccer?" asked a stranger's voice behind me.

Still walking, I half turned my head to see if someone was talking to me. I saw a young man looking and smiling at me, walking as close to me as a shadow. I looked ahead again, feeling my heart bouncing all over my body, trying to spot a bar or a store, any place full of people. As I was beginning to think about running to a fruit stand on the other side of the street, I felt the stranger's hand on my shoulder.

"You don't recognize me, do you, Marcelo?" the stranger said and opened a large white smile. "I mean, *t-i-o* Marcelo," he said pretending he was correcting himself.

Only the street kids call me *tio* Marcelo.

"Pelé!" I finally said recognizing him.

"It's me," he said starting to pull me toward him.

I was getting ready to hug him too but he suddenly put one hand on my chest and stepped back, looking around us without moving his head much.

"I didn't recognize you at first, I must admit," I said quickly shaking his hand instead.

He seemed happy to see me again. "I know! I saw the scared look in your face," he said enjoying himself.

I smiled. "I thought I was about to lose my backpack."

"Nobody would steal this old backpack," he said and we laughed.

Then I thought I may not have recognized him in those smart clothes. He must have noticed my eyes checking him out.

"Yeah, you see, I don't wear those ragged clothes no more," he said fixing his red shirt tucked into his beige trousers.

"You're looking sharp. Did you win the lottery or something?"

"I guess you could say that," he said with a sly smile.

"I haven't seen you in downtown since I started working again with the kids," I said wanting to change subject.

"I've being doing some business here in Paradise for a while now. I was getting too old to live on the streets, if you know what I mean. Nobody was giving me money or food no more. Then one of the juvenile officers found out I had turned 18 and said that he was just waiting to catch me doing something wrong to send me to jail. So I moved back here and started to work for some guys I knew. Now I have my own . . . business."

"Have you been playing a lot of soccer?" I asked trying to go back to familiar grounds. "You used to love it. You used to play all the time in those days."

"No. I don't have much time for that no more. We used to have a lot fun back then, huh?! Do you still play on the street with the kids?"

"Nope, they seem to have lost interest in that. Too busy after crack, you know."

"Yeah. Remember that night you spent with us, in that abandoned house we used to live in? We barbecued some bad meat at 4 in the morning, drank some cheap wine, then chatted till dawn."

"Yes, I remember," I said noticing a young man lurking around us.

Pelé saw the guy too. "I can't talk right now," he said to the guy.

"I really need to talk to you, Pelé, just for a minute," the young man said approaching us.

"Not now!" Pelé said firmly. He looked at me uneasily.

"I really need to buy a stone, now, please," the young man said grabbing Pelé's arm.

"I need to get going," I said offering my hand to Pelé. "We'll catch up later."

"Okay," he said pushing the young man away from him and shaking my hand.

I could hear Pelé scolding the young man as I walked away hurriedly. The next thing I heard about Pelé, at the end of that year, 1996, is that he'd been shot dead over a territorial dispute in Paradise.

Notes

1. Translation of Vinicius de Moraes's poem.
2. My master's thesis (2002), "The fans' greatest love: *Torcida jovem amor maior*," was a critical ethnographic project, where I worked

with soccer-fan members of the fan club Torcida Jovem, in Campinas, Brazil.
3. This is a slang expression for "looking for trouble."
4. Ponte Preta's biggest rival, whose stadium is just a couple of blocks away.
5. On this day, Guarani and Ponte Preta were playing different teams at the same time. The fans met in their way out of those games.
6. "Near Guarani's stadium, the Ponte Preta fan, João Fernandes, fired four shots toward Guarani's fans. The shots reached Wagner Lopes (23) and Luis Gouveia (24). Wagner had surgery and is doing well. Luis is already at home and is well too. João, who was imprisoned by the police, said that he was just defending himself (*Lancenet: O campeão da rede*, Brazilian newspaper, 09/11/01. http://lancenet.ig.com.br/).
7. Ellis and Bochner (2000) go on to state: "a personal narrative, the project of telling a life, is a response to the human problem of authorship, the desire to make sense and preserve coherence over the course of our lives. Our personal identities seem largely contingent on how well we bridge the remembered past with the anticipated future to provide what Stephen Crites (1971) calls 'a continuity of experience over time'" (p. 746).
8. According to Russell (2002), purple leisure activities are those that participants enjoy but are harmful to society.
9. In short, a feminist communitarian ethic, according to Denzin (1997, p. 277), is a model that "seeks to produce narratives that ennoble human experience while facilitating civic transformations in the public (and private) spheres. This ethic promotes universal human solidarity. It ratifies the dignity of the self and the value of human life. It is committed to human justice and the empowerment of interacting individuals. It works to build covenant rather than contractual bonds within the local community."

Chapter 6

BETWEENNESS IN SEXUALITY

STORY 9

A PLACE FOR RECOVERY

Wednesday, February 14th, 1996. Marga and I had just crossed Rosario Square and were walking down Barão Street looking for Katia when we ran into Jaca. It was the end of the afternoon, and this narrow street in the middle of downtown was crowded with cars and pedestrians, people leaving their jobs, people going to shops and bakeries, some heading for the many bars and cafes with tables outdoors, and who knows what else. Marga introduced me to Jaca as a fellow street educator and then told me they had known each other since he started sleeping in the streets of downtown. "When we were still happy with glue," he said with a sly smile.

"And we thought *that* was bad," Marga said.

"Yeah . . . sometimes I wonder what's gonna come after crack," Jaca said affecting an air of preoccupation.

"Don't even joke about that," she said gently punching him in the arm, and they laughed.

Marga wanted to know where Jaca had been for the last few months. She had heard he had gone to a Catholic recovery center in the south of Brazil. As we stood between two cars parked along the sidewalk, Jaca, a young man almost leaving his teen years behind, told Marga it was impossible for him to quit smoking crack without leaving town, where most of the people he knew were somehow involved with drugs. "The streets crack you down," he said with a smile, rubbing his shirtless thin chest.

He went on telling us in his streetwise vernacular how he had found this place in the south, in a rural area, away from urban centers, through the local Catholic organization. He said he'd gotten clean and stayed that way for over 3 months, that he was happier and wanted to settle down in that area to start a new life. But he got the news that his girlfriend, who had stayed in the streets of downtown when he left, was pregnant with his child, and so he came back to be with her.

"And things are getting worse now," Jaca said.

"Yeah, I heard it's getting cheaper," I said timidly.

"And it's easier to find it," added Marga.

"That, too," said Jaca looking at Marga.

"Crack makes the kids more desperate to get money," said Marga.

"That, too," Jaca said.

"So they get into more trouble," said Marga.

"That, too."

"What are you smiling about?" Marga, looking a little surprised, asked Jaca.

"Nothing," he said, laughing some more.

Marga crossed her arms in front of her chest, tilted her head to the side, placed her big brown eyes on Jaca's, and smiled with one corner of her mouth.

"It's nothing really, Marga," Jaca said, "it's just that I heard Celi got into some real trouble with some dealers the other day."

"What kind of trouble?" Marga's face tightened up suddenly. I think my face took a similar expression. We had just been talking about the dangers of getting too involved with crack dealers, how the kids would be entering yet another universe where all sorts of abuse went uncared for by public eyes. Most of the kids we knew, if not *all* of them, were already constantly harassed by the police and private security guards downtown, even when they, the kids, were not breaking the law. To make things worse, the kids' apparent preference for language normally considered foul, and the increasing number of elderly people losing their wallets and purses to kids' quick hands, didn't exactly gain any sympathy from downtown residents and workers. And now they were beginning to owe considerable amounts to drug dealers. Unlike the police's and security guards', we didn't know the dealers' methods of retaliation; and not knowing had made us fill our minds with terrifying images. Now Jaca was about to fill our hearts with some of the same images.

"Celi was gang-raped by a bunch of dealers down in the Old Quarter," Jaca said now unsmiling. "She went there after crack, and they did her right there, in front of some guys I know. That's how I heard 'bout it. Some of my buddies saw the dealers raping her, one after the other. And they said they're gonna do it again if she don't pay 'em."

Marga and I stood there in silence, looking down. I glanced at Marga out of the corner of my eyes and saw a tear coming down her cheek. Jaca made a sound and we looked at him.

"You know how she is, Marga. She's got a big mouth, disses everybody with her tough-guy attitude. She started pulling that shit again with the dealers, and they decided to teach her a lesson or something like that. If I is Celi, I'd be very careful out here on the streets these days, you know, till those dealers get some bigger problems and forget 'bout her, that she owes them money and got a big mouth. Jaca patted his bare brown chest again. "Well, I gotta go now."

"When did that happen?" Marga asked.

"I don't know. It coulda been this past Sunday, or Saturday, maybe Friday."

"Stay away from the damn *stone*, you hear me?!" Marga said to him firmly, but more like a friend than a parent would.

"No worries, Marga, I'm taking it easy now," he said lifting his chin a little.

"At least keep it away from your girlfriend. You know what crack can do to pregnant women and their babies?"

"No worries, Marga, we're keeping it clean." Then he shook hands with me, kissed Marga goodbye, and left with a smile, his front teeth brownish like teeth in a mouth that smokes a lot of crack. Marga and I stood there watching Jaca look smaller by the step.

"Celi . . ." Marga covered her mouth with her hands. "The bastards!" she said looking at nothing, her eyes moist again.

I put a hand on her shoulder and we slowly started to walk to nowhere. I put my hand back in my pocket and we walked like this for a while. "Do you think this is why Celi suddenly seems to want to go to that recovery place?" I asked after a long silence.

"Maybe . . . she looked scared last time I talked to her. Poor girl. . . ." Marga's face was twitching all over, sometimes her eyes, sometimes the corners of her mouth, other times the jaw muscles.

Marga and I had been trying to get Celi into some sort of recovery program for a few weeks then, but always without success. At first Celi looked for Marga and asked her to find a place. Marga was excited, saying that it was the first time that Celi had asked for help of that kind, and I joined her in trying to find a place in town. The options weren't many, especially because Celi had already spent time in the two religious shelters for children and adolescent drug addicts in Campinas. And neither Celi nor the folks working in the religious shelters wanted to spend time together again.

Marga had heard about a recovery place near Rio de Janeiro, the SN Center, where another girl she knew—Marta was her name—had spent time and gotten clean. Marga had tried to talk Celi into going to that place a few times. In the beginning Celi had said a firm no, that she didn't want to go anywhere out of town, that she wanted to be around her friends. Marga persisted and Celi then said she would go. Celi wanted to know what kind of place this SN Center was. When Marga told her that it was in Rio de Janeiro (I noticed that Marga didn't specify if it was the city or the state), Celi opened a big smile and said she would go. Celi continued to drill Marga with questions about the place, but when she heard it was not in Rio de Janeiro *City* but state, and that it was on a farm, with cows, chicken, sugar cane, and miles of orchards and vegetable gardens for the patients to care for as part of recovery, Celi angrily told us off. Neither Marga nor I saw her for days after that. Marga called the SN Center anyway but was told that nothing could be done until Celi decided to approach them, that the first step was to go to an interview at the Center's office in town.

Before I realized it, during our aimless walk Marga and I had arrived at the cathedral, in the heart of downtown. We sat down near the top of its many front steps next to some old ladies and men, a young couple exchanging silence and looks, and some homeless men lying down in the shade at the bottom of the steps. I saw some young kids running after a half-filled party balloon, their feet shoeless, and Celi came to my mind again. I'd run into her the day before, Tuesday, in front of the Brazil Bank a block east of the cathedral, and I'd thought it a little strange when she told me she wanted to go to the Center, with cows, vegetables, and everything else. I forced myself to take it seriously, but it didn't work. She asked me what she had to do to go there. I told her without details.

"We need to get her out of here," Marga said breaking the silence, getting up and starting to walk fast again. I followed her. We went straight to the small house she and her husband use to run their Reading Club business—and where the street educators of the National Movement for Street Kids meet every now and then. Marga started to make phone calls to people at the SN Recovery Center, to friends working for the City Hall's Children's Council, and to anybody who she thought could help get a spot at the SN Center for Celi, and fast.

In less than two days, Celi and I were on the bus to Rio de Janeiro, with a change of busses in Sao Paulo City. We got on the bus in Sao Paulo at midnight. Celi slept the whole 6-hour ride from Sao Paulo to Rio. I had to stay awake the whole time for fear of not waking up in time to get off some 50 miles before Rio de Janeiro City. To keep myself awake in the hot and stiff air of the full sleeping bus, I started to think about the hassles of the last two days . . .

The day after Marga and I talked to Jaca, I went downtown early in the afternoon trying to find Celi. I wanted to talk to her right after she woke up, when she was usually slow and uncracked. At 1 P.M., I arrived at Rosario Square, one of the areas where she had been sleeping lately. I looked for her in the usual places: under the metal trailer that served as a newsstand for a local Spiritist publisher, behind the popcorn cart, on top of the marquee that went around the Square in the shape of a U, behind the wooden benches where retired folks sit down to talk, play cards, or share silence. Not finding her or any of the other kids, I thought of walking to Marga's apartment building. I had heard that some of the girls were sleeping on a hidden corner in front of the building sometimes. Marga's place was six blocks from Rosario Square, in a quiet narrow street on the outskirts of the downtown area, and I headed that way.

When I got there, I saw two bodies lying next to each other on the corner and recognized Kleo and Regi. I was surprised to see Regi there. She had been living with her older sister for over 2 months, coming downtown only to go to her job, as a maid for a Baptist family, and to see the team of therapists working with young recovering drug addicts down at the municipal Children's Health Center. I called her name softly at first, then louder and even louder, but she didn't move. Her thick curly hair was neatly pulled back in a ponytail, her clothes were clean and looking new, and she still had some red nail polish on her fingernails. The black skin of her face and arms looked smooth and cared for, and I figured that must have been her first night back on the streets. I bought a plate of rice, beans, and sundried meat to-go in a self-service restaurant across the street, walked back to where they were sleeping, and set the plate down between their heads. It didn't take long for them to open their eyes, look at the plate of steaming food, and smile at me.

"Good morn . . . afternoon beauties," I said returning their smiles.

"Hi *tio* Marcelo," Kleo and Regi said almost at the same time.

"It must be late, I'm so hungry!" Kleo said sitting up. She picked up one of the plastic forks I'd stuck in the pile of rice and started to eat.

I looked at Regi as she sat up rubbing her face and eyes. She caught my eyes staring at her and turned away, smiling. "Hey Regi, why don't you get a bite? I bet you haven't eaten since you left your sister's house," I said still staring at her, with a smile as wide as I could manage.

"I'm still living there, *tio*, don't look at me like that," Regi said putting her hands to the sides of her hips. "I hooked up with some of the girls last night on my way home from work, you know, I haven't seen them in a long time and I wanted to have a good time with them, and . . . here I am," she said shrugging. "But I'm going home today, it's true! I'll go home tonight, I promise you," she said now pursing her lips and looking at me out of the corner of her eyes.

"I'm not saying anything, Regi, eat something." But she was right, I was reproaching her behind my smile. I didn't want to, but couldn't help it. She was the one, out of all the kids, I thought could find a dignified life, get out of the streets of downtown. Looking back, I guess I was upset because she showed me how much more complex the business of getting out of the street really is.

"Have you guys seen Celi?" I asked after a while.

"Yep. She got picked up by the Juvenile officers this morning, just before we came here to sleep," Kleo said eating, without looking at me.

"You didn't sleep the whole night?"

"No, Celi was too scared of the dealers to fall asleep in the dark, you know, so we kept on the move the whole night, trying to have fun here and there. When the day came and the streets were getting crowded with people, we started to head this way. That's when the officers saw us from their van, they stopped, and started to chase us. There were two of them. We ran fast but they caught Celi. She's probably at the Juvenile Court now." Kleo stopped chewing and looked at me. "Are you gonna get her out, *tio*?"

"I'll try. Do you know why they were after her?"

"Who knows . . . maybe somebody called them saying that we were disturbing the peace, who knows, it's always something or the other," said Kleo.

"We're trying to take her to that place in Rio, you know the one on a farm?" I said.

"Yeah, where Marta was," said Regi licking the meat sauce off her fingers.

"That's right," I said.

"Can you take me there too, *tio*?" asked Kleo.

"You want to go now?" I asked.

"No, not now. Next week maybe?"

The three of us looked at each other for a brief moment and then laughed. They always had some business to finish in the streets before they could go straight, it seemed to me. We talked a little longer until they were done eating, and I left for the Juvenile Court.

When I got there, I saw Celi sitting across the desk from an officer who was typing some kind of report, making something up, I thought. I asked to see one of the social workers, saying it was about Celi. While I waited, I walked over to where Celi was, greeted the officer, and asked her if she still wanted to go.

"Of course, *tio* Marcelo. I was trying to tell them that and they took me here anyways. . . . I'm starving," she said affecting an intensity I had only seen when she was asking pedestrians for money, rapping her spiel about a little brother or sister starving. I stroked her hair and looked at the officer sitting in front of us.

"She told me she was going to a recovery place this week, but I didn't believe her, you know, she's said that before and the next day we see her causing trouble around downtown," said the officer inserting an empty form in the typewriter.

"This time is for real, isn't it Celi?" I said looking down at her.

She moved her head up and down several times looking at the officer.

"I came here to get authorization from the judge and talk to the social workers," I said. The officer looked up at me from the typewriter, then looked at Celi and went back to his typing without saying a word.

Just then the clerk at the front desk came over and told me that I could go in. I asked Celi to come with me, she looked at the officer, and he nodded yes. After I had given a rather long explanation to the social worker about the situation, she said she was glad I was doing something for Celi.

"We don't know what else to do for her. We have tried everything we could, but she always lets us down," the social worker said looking at Celi, who sat there quietly, staring at the floor. "I will send a request for an authorization up to the judge. You can wait upstairs by his chamber," she said getting up.

After more than an hour of waiting for the authorization, Celi was growing impatient, threatening to leave every 5 minutes or so. I was getting impatient with her impatience, wanting to remind her that it was for her own benefit and that controlling the drive for immediate gratification was one of the first steps to recovery. Instead, I went outside to get her a hot dog and a soda, and kept repeating to myself that this was the most difficult stage, that if I could keep her on my side until we arrived at the recovery place in Rio, she would be on her way to recovery from crack addiction. And perhaps be free from the street, and real nightmares.

After I got the authorization allowing me to take Celi to another state, and after Celi heard everyone in the building say to her that this was her last chance to change her life before she turned 18 and was sent to jail, we walked out of the Court and took a bus to the Reading Club, where Marga was waiting for us with the news that she had gotten an appointment for an interview with the SN people the following morning. The rest of the afternoon Celi stayed there with Marga. We wanted to keep her away from the streets, lest she change her mind and disappear again. In the meantime I went around from office to office in the City Hall gathering signatures and documents assuring that the Children's Council would pay for Celi's stay at the center.

That night Celi slept at Marga's apartment, breaking an unwritten but highly respected law that prevented street educators from giving shelter to street kids under any circumstances. Needless to say, this later caused a lot of jealousy and hard feelings from some of the other kids toward Marga and her husband when the word got around, through Celi herself.

The following day, Friday, early in the morning, another street educator and I took Celi to the interview at the SN office in Campinas. There was more waiting and lots of impatience, and I kept buying popsicles for Celi. But by noon, we were leaving the SN office with a spot guaranteed for Celi at the recovery place in Rio, as soon as we could get her there. Marga and

I spent the afternoon calling or going to several charity institutions around downtown, asking for clothes, shoes, and other stuff Celi was going to need in this new phase of her life, like having her own toothbrush.

Except for the few times she complained about waiting for appointments, Celi was very agreeable during those unusual two days. She seemed calm, and was definitely quieter than her usual self out in the streets. Marga thought it was a sign that Celi really wanted to get clean this time. I agreed with Marga then, but now, as I try to keep myself awake inside this quiet and stuffy bus, I look at Celi sleeping in the seat next to mine and wonder whether she will ever get used to a farming life, whether she's even mature enough to follow the 12-step program we found for her. But it's 5 A.M. and time to stop wondering and get off the bus, almost 50 miles from Rio de Janeiro City.

Celi and I took another bus, on the other side of the road, which left the main highway and started onto dirt roads cutting the green fields of cattle and sugar-cane farms. We got off the bus near the recovery center but still had to walk for several minutes before reaching the farm's entrance. Celi and I stood there, looking around the hills and the vast plantation.

"Is this the place, *tio*?" Celi asked me frowning.

"Yes! Isn't this a beauty?" I said looking at the sun rising in the horizon, thinking that I would like to spend some time surrounded by all that nature.

"I don't like this . . . where is the town?" she asked looking around without smiling.

"The nearest town is several miles from here." I looked at her seriously. "Staying away from cities, urban life, you know, changing the scenario is important for the beginning of recovery."

She looked at me and said she wasn't staying there. "I think we'll have to wake them up," I said unlatching the wooden gate, grabbing her bags, and heading for a little white house 50 yards uphill. Celi followed me; I didn't look back and kept hoping she wouldn't stall on the way. I woke up a man who turned out to be the manager of the place. He was friendly, said he was expecting us early in the morning, and made us coffee. He must have seen the hesitation in Celi's face and in less than 10 minutes he had a sponsor for Celi and was already escorting me out of the farm, toward the way I had just come from.

Back in Campinas, some people seemed happy, others just relieved, that Celi had stayed in Rio. I was asked by the kids to re-tell the stories of our trip to Rio several times, and Dalva, Grace, and Kleo asked me to take them there, too. But in less than 10 days, Marga got a call from the manager of the recovery place saying that we needed to go pick Celi up. He said she was not adjusting, that she was actually causing trouble there, getting into fights with the other "guests" and not doing her tasks around the farm. When Marga tried to reason with him, arguing that she had no other place to go other than the streets, he said that Celi had already tried to run away, and that she would be in even more trouble if she went to Rio de Janeiro, the nearest big city around. I left for Rio before the end of the day.

"Hey *tio* Marcelo! I knew you would come to get me," Celi said hugging me tight.

"What happened, Celi?" I asked unhugging her.

"I don't want to stay here anymore, I'm feeling fine already, haven't smoked crack for almost a month."

"Ten days," I said keeping a straight face.

"I feel like I don't need recovery anymore . . . I reached se-re-ni-ty already!" she said smiling large.

I smiled back at her, shaking my head. Then I saw the manager coming toward us with two large bags in his hands.

"Perhaps she isn't ready for this yet," he said shaking my hand and setting the bags by Celi. "She is welcome to come back when she feels she is ready."

"I'm okay, *tio*, I swear. I won't go back to the streets. I'll go straight to my aunt's house. I don't want to smoke crack no more. I will get a job and go back to school. And I'll just go downtown to visit Dalva and the other kids." Then she grabbed her bags and started to walk toward the dirt road.

At the beginning of our trip back to Campinas, Celi told me only good things about the farm, her sponsor, and the activities. Then she started asking about the girls and boys in the streets, saying that they should do like her and get clean before it's too late. I told her that things had gotten worse, more violent, since she'd left, and I wasn't lying. Celi didn't say much after that other than complaining that the way back was much longer than the way from Campinas to Rio. I drew her a map to show that the distance was the same, that the roads run parallel all the way, but she didn't buy it. I then told her that if she fell asleep, we would get there faster, and that seemed to make more sense to her.

We arrived in Campinas at 10 P.M., more than 24 hours after I had left for Rio. I woke her up and asked where we were going to take the bus to her aunt's house.

"You don't need to come with me, *tio*, you have done enough for me," she said looking concerned.

"I insist. It's late and your aunt may not let you in the house. I want to explain to her what's happening."

"No need for that, really," Celi said and started to walk toward downtown.

"Where are you going?" I asked, grabbing one of the bags and running to catch up with her.

"I just want to say Hi to Dalva before I go to my aunt's."

"Celi . . ."

"Don't worry, *tio*, I just want to say Hi," she said without looking at me.

We walked in silence to the municipal bus terminal, where many of the kids hang around at night, and where Casa Aberta used to be. She stopped in front of the former Open House and asked me to go inside to talk to someone about leaving her bags full of clothes there for a while. I did what she asked and when I came back out Celi was gone, only her two bags were still there. Marcio, the resident assistant in the center, who had come back out with me to talk to Celi, shook his head and chuckled, "That's the Celi I know. I'll keep her bags here, she'll come for them tomorrow." I walked home slowly.

The next day Marga told me Celi didn't have an aunt in town. Two days later I saw Celi walking down Rosario Square with Dalva and Kleo. She was wearing the same clothes she had on the last time I'd seen her, only they were dirtier and her new tennis shoes gone. The same day I learned from other kids how happy they were with the stuff Celi had exchanged for her two bags of clothes.

ACT 6

MADE FOR SEX

Mister Miguel

I was less than 1 year old when my family moved to this new neighborhood. It was a city project for low-income families to achieve the dream of their own house. The neighborhood was in the boarder of the city, surrounded by farms on the west and by old poor houses (where the real poor ones lived) by east and south. My parents bought one house, and my grandmother also bought one a block north from ours. After a year, my dad could not pay our mortgage so we lost the house and went to live with my grandma, my dad's mother. After another year or so, my mom could not get along well with my grandma, and then we move to another part of town, paying rent, of course. I was 3 maybe 4.

I have only two memories of this time. First I remember the day, when my dad brought a TV home. It was a black and white one and it stayed 1 month with us, until we had to sell it to pay the bills. The other memory that I had is about the day that Mister Miguel's wife passed way. I can recall the image of walking in the sidewalk and seeing Baby Rejane crying through the small window. Mister Miguel lived three houses east from us. His family was the only black one in the new houses. I remember my grandma explaining to me that Rosa, Miguel's wife was called by Jesus, and so she was going to live in the heaven. "But, who is going to take care of Rejane? I asked. "Life" said my grandma. I did not get her answer, but I did not dare to ask for more.

Later in life, my parents got divorced, and my sister and I came back to that neighborhood to live with my grandma. It was a strange place. There were two set of not so new houses. Not for people aspiring middle-class status but for people who used to have that status. Those houses were surrounded by old smaller ones, the kinds that were put together without any kind of order. They weren't painted, and one could see the variety of material had been used in their construction. Roni's (you and I are going to meet him) house was a good example. He had nine brothers and sisters, and so his house was always in a construction stage. When I moved back, his family was adding a new room in the back, which was half cement and half pressed wood. I was 7 or 8, do not know for sure. In my first morning there, I went out to make new friends. I met Roni, one of my buddies in the next years. We began to talk, measuring ourselves the way kids do when they meet a new possible friend, when a group of old kids (12/13 years old) headed by a huge one, passed running in front of Roni and me.

Celita

"Who are they?"

"The big one is Juca Baleia (*baleia* means "whale" in Portuguese), the others are kids from around here." Told me Roni.

"What are they doing?"

"Come and see." And Roni begins to run toward the kids.

I could see Baleia and the others arriving at Mister Miguel's house. The house, as well the people who lived in it (Miguel's family), were pretty much beaten up, life had not been easy on them both. They kicked the door and entered the house with Roni and me following them with a "safe distance." Mister Miguel had four children, Rosa 15 (named after her mom), Little Miguel 14, Celita 13, and Baby Rejane, who was 4.

When we got inside the living room two or three kids were beating little Miguel.

"Stop crying your fucking *negão*, or I am gonna put my dick in your mouth, motherfucker!" Said one of the kids to Little Miguel.

Baby Rejane, she was not a baby anymore, was crying in one corner. The others were all over Rosa and Celita. Some were masturbating, and others were undressing the girls. Celita's breasts were outside her bra. It was the first time that I was seeing a woman/girl breast. I had my eyes fixed on them. And I was hearing things like:

"Come on; give me your little pussy. You gonna be a whore. It's a matter of time. Why don't begin with me. I gonna be nice with you."

The girls keep fighting and the kids are getting mad.

"Your fucking whore, you like this. You are made for this." The kids keep going until they get their pleasure, cleaning their penis in the girl's face. Then, they leave the house. I heard Baleia saying:

"It's a matter of time. Very soon we gonna have their pussies."

Mister Miguel

I was excited and scared. My friend Roni stayed all that time with his hand touching his young penis inside his shorts. We did not know what to say to each other. Finally, Roni broke the silence.

"Those kids do it everyday. The girls like it, you know. They are whores."

What is ironic is that Roni and most of the other kids are black, too. "They are made for this. When I get some hair in my dick I gonna do the same."

I got what Roni was saying to me. Rosa and Celita were "easy black girls." They were "good for sex." I would never have girls like them as a girlfriend. They were for sex. And I, I was learning life in the streets.

Around 5:30/6:00 P.M. I was with my grandma in front our house, when I saw Mister Miguel coming from work, hiding his bicycle. My grandma said "hi" to him, and they exchanged few words. I was just a kid, but I was impressed with the look in Mister Miguel's eyes. He did not make an eye contact with my grandma. From time to time he would look up at her, acknowledging that he was following her. Every time that he looked at grandma, his eyes were saying, "I 'm sorry for my kids. I'm sorry for living in your neighborhood. I'm sorry for making your new neighborhood look dirty."

When I moved from that neighborhood I was 16. The poor ones had moved a couple of years before me. Rosa and Celita had three kids (each of them) with no father. Little Miguel was an alcoholic who sleeps in the front yard of his house. He usually arrives home so drunk that he was not able to get inside his house. Baby Rejane was already pregnant.

Cláudio

That night, the night that I saw Celita's breasts, I dreamed of them. Later in life, when sex becomes important to me, Rosa and Celita were all over my thoughts. Sex was dirty and so forbidden with the "good girls." But fortunately, for boys like me, we had the "easy girls who are made for sex."

Rape? No way!

Angela was a good-looking girl in my neighborhood. She had two little brothers: Naldo and Andrezinho. She was 12 the same age of my sister. They used to play together when they were younger, but not anymore. Now both of then were teens, a dangerous age for girls. Puberty with its sex appeal might get girls in trouble. The thing that was "wrong" with Angela was that her mother was single and worked at night. That was enough for the people in the neighborhood to make assumptions. Angela's mother must have been a prostitute. At least, that was the rumor in the "hood," and she probably was, but that is not the point here. What counted is that this was the reason why she could not play with my sister anymore.

Angela is not black like Celita. She has a different color that best shows the mix of races that exists in Brazil. Some people might say that she is kinda dark, while others say that she is kinda blond. But everybody in the "hood" would say that she is the daughter of a whore, and pretty hot. And that again, is what counts, period. That makes Angela, like Celita, good for sex.

Kids in the neighborhood know that, and so do I. We hang around the corner of her house, waiting for her to come back from school. "There she is." Says someone. Then, the kids bump into her body, trying to touch her breasts and butt. I keep looking to this. I admire the way that Angela fights with the boys (too much of middle-class on me). "What a girl," I say to myself. I do not participate in this act, but I am not brave enough to help her. I wish she could be my girlfriend, but what the hell? Her mom is a fucking whore. She is no good for me. If I only know that later, I would listen to the same comments about myself, that I am no good for "family girls." More than twenty years later, on my wedding day, I heard people saying that I am no good for my wife.

But back then, all of this seemed "natural." I never, ever, heard the word rape related with girls like Rosa, Celita, and Angela. Of course not, they are made for sex. Even what happens with Andre seems to be natural, and the worse, if it is possible to have one, it never has been told before as a rape.

He is just 5, for God's sake

He is five years old

His name is Andre, little Andre
Andrezinho . . .

Remember, he is five.
Andrezinho, Andrezinho . . .
He is playing in the street
He is just a kid,
Remember, he is five.

Old kids are coming
They grab Andrezinho by the ears
They pull his head toward their penis
Two words are said to him:

"SUCK IT"
Remember, he is five.

Andrezinho poor Andrezinho
His young ears are full of this sound
"Tell your sister, till she gives to us what we wanna you are going to be our pet."
Andrezinho is a pet
Hey people, he is five.

Andrezinho is five
But not an ordinary kid
His mother is a prostitute
So his pretty sister is a prostitute to be
But he . . . he is five.

Poor brave Andrezinho
He fights back
He doesn't dare to look for help
Spiting month
Throwing stones, he courses to the world:
"Motherfuckers, motherfuckers, motherfuckers"
Hey people, this kid is five.

Poor little brave and raped Andrezinho
Who is going to help you?
Not me, I watch the whole thing
I go to a store nearby and steal two toys
A small soldier and a fire truck
Remember, he is five.

Little, little, little five-year-old boy
He takes the toys without looking at me
I just hear an angry voice
"That bitch, why in the hell she doesn't give what the bastards wanna?
I HATE HER!"
And remember, he is five.

Andrezinho, Andrezinho, my dear Andrezinho
Why in the hell your prostitute, bitch, whore mother give you a name?
Why GOD, isn't he a dog?
Andrezinho, my dear raped Andrezinho, I got news for you:
You're a nobody sonofabitch.
But remember, he is five.

Andrezinho, Andrezinho
He is playing with the stolen fire truck
Of course he is
Jesus Christ, he is just five!
He sees the kids coming
He looks for an escape route
He runs for it
Run, run MY little nobody
Fuck! He's coming back ...
He forgets his stolen fire truck
He is coming back for that fucking toy!
I forget that he is five.

MY raped nobody not dog Andrezinho
Kids grab him by the ears
He has a dick in his mouth,
And other and other
He's suffocating with semen
And please, don't forget: He is JUST five.

MY dear, dear brave Andrezinho
Are you able to fall into the world,
Like the Kittredge kid?
He is not able to give me an answer ...
MY little nobody is gone ...
(Pay attention people, he's MINE now and we are redeeming each other now)
Are you, brave Andre, able to go falling into the world?
A world that fills your young mouth with penis and semen?
A world that somehow fails you?
FOR GOD'S SAKE HE IS JUST FIVE!
ONE
TWO
THREE
FOUR
FIVE, FIVE!

STORY 10

STOLEN ROMANCE

I had already heard a lot about her when I first met Rachel, while she was still living at the Mission for girls. The girls often told me stories about

CHAPTER 6

Rachel acting more like a boy than like a girl. She spoke like a boy and fought like a boy, they said. She always hung out with boys but really liked girls, "if you know what I mean," Celi told me once, enjoying herself. "She doesn't like anybody, she's a mean bitch!" someone else said.

The boys were afraid of her, too.

But every time I visited one girl or another in the Mission, I would have good conversations with Rachel. She sure had a quick mouth, and her wit was invariably sharpened at someone else's expense, often at mine, too, but she seemed kind toward Berta, the manager of the shelter, and protective of the smaller girls. She seemed to be doing so well at the Mission, going to school in the mornings and helping with the many household tasks in the afternoons, that I thought I'd never see her on the streets of downtown. But I was wrong.

Rachel got into a fight with a new girl in the shelter and left for the streets. Berta couldn't do anything to stop her, for the shelters have no legal power to keep kids locked up. For several months I saw Rachel terrorizing downtown, stealing, beating up on other girls and boys who said she was a lesbian, always full of energy, much of which was used to harass and taunt passersby and other kids.

This particular day I went to Rosario Square to find Rachel gloomy, really withdrawn, indeed, lying all by herself in a corner while the other kids were clowning around in the hot afternoon. I made a remark to Dalva about how quiet Rachel was that day.

"I think she is like that because of Alema, you know, the boy she is always with. I think she likes him, like a boyfriend. But he's been hanging out with another girl lately, and Rachel has been like this ever since," Dalva said smiling and shaking her head.

After a few minutes I saw Alema (I'd talked to him only once before), a tall black boy in his late teens, walking toward us. I looked at Rachel to see if she had seen him. She had. She got up and came to where a bunch of us were. Rachel tried to get his attention several times, but he never acknowledged her. This went on for almost one hour, then Rachel went back to where her blanket was and lay down.

Alema walked over to where Rachel was lying down, teasing her about this and that. It was Rachel's turn to ignore him. That's when I saw Alema walking toward a car stopped at the red light near the corner where we were all hanging out. Alema reached inside the car, through the driver's open window, and turned around quickly. I saw the woman waving her hands, yelling something and driving away, pushed by the intense traffic behind her.

He walked back toward where Dalva and I were standing, showing a golden watch and a gold ring, smiling at us.

"Get away from here, you crazy punk! You're gonna get us arrested," Dalva said firmly.

He smiled at me, looking proud of his feat. I stared at him seriously. He then walked over to where Rachel was and lay down next to her. She acted uninterested but let him slide the gold ring down her finger. He had stolen the ring for her, I heard him say as he caressed her thighs. She started smiling. She motioned for me to come and see the ring. I shook my head no from where I was, mad that Alema had exposed all of us like that, afraid that the police would soon come, but too curious about their making up to leave the area. I watched them as they spoke in each other's ears. In no time, Rachel was mocking everybody again.

Chapter 7

BETWEENNESS IN INDIGENOUSNESS AND POSTCOLONIALISM

STORY 11

OLD-FASHIONED NIKES

The day was unusually hot for that time of the year, and the bright sunlight seemed to have inflamed the kids. They were all over the place, begging for money at the surrounding stoplights while playing soccer with empty soda cans on the sidewalk, chasing one another down the streets swaying around the moving cars and speeding buses, sometimes just disappearing from my sight. I had been hanging around for more than three hours when Lico, a fast-speaking young boy, sat by my side on the edge of the sidewalk.

"Don't you live in the United States?" Lico asked.

"Yes, I've been living there for a while now," I said expecting him to ask something about the fragments of American culture he'd seen on TV during the soccer World Cup '94 that had just ended.

"So how come you are wearing these old-fashioned Nike shoes?" he said opening a big smile.

"But I just bought them before I came to Brazil three months ago!" I reacted, surprised, looking down at my black Nike cross-training shoes.

"And you bought this old model anyway, huh?" Lico said, now rolling backward with laughter. Two boys who had been kicking cans around a few yards away walked toward us smiling and looking at me.

"Why didn't you buy an Air Jordan?" said one of them.

"What's the difference?" I asked.

The three of them were soon, all at once, saying things like having better cushioning, jumping higher, protecting joints, enhancing performance, and moving really fast. I felt like I was in a Nike commercial. Before I could ask how they knew about all that, the kids were already chasing one another, making dunking moves in the air and sticking their tongues out. In seconds they were on the other side of the swarming avenue.

STORY 12

"SHE COULD BE LIVING IN ITALY NOW . . ."

"You could have given the money to me instead," she said smiling.

"You're already too grown up to be riding the bus without paying," I said. "Plus I brought money to pay for your ride."

"But I always sneak in without paying, and most bus drivers don't say anything," Lara said.

"You want to get out of the streets, get a job, be treated with some respect. You can't keep on crawling into busses, hoping people will pretend not to see you. You want to be treated like everybody else, so you gotta pay like everybody else," I thought to myself. "It's a good practice for when you get a job and have money" is what I actually said returning her smile.

"I hope I *will* get a job," she said looking away.

We were quiet for the rest of the ride to the Juvenile Court House, hanging on to the greased handrail next to the exit door, saying something only when one of us lost balance during a curve or a sudden stop.

We got off almost in front of the Court House building. As always, there were official vans and police cars parked right in front of it. There were a few officers talking and laughing on the sidewalk. We were walking past them when Cacho, a tall and curved man who has been a Juvenile officer for years, saw us. He took the pipe out of his mouth, looked at me, nodded, and gently grabbed Lara's arm. "What did she get herself into this time?" he said looking at Lara. The other officers laughed, and he smiled. She shook his hand off her arm, told him to bug off, and kept on walking toward the front door. The officers' laughter was louder this time. "She hasn't done anything wrong," I told him and hurried to catch up with Lara at the door. "She has, she always does, watch out for your pockets," we heard him shout from outside as we went in, her head shaking, my right hand on her left shoulder.

I think we couldn't hear the officers laughing again because of the noise in the front desk area. There was a commotion in the officers' corner, where the cell is located, and we could hear a woman yelling something about her son being hurt. There were several women with kids of all sizes sitting on the chairs set against the surrounding walls, waiting to be seen by the social workers and psychologists housed on the first floor, or just waiting.

We knew the drill. I had been there many times and Lara even more. "Hi there," I said to the two women behind the front counter. They smiled at me, and we made some small talk about how busy the place was. Then the older woman looked at Lara, smiled, "You in trouble, girl?" Lara shook her head, and the women must have thought she was answering them. "What's up then?" the older one asked, looking at me.

"We need a copy of Lara's birth certificate, and she thinks you might have one in her file."

"I'm sure we do. Such a thick file," the older one said with a smirk.

I turned to look at Lara, but she was already a few feet away talking to a young boy sitting on a chair next to the officers' corner, handcuffed.

"She's a good girl," said the younger one from across the counter, "she's just had a tough life."

"Who hasn't?" snapped the older one. Then looking at me, speaking softly again, "Who hasn't, huh?! Who hasn't had a tough life, you tell me. Don't you agree?! I'm telling you, life is not easy, no way mister, don't you think so?! See the boy Lara is talking to? A newcomer, says he just ran away from home, first week on the streets, and already in trouble, caught stealing a purse from an old lady. Think he wants to go back home?! No mister, he won't even tell the officers where home is. It must be bad at home, I reckon, but to prefer the streets! He's in for a tough ride, if you know what I mean, no home can be that bad. He'd better go back home, if you ask me. Don't you think? You'd better get going, upstairs, talk to the secretary at the documentation office."

I motioned Lara to follow me and headed to the second floor, glad the older woman hadn't paused between questions. Upstairs there were more women with kids sitting on benches waiting to see the Juvenile Court Judge or the state attorney working under him. Lara and I walked to the office where the documentation crew worked. All the clerks seemed busy, some typing, some chatting away. I waited until the head clerk, a woman in her late 40s, made eye contact with me from her desk. She was the most helpful person in that office, and very pleasant. She took a sip of her coffee, folded the newspaper neatly, and came to the counter.

"Hi there, you always come when we are most busy," she said with a smile. Then she looked at Lara, and the smile was gone.

"We were hoping that you would have Lara's original birth certificate in your files," I fired quickly before she had time to ask what Lara had done wrong. "Lara is trying to get a job, and she needs to have an ID, and to get the ID she needs to show her birth certificate at the police department."

"You want to get a job, huh? Why don't you talk to the people at the City Hall's Youth Project? You don't need an ID for that." She was amiable.

"I don't want to deliver newspapers or be a messenger between offices in downtown." Lara was polite but curt.

"And why not? You feel you are too good to do those kinds of jobs?"

"No, no, no, ma'am. That's not it. You see, these jobs that the Youth Project finds for us pay less than a third of the minimum wage, and I cannot live on that, right? And you can only work on these jobs till you turn 18 years old. I'm already 17. Then what? I need to learn skills for jobs that will give me enough money for rent and all that. I want a job that will pay minimum wage so I can rent a small room, buy food and clothes, you know, live a normal life."

I was genuinely impressed by Lara's moderation and determination. For a few weeks she had been saying that she wanted to get a job, to make money, to rent a small room of her own. She then asked for my help in getting her ID, and I began to believe that she was serious, although a little dreamy I thought, about leaving the streets and getting a job. Hearing her speak now made me think that she was actually going to do it. I think the head clerk was impressed as well, at least for a brief moment.

"Very well. So, what do you need then?" the head clerk said looking at me. I looked at Lara.

"The birth certificate, the original," Lara said, swiftly cutting the air with her hands forming a rectangular shape.

"Oh yes, the birth certificate," the head clerk said softly looking at Lara's hands. She paused for a second or two, her eyes looking distant. Then she looked up, first at Lara and then at me, turned around and ordered a young male clerk to hang up the phone and get Lara's file.

After a few minutes the male clerk returned and said he couldn't find Lara's file. "Have you looked in the 'lost cases' cabinet?" the head clerk asked. As she looked at Lara gravely, the male clerk went back to where the file cabinets were.

"I've known Lara since she was 3 years old, when her mom was taken to jail, I don't know what she did, and we had to find an institution for her to live in." She was matter of fact.

"What do you remember from when you were little?" I asked Lara.

"I d . . .," Lara began but was interrupted by the head clerk.

"She's been trouble for us ever since. She picked fights with everyone and has been thrown out of almost every institution in town." Her tone of voice was ever gentle.

"That's not true!" Lara replied.

"We've done all we could for her," she said pointing with her chin at Lara, who was staring at the head clerk with her big brown eyes.

"But she's young and has lots of time to change her life," I said.

"She always manages to bring things down on herself," she said as the male clerk handed her a manila folder containing what looked to be hundreds of pages.

"But now she's more mature," I said hoping we could find the birth certificate quickly.

"If anybody has her original birth certificate, it's us." The head clerk set the heavy manila folder on the counter between us, everything upside down from where Lara and I were standing, and she started flipping the pages so fast that I couldn't make out a single word.

"Why are there so many papers, *tio*? What do they say about me?" Lara asked me.

"These are the records for every time she got in trouble or she moved from one institution to the next," the head clerk said glancing at me briefly, still flipping.

She suddenly stopped on a page with a few pictures glued to it, shook her head, and tapped one of the pictures with the tip of her index finger. "This is the best example of what we [we?] were talking about. Through us, an Italian couple had made all the necessary arrangements to adopt Lara; they came all the way from Italy to get her, but she didn't want to go. You see what I'm saying? She could be living in Italy now! But she threw that chance out of the window." She said the last words looking at Lara, her tone still gentle.

I looked at Lara, and her light brown skin was blushing a little, her lips arched in a shy smile. She asked the head clerk to see the pictures; she said she couldn't remember what she looked like when she was young.

"That was in '89, Lara was 10 years old then. The couple seemed to be good people and were extremely disappointed that Lara didn't want to go with them," the woman said as we looked at the photos.

"What made you not wanna go?" I asked Lara.

"I was scared."

"She was dumb."

"I couldn't understand what they said."

"She turned her back on her only chance to lead a decent life."

"I was scared," Lara said still looking at the pictures.

"You know how hard it is to find adoptive parents for kids as old as 10; we did and she blew it," said the head clerk looking at me, shrugging.

"I would go now," Lara said smiling to the head clerk, who looked at Lara without smiling back. "Can you get in touch with them now and say that I'll go?" Lara's smile turned somewhat mischievous.

"Too late." The head clerk took the manila folder back and started flipping pages again.

I asked Lara to tell me what she remembered from that time, from the encounter with the Italian couple and her fears. She told me about a fancy hotel room, not understanding what the couple was saying to her, crying, not wanting to leave her friends at the institution she was living in, yelling at the couple, running away from the hotel room. Lara said she wished she'd gone with them back to Italy, "wherever that is." She thought they were rich and that she'd have nice clothes, her own TV set in her own bedroom, that she'd travel and wouldn't need to work, that she'd be able to eat steak every day, "for lunch and for dinner." I told her she could still do that if she got a job; she fell silent. I'm certain that, at 17, she understood the difference between being raised in a wealthy family and getting by on a low-skill job's paycheck better than I did.

"Can't find her birth certificate here," the head clerk said closing the manila folder.

"Let's get out of here, *tio*, forget this job thing." Lara stormed out of the office. I went after her.

ACT 7

UNSPEAKABLE TRANSGRESSIONS: INDIGENOUS EPISTEMOLOGIES, ETHICS, AND DECOLONIZING ACADEMY/INQUIRY

I: Invented Roots, Different Nationalism

I look at this ad for a joint position on gender studies and American Indian studies. I look further. I go to the website, and then I see this picture of this professor. He has long hair, as I do; he looks white, at least for my eyes. However, the page mentions the ethnicity/tribe to which he belongs.

Later in the day, talking to another professor, I mentioned the job ad.

"Forget it. You are neither native nor American."[1]

Am I not? America is how the empire names itself. I forget that the other America(s) is named Latina/central/south. I am from South America but not *the* America. But what happens when "history" and "heritage" are nowhere to be found or claimed and granted.

I was raised mostly by my grandmother, Alda, and her sisters, aunts Zeze and Ana. I remember them telling me stories about their grandmother, a very short and very dark woman who was a native. Their grandfather took her from her people, but as they rush to say, he married her.

"But aunt Ana, your eyes are blue." "These come from my grandfather."

Aunt Ana was the only person with blues eyes in my family. Today, January 4, 2007, she is turning 90. I spoke with her early this afternoon. Next week, Dani is going to visit her with our kids. Aunt Ana is really excited about seeing them, especially Francisco, who has the same name and blues eyes of her grandpa Chico.[2]

On the other side of the tree, there is Grandpa Geraldo, my mother's father. He died when I was 3 or 4. I do not remember him. I've seen pictures here and there. Grandpa Geraldo was something, but neither black nor white. He was . . . colored. There are many stories about this man.

I might tell some in another occasion. For now, I am going to tell just one.

My Grandma Antonia was the sister of uncle Venancio, the big farmer in the region, the patriarch of the family. She was very white, as if we can measure the unmarked. She fell in love with Geraldo. The problem was that Geraldo was just someone who grew up among the peasants who work in the farm. He was not good for her. For what I've been told, Geraldo wanted everything but getting married.

However, Grandma Antonia was a stubborn woman. She decided that if she wasn't going to marry Geraldo, she would not marry anyone. The legend is that when she turned 30 years old, Venancio gave up. Better to have Antonia as Geraldo's wife than single. The legend also says that he could not stand to see his sister suffering anymore. Hence, Venancio "bought" Geraldo to marry his sister. Geraldo and Antonia got married and had two children, a dark one, my mother Helita, and a light one, uncle Paulo. Antonia died when my mother was 5, and she and little brother went to live with Venancio, his wife and four children. Geraldo went on to live his life, showing up from time to time in my mother's life.

But who was Geraldo? He was—ethically and racially—something. What he was, comparing to Wolf's European peasants, part of the people "without history"(Scheper-Hughes, 1992, p. 90) I can trace the white arm of my heritage but not the dark one. I do not know the names of Geraldo's parents. This is a good example of the myth of "Brazilian Racial democracy"(Freyre, 1936). Geraldo was the *caboclo*[3] and/or the matuto,[4] the product of colonial rape and also my grandfather.

I can claim a "native" identity, but can I be granted one in our institutionalized system with its categories? This goes to the heart of Foucault's concept of power and knowledge.

But this is not about me, as a white male scholar who lives in a privileged position, trying to appropriate an otherized identity. My experience is never alone in the world. It is about "those people without history," described by Nancy Scheper-Hughes in her powerful book, *Death without Weeping: The Violence of Everyday Life in Brazil*, as:

> "The *matutos*' faces are browner; their bodies are smaller and slighter. One might see them as tough and sinewy, but that would be at variance with their own image of themselves as weak, wasted, and worn-out. One can see both the Amerindian and the African in their eyes, cheekbones, hair, and skin, although the African predominates.... These people are the descendants of a slave runway slave-indian, caboclo, population. Yet, they do not think to link their current difficulties to a history of slavery and race exploitation.... They call themselves *os pobres* (the poor), and they describe themselves as *moreno* (brown), almost never as *preto* or

negro (black). They are 'brown,' then, as all Brazilians, rich and poor, are said to be 'brown.' In this way the ideology of a 'racial democracy' goes unchallenged, uncontested, into another generation." (1992, p. 90)

I grew up among them. Remember Roni? "They also have been my maids, caretakers" and "easy girls made for sex" (Moreira, 2007). And yes, through my whiteness and heterosexuality, I discriminated them, I oppressed their marked bodies, I otherized them, and also, I studied them. Conde is dead. It is about going against the code and recoding of race and ethnicity in popular culture and elsewhere (Dimitriadis and McCarthy, 2000).

"Quite clearly, the increasing complexity of popular culture, and its coding and recoding of race, demands similar efforts, efforts to use our lives and experiences as resources to conjure up communities with moral and ethical imperatives. . . ." (p. 186)

I am from Brazil, the country of slavery and migration; the "stage" for the genocide of black and natives; the huge internal migration that never seems to end; the country of the *Nordestinos*, the people from the Northeast.

The migration in Brazil is marked from rural to urban. People who live in the dry arid areas of the Northeast generally don't have enough water for their subsistence and need to walk long distances to obtain it. Many times these people, who are generally poor, give up and go to live in the city, São Paulo and Rio de Janeiro being the main destinations.

"In 1940 only 6.3 million persons (15.3%) lived in the cities of 20.000 or more. By 1970, six cities accounted for more than 80% of Brazilian urban population (52.9 million)." (Wagner and Ward, 1980, p. 250)

The Nordeste *is the poorest region of Brazil, with the worst living conditions in the country, primarily in the rural areas. Education and health care are nonexistent; suffering from hunger and malnutrition are common conditions that afflict people living in these areas; illiteracy and child labor are alarming, as is child prostitution in major cities. In São Paulo and Rio de Janeiro, as well as many other parts of the metropolitan areas of Brazil outside the Northeast,* Nordestinos *are often despised, even hated, by people of the middle and upper classes, who claim that the* Nordestinos *are responsible for many of the social problems of the city. They are, after all, the "Latinos" of Brazil.*

Baianos *(persons from the state of Bahia),* Paraiba *(name of one of the states in the Northeast),* Pau de arara *(Parrot's perch—an allusion to how* Nordestinos *are transported in old and dangerous old trucks and buses to the sugar cane plantations around the country; it also became the informal name of a device of torture used by the police for punishment or confession in Brazilian's detention centers),* cabeca chata *(an allusion to the big size and form of the* Nordestinos' *heads in relation to their bodies),* arataca *(a kind of trap to hunt wild animals, an allusion to the lack of food that urges the* Nordestinos *to hunt for survival),* favelados *(people who live in the* favelas/*slums)—these are all derogatory names for* Nordestino *migrants to the industrialized south of Brazil. All these words and expressions are synonyms for criminal, lazy, dirty, ugly, sexual deviant, stupid, and so on.*

This story is an old one. *Nordestinos* come without much money, trying to escape the hunger, the drought, in hope of a better life and are rejected by most employers because of their low or nonexistent education. Quickly realizing that the big city is as bad as or worse than the *sertão* (hinterland, back country, remote dry interior of the Northeast), they end up in *favelas* . They are the *retirantes*, refugees from the countryside, "driven or expulsed ones and *flagelados* (the afflicted), who crossed barren wastelands that even birds and small mammals had deserted. . . ." (Scheper-Hughes 1992, p. 68) In my last "fieldwork" (I hate this word[5]) in the *favela* of Parque Oziel, a relatively "young" (9 years old) settlement, I was able to see the clash between families and people who have been in the city forever (3–4 generations) and the ones "fresh" from the *sertão*. However, the people without history do have one: 500 years of colonization and massacre.

> Conde is dead.
> Conde was beaten to death.
> He was 26 years old.
> He was a black soccer fan.
> Conde is dead, but Zezao is alive.
> When I first wrote about Conde, I named him Zezao.
> Yes,
> I changed his name.
> I was/am the powerful researcher.
> And Conde?
> He was just the subject.

I could not have done the study for my master's thesis without Conde. I got my degree, and what did Conde get? Rony, my best friend in my childhood was, as my Grandpa Geraldo, everything but white.

I, we, need more than that. Postcolonial, Third World Feminism, Indigenous theories give us that. I am not the white man trying to negate the identity the Others have fought so hard to conquest and to keep. Based on those concepts, I am, as an allied Other, radically and at the same time humbly, trying to expand the possibilities of life. I build on Linda T. Smith's words:

> "The desire for 'pure,' uncontaminated, and simple definitions of the native by the settler is often a desire to continue to know and define the Other, whereas the desire by the native to be self-defining and self-naming can be read as a desire to be free, to escape definition, to be complicated, to develop and change, and to be regarded as fully human. In between such desires are multiple and shifting identities and hybridities which much more nuances positions about what constitutes native identities, native communities, and native knowledge in anti/postcolonial times." (2005, p. 86)

Smith alerts us that the desire for "pure" is one (of many) factor that makes the "native" complicated. She acknowledges that many natives live the contradiction of being a member of an oppressed colonized community that still "remembers other ways of being, of knowing, and relating to the world" (p. 86). However, "when the foundations of those memories are disturbed, *space sometimes is created for alternative imaginings to be voice, to be sung, and to be heard (again)*" (p. 87, italics added).

I am trying to help the creation of this Smith's space—not negating it, but in collaboration with the work that is being done in Brazil (and beyond) by natives and non-natives to empower the ones who have survived the massacre and are officially recognized and also identified with the indigenous population in Brazil. According to the official word in the Brazilian government there were still 350,240 natives (0.22% of the total population) distributed in 227 ethnicities with 175 different languages and dialects being spoken all around the country, but mostly concentrated in the state of Amazonas (25%) (1999, IBGE-Brazilian Institute of Geography).

There are beautiful and powerful works being done in Brazil, such as those of Gersem Luciano Baniwa—from the Baniwa Tribe—the first Native Brazilian to get a Masters degree in anthropology at the Universidade Federal de Brasília. He also was the first president of the Federação das

Organizações Indígenas do Rio Negro–(FOIRN). Gersem fights for the legalization of land for natives and the inclusion of system of quotas (a version of affirmative action) that would help native Brazilians to get access to higher education.

Trinh T. Minh-ha, in *Woman, Native, Other*, lay out beautifully and powerfully what I am trying to say here. It's worth (another) long quote.

> "A critical difference from myself means that I am not I, am within and without i. I/I can be I or I, you and me both involved. We (with capital W) sometimes include(s), other times exclude(s) me. You and I are close, we intertwine; you may stand on the other side of the hill once in a whole, but you may also be me, while remaining what you are and what I am not. The differences made *between* entities comprehended as absolute presences—hence the notion of *pure origin* and *true* self—are an outgrowth of a dualistic system of thought peculiar to the Occident (the 'onto-theology' which characterizes Western metaphysics). They should be distinguished from the differences grasped *both between* and *within* entities, each of these being understood as multiple presences. Not One, not two either. 'I' is, therefore, not a unified subject, a fixed identity, or that solid mass covered with layers of superficialities one has gradually to peel off before one can see its true face. 'I' is, itself, *infinite layers*. Its complexity can hardly be conveyed through such typographic conventions as I, i, or I/i. Thus, I/i am compelled by the will to say/unsay, to resort the entire gamut of personal pronouns to stay near this fleeing and static essence of Not-I. Whether I accept or not, the natures of *I, i, you, s/he, We, we, they,* and *wo/man* constantly overlap. They all display a necessary ambivalence, for the line dividing *I* and *Not-I, us* and *them,* or *him* and *her* is not (cannot) always (be) as clear as we would like it to be. Despite our desperate, eternal attempt to separate, contain, and mend, categories always leak." (1989, pp. 89–94)

My intention here is not, by any means, to stand against the creation of ethnic departments in higher education. Nor it is against the social movements originated in these spaces. My intention is to challenge categories of knowledge that also relay in "knowledges" and social constructions, created by mechanisms of colonization even when they are created for the empowerment of the oppressed in many circumstances. The uncontrolled desire to understand and control the Other. These are too American. I learned from Audrey Lorde that "the master's tool will never dismantle the master's house. They may allow us temporarily to beat him at his own game, but they will never enable us to bring about genuine change." (1983, p.112)

There is the need to radically break with the colony/metropolis apparatus. There is no innocent time, or home for that matter, to look for. As Chandra Talpade Mohanty suggests in her reading of Minnie Bruce Pratt's autobiographical narrative "Identity: Skin Blood Heart"[6]:

"the tension between the desire for home, for synchrony, for sameness, and the realization of the repressions and violence that make home, harmony, sameness imaginable, and that enforce it is made clear in the movement of the narrative by very careful and effective reversals that do not erase the positive desire for unity, for oneness, but destabilize and undercut it. . . . It depends on acknowledgement not only on her ignorance and her prejudices but also her fears, above all the fear of loss that accompanies change." (2003, pp. 102–103)

Diaspora always includes some kind of loss. Home, land, identities. . . . Hope, care, and love are to be found in the no home/innocent space; in the space that is not here/not there; the space that "does not exist," because it has to be created.

In this performance, these written lines in the pages above, what I am trying to do is to build in Hommi Bhabha's suggestion that "the colonial encounter is not repressive but productive of all kinds of effects the colonizer did not anticipate" (Dimitriadis and McCarthy, 2001, p. 55); building is his concept of hybridity, but not only as the "acceptable and regulated" mix of races, forced mostly through rape and destructive systems of domination, but ones that goes beyond the biological and scientific constrains.

Borrowing from Bhabha:

"Hybridity is the sign of the productivity of colonial power, its shifting forces and fixities; it is the name for the strategic reversal of the process of domination through disavowal (that is the production of discriminatory identities that secure the 'pure' and original identity of authority). Hybridity is the revaluation of the assumption of colonial identity through the repetition of discriminatory identity effects. It displays the necessary deformation and displacement of all sites of discrimination and domination. It unsettles the mimetic or narcissistic demands of colonial power but reimplicates its identifications in strategies of subversion that turn the gaze of the discriminated back upon the eye of the power." (1994, p. 112; quoted from Dimitriadis and McCarthy, 2000, p. 55)

Hybridity in this stance "is a radical disturbance of both 'self' and 'other,' an encounter that leads ultimately to unanticipated, maybe even unspeakable, transgressions" (p. 55).
Where do I want to arrive with all these words?
In Anzaldúa's notion of a different kind of nationalism, her "Invented Roots" and "New Tribalism." Below is how, in a conversation with Ines Hernandez-Avila, edited by AnaLouise Keating, Gloria Anzaldúa explains her ideas:

> "It's actually the white Anglo dominant culture that privileges the white in us, that tries to erase, to hide the fact that we have African blood, the fact that we have Indian blood, and only a very small percentage of Spanish blood." (Anzaldúa, 2000, p. 181)
>
> "GEA: Another thing I want to touch on and see what you think is what happens when our sense of tribe and identity changes, when it expands to include a new kind of tribalism. . . . Chicana feminists, artists, *activistas*, and intellectuals, many of us dykes. We looked for something beyond just nationalism while continuing to connect to our roots. If we don't find the roots we needed we invent them, which is fine because culture is invented anyway. We have returned to the tribe, but our nationalism is one with a twist. . . . It's saying, 'Yes, I belong. I come from this particular tribe, but I'm open to interacting with these other people.' I call this the New Tribalism. It's a kind of mestizage that allows for connecting with other ethnic groups and interacting with other cultures and ideas.
> IHA: They look at . . . and say, 'Oh, you're not the real Indians. . . .' And you go, 'wait a minute. Who are you to tell me that I'm not real?' . . . It comes back to the whole idea of tradition. Tradition is not static, it's dynamic and it's always been dynamic. Otherwise it would have died." (Anzaldúa, 2000, p. 185)

I have the duty
To manipulate and transform
The tale of colonization
Using my life as source to show
With a political propose
An experience
To expand the sacredness of life

II: Unspeakable Transgressions

Are we crazy?
Are we insane?
We should be ashamed—me included(ing)
I've been in both ends of the window
The beggar, the giver
Probably the taker
Really really
Look at the pictures
Pictures that I probably cannot "legally" use

Define race and ethnicity for me?
The minority of no white that take in the majority of Other's lives
And no, I am not trying to claim 1/564 of my blood is native
To legitimate a position that justifies my job's application
Please
With yours and mine well intentioned writing books
Am I the only one?
Are they?

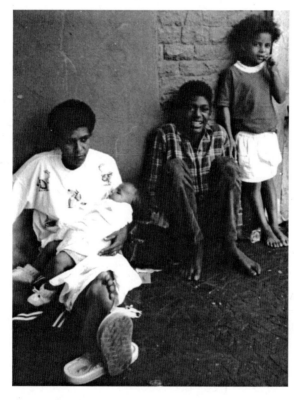

It is a dissertation . . . and I know that I am supposed to come with answers
    . . . and instead I am coming with questions . . .
Am I supposed to have anything figured out?
Let's us forget all the bullshit
People keep me telling about my anger . . .
Looking . . .
Look!
At the fucking pictures . . .
They still are at the end of the gaze and
I know
I'm not helping much

Want me to explain?
Wanna me, with my broken English to explain?
Look at the fucking pictures

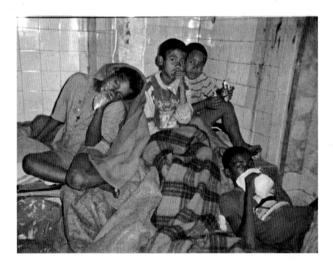

And
For God—not white and not male—'s sake do something
Stop
Stop right now the cynicism—because I'll not stop—because that's the only
    way to justify my minivan that I do not have yet
Is it?
How in hell do we claim and get granted whatever we decide to be?

We
The product of the Colonial rape
Thank you Anzaldúa
Aren't we, after all the scooping, building our stuff in the same way that THEY BUILT their own?

There's no ice cream here people
Haraway told us
ALREADY
We are dealing with people's lives

You are not crazy . . . I'm the crazy one
I am the one that like in the good movie
Is
"Lost in translation"
For everything
Lost and fucked up
And
Blessed
'Cause I survived
Hey, I'm a white male, life gets easy on me
Because
After all, I believe
And don't ask me what the "all" is
I believe and
Live by and raise my children believing
In the possibilities of imagining the
Human

Because, like the great white fairy tale, in the Kevin Costner's[7] movie, people will come
You better believe
YES THEY WILL!!
But not for baseball

Some people write about theory
I write about bathroom and shit
Refusing
The colonizing need for understand
That is on us

III: In Purity

> "I am from an island whose history is steeped in the abuses of Western imperialism, whose people still suffer the deformities caused by Euro-American colonialism, old and new. Unlike many third world liberationists, however, I cannot claim to be a descendent of any particular strain, noble or ignoble. I am, however, 'purely bred,' descendent of all parties involved in that cataclysmic epoch. I despair, for the various part of me cry out for retribution at have been brutally uprooted and transplanted to fulfill the profit-cry of 'white' righteousness dominance. My soul moans that part of me that was destroyed by the callous instrument . . . the gun, the whip, the book. My mind echos with the

screams of disruption, desecration, destruction." (Rosa Villafane-Sisolak, from an unpublished paper, quoted from Anzaldúa, 1990, p. xix)

"Is she talking about me?
No, you moron.
Is Brasil an island?
Hey Thug, that's enough. Shut up."

Story 13

Nike Cap

It was the 20th of May, 1994, my third day out on the streets of Campinas. Magali, a street educator who was my mentor in the realities of street life, and I were walking to a viaduct where kids usually hung out, when we saw someone sitting alone by the creek that ran between two busy avenues. As we got closer Magali saw it was Lucio, a 13-year-old boy whom she'd known for a couple of years. His eyelids were heavy, and his hands and face were all dirty from the pink nail polish he'd been sniffing. His arms moved slowly around Magali's neck when she leaned forward to give him a tight hug. I stood there just watching those two kiss and hug. Magali introduced me to Lucio as a friend of hers. I shook his weakened hand and sat down in front of him, a little uncomfortable with his suspicious gaze toward me. They hadn't seen each other for a few weeks, and Lucio was telling Magali his latest adventures between one sniff and another.

"I'll leave now if you don't stop sniffing this shit," Magali said calmly but firmly.

He smiled at her and put the plastic bag with the nail polish away. I just listened while they talked. Lucio looked at the bag Magali had on her lap.

"What do you have in there?" he asked.

"Some games," she said taking them out of the bag. "Wanna play dominoes?"

After we'd been playing for a while, Lucio began to look at the cars and people that were passing by. He'd won again and, looking at me, asked if my Nike cap was imported.

"No," I quickly lied embarrassed.

"Can I see it?" he asked, trying to hide a smile in the corner of his mouth.

I gave it to him, sure that I wouldn't be caught lying, because the Nike tag inside the cap, whose English words would have been a giveaway, had fallen off a few weeks before. Lucio took my cap in his hands and started counting the stitched sewing lines on top of the visor.

"It's imported," he said handing the cap back to me.

"How do you know?" I asked surprised.

"It has eight lines on the visor," he said collecting the domino tiles from the floor.

"So, if a cap has eight lines sewed on the top of the visor it's got to be imported?" I asked, still baffled by this kind of knowledge.

"Yeah. Everybody knows that!" Lucio said frowning, which I read as a sign of disdain for my ignorance.

Lucio and Magali began to talk about something else. I was still puzzled by his ability to identify a foreign commodity. I wondered whether it had been a good guess or he really could make that distinction based on such a small detail.

I was out on the streets again the next day, and another boy, whose name I never learned, asked to see my cap. Again the sewing lines on the visor of my Nike cap were being carefully counted.

"This is an imported cap," he said placing it back in my head.

Notes

1. I am not implying that the views of America or being native that I discuss in this section are shared by the professor I saw in the picture or by his department. Moreover, not even knowing much about them, I believe that their views are the opposite. I do not intend, in any way, to criticize the professor or the department.
2. *Chico* is short for Francisco in Brazil. Naming my son Francisco was a coincidence. I had totally forgotten about "grandpa Chico" until being reminded by aunt Ana. She was so happy that I never told her about this.
3. A copper-colored, "civilized," or mestizoized Indian; person of mixed and white ancestry.
4. One who comes from the *mato* (jungle, forest); rustic country person;
5. That is why I intentionally use this word here.
6. In Minnie Bruce Pratt's narrative, she identifies herself as white, middle-class, Christian-raised, southern, and lesbian.
7. *Field of Dreams*.

Chapter 8

BETWEENNESS IN KNOWLEDGE PRODUCTION

STORY 14

FIRE IN THE MISSION

Judge E. had sent a message through one of the juvenile officers saying he wanted to see me. I had been trying to get an appointment to see him for months, unsuccessfully. I went to the Juvenile Court on the same day, even though I had no clue why he wanted to see me, or how he knew about me.

As I walked into the busy lobby, I saw Dan and Carlos sitting near the officers' desks, handcuffed to each other. I had first met them during the winter of 1994, nearly two years earlier, each hanging out with a different crowd and in a different area of downtown. They were both 14 years old at the time.

Dan was then a sort of leader in a group of ten to fifteen boys who were living in an abandoned building next to a busy intersection of large avenues on the outskirts of downtown. Dan, a light-skinned mulatto, was bigger and stronger than the other boys, and often more daring in their daily adventures. I hung out a lot with that group in 1994, and Dan was the last one to warm up to me, and even then I didn't think he liked me much. He seemed suspicious of everybody, including the street educators who visited them daily. But on my last day with them, before I left the field and went back to graduate school, Dan surprised me with his affection (though without losing his candidness!). "That's not right, *tio* Marcelo! You make us begin to like you and then you leave us here," he let drop as I was saying the last goodbye to the boys. I'm trying to come up with a response to this day.

Carlos, a white boy, used to hang out with two older teens, cleaning the windshields of cars stopped at red lights. Sometimes they would get a few coins for the job; most of the time they got yelled at, or not even acknowledged, by the drivers. Carlos was always kind and talkative and seemed eager to leave the streets. In spite of being homeless, he had gone back to school and wanted to get at least a high school diploma. One cold night I saw him working alone and stopped to talk to him. We talked about school for a while. He didn't like the torn down building, but liked his Portuguese teacher. That day his teacher had asked him to read his short essay in front of the class, prefacing that it was the best essay of the class.

"She said it had a few grammar mistakes, but that it was very good. She makes me want to go to class. You know, sometimes it's hard to get to class on time. And when my clothes are all dirty and I smell bad, I don't go at all," he said showing a missing front tooth through his smile.

"How do you get up early in the morning?" I asked realizing my own absolute dependence on my alarm clock.

"I try to lie down in a place where the first beams of sunlight will reach my face and wake me up. I usually miss class on cloudy days," he said smiling again. "You wanna see my essay?"

"Would love to," I said, glad I didn't even need to ask.

To be a Brazilian . . .

. . . Is to live in a country where most of the families don't have houses to live, don't have jobs, and are starving.

Where the politics is a game of power and influence. This is the opinion of most of the Brazilian people. The politicians use all the races (Black, White, Indian) to continue savoring luxuries, trips in the vacation seasons; all that paid for by us, you and me, who are underpaid workers.

It's necessary to dream, love, and fight for a Brazil more honest and just.

by C____ V____

I finished reading Carlos's essay for the third time and started watching him at work, dipping the mop in a bucket half full of blackened water, walking up to a stopped car with a smile, pointing to the windshield with the dripping mop, and seeing the driver's index finger move sideways on the other side of the windshield, declining. Or the driver would quickly close the window and lock the door when Carlos walked toward the car.

Carlos then would smile or shake his head and walk to another car. In the half hour I watched him work that night, I counted more scared and disgusted faces than I'd seen in all my life.

I stopped to talk to him more often after that night. We talked about many things, like school, girls, America, soccer; but one conversation in particular has never left my mind. It was mother's day, in May, and he said he'd been thinking about his mom the whole day.

"I miss her," he said.

"Did you go visit her today?"

"I can't go to her house. Last time I was home I broke a chair on her boyfriend's head. He was beating her up, the drunk bastard, he always did, he came home loaded every day. I heard her crying and tried to stop him. We started to fight, but he was drunk and kept falling down. I hit him really hard on the head with that chair, yes I did. Then my mom started to yell at me, saying that I had killed him, that I was a no-good. I couldn't believe she was defending him, you know, I got so mad that I left home right then."

"Did you try to go back?"

"Yeah, I went back the next day, when I knew the son of a bitch wouldn't be there, but my mom said that what I'd done was wrong, that the son of a bitch is the man of the house and I need to respect him. Fuck that! I got mad at her and left, for good."

"Maybe she's changed her mind now," I tried to be encouraging.

"No, she knows where I am. People from her neighborhood see me here every day."

We were silent for a while and then started to talk about something else.

I hadn't seen Carlos since that mother's day, but we recognized each other right away. I was surprised to see him with Dan. I walked up to him and he stretched his cuffed hand toward me, dragging Dan's hand and attention with him. Carlos and I shook hands and smiled at each other.

"Hey, *tio* Marcelo!" said Dan, looking surprised to see me.

"It doesn't look like you guys are doing too well," I said shaking hands with Dan, too.

"It's all right. It's always the same thing, you know, they bring us here, tell us how bad we are, how we're gonna grow up to be scumbags. Then they let us walk out. They don't even bother to take us to our families anymore." Dan's voice was much deeper now, his hands looked huge on his knees.

"Why did they bring you here this time?" I asked.

"They caught us with a walkman we'd taken from a rich boy near the cathedral," Dan said casually.

We talked some more and they told me about their latest escapade. Two weeks before, they had been taken by the juvenile officers to the Mission for Boys, a shelter run by the Baptist church that serves some twenty-five economically underprivileged kids younger than 18 years old. Both said they were happy with the idea at the time, tired of sleeping on concrete, eating what others chose to buy for them, and the endless hassle from life in the streets.

But they encountered trouble from the beginning. Some of the boys already living in the Mission spread toothpaste on the few clean clothes Carlos had brought with him while he was having his first breakfast. Then, when they were playing soccer in the backyard, one of the boys started a fight with Carlos. Dan butted in and slapped the boy around, telling the other boys they would get the same treatment if they messed with him or Carlos.

"I went to school in the afternoon and even started to like the idea of going to school, you know, there were some babes in my class," Dan said smiling. "But when I went back to the house after school, tio Tom started to yell at me. I figured he had heard about the fight in the morning, and I tried to explain that the boys'd started it, that I had to defend myself. I told him that Carlos had nothing to do with the fight. He had!" Dan said looking and smiling at Carlos. "I knew he really wanted to stay there, so I lied."

"But *tio* Tom said he didn't care who had started the fight. He said I was new there and had to learn to respect the ones who'd been there longer. He was yelling all the time, like I was a soldier! He even tried to hit me. I told him to fuck off then. I wouldn't put up with that, you know. That's why I left home in the first place. So I set some mattresses on fire and left the damned place."

I had no trouble believing every word Dan said. Tom, the head of the Baptist Mission, had threatened me with words a few weeks before, when he accused me of bringing Grace, Dalva, Regi, and Kleo to his office only to threaten him and his assistants. In fact, I'd gone to his office to return the copy of Dalva's birth certificate that his assistant, Berta, had given me that morning. The girls had seen me walking to his office and joined me. But the girls, who had all been to his shelter for girls before, didn't like Tom and let him know that, in his own office. Afterward he let me know what would happen to me if I brought them there again.

Carlos then told me he'd left a week after Dan did, unhappy with the strict rules and schedules in the Mission. They were both sleeping on the streets but told me they were not smoking crack.

"Only a drag here and there so the guys don't get on my case," Dan said and we all smiled.

We said goodbye, sure we'd be running into each other soon now that they were back on the streets, and I went to see the judge.

Judge E. must have heard that I was associated with an American university and doing research, for he talked at length about the need to support the few institutions working with street kids in Campinas. He talked about how these institutions need to be represented in a positive light so they can attract more money from international agencies and foundations. He talked about other needs, too, but I'd stopped listening to him when he suggested that I give special attention, "in whatever I write," to the excellent work carried on by the Baptist Tom and his missions.

ACT 8

LIFE IN SO MANY ACTS

Act 1: Life 1—USA

I am walking on Sixth St. toward Green. Even without looking or moving my head, I am aware of the car that is parking on my right side. It was a beat up blue car. It had been in a crash that damaged the left front corner. The headlight is missing. I am also aware of the guy that gets out from it. White, early 20s, a worker of some sort. His clothes are dirty with old paint. He is close. Too close, at least for Americans. He is walking behind my back, right to left, again, too close. My left side is tensing up. My elbow is ready to move. I can tell the exact moment I should move. I can picture my elbow splashing his nose . . . blood everywhere . . . his look of surprise and fear. . . . But, I do not move. The guy passes by me, and I am going to meet Dani in the coffee shop. I am in Champaign, it is 5 o'clock afternoon in a spring day.

Funny though . . . It is on me. Sometimes, I am more sensitive to my body's reactions. I like to play with it; to exercise my senses, as I, lousily translated, named it. I know I am safe. Here in Champaign is the safest I had ever felt in my life. No need to "watch my back". Growing up in a poor neighborhood in Brasil was a different story. Same with doing fieldwork in the streets or in the *favelas*. On the one hand, growing up, on the other, fieldwork, in both cases looking for, expecting the same different violence, from the same different bodies.

    Knowledge versus experience
    Am I the thug/colonized?
    Or
    Am I the respectable grad student/colonizer?
    Please, tell me.
    Scientists of the world, help me here. Can you, with your theories, separate one from another?

The thug from the student?
The many from the other many, in my one body?
I heard you are good at this.
And so am I, or I'm supposed to be, because, I am a trained grad
 student.
Not so fast . . .

Act 2: Life 2—Brasil

I open the door of the car. It was a gooooood dinner. Funny . . . All this beef tastes like home, but few times could I have all this beef. Before I get in the car, I look up and see my friend's car on the other side of the park. There is a new way to get on the expressway, and I need to follow them. Nope, don't want to get lost.

I get inside the car. Keep the door open, using the inside light to find a candy. I know I have a candy somewhere here. Here it is. Using my left hand, without looking I try to close the door. The door is not closing. . . . Still without looking I pull harder. I finally look and see a leg holding the door.

Leg?

Then it hits me. In a split of a second. Fuck! I don't look up. Don't need to. My senses are all on alert. Fuck, fuck, fuck! In one move, I kick the door open. At the same time, in the same move, sensing the gun on my left, using my two hands, I throw a bump in the chest of the guy.

Hard.

Making sure that my left arm is in place to take away the good shot he has. Feeling both feet firmly planted in the ground, I looked up.

White, male, young, nice clothes, surprise!!! Middle-class looking guy. Stereotype . . .

I look at the guy. Eye contact. Surprise in his face.

"Get in the car." With the gun almost touching my chest.

Fast. Really fast.

"Now! Or I'm gonna shoot you."

I'm looking the guy in the eyes. There is a little tremor in his hand. God! I wanna make a move. I like my chances. I wanna beat this motherfucker so bad. Anger! Scared Shitless. Desire for blood. Any blood.

Fast. Really fast.

I get this image. I see my kids. It's like they invade my whole body.

Cannot write this.

Fast. Really fast.

Still looking at the eyes.

"Take the fucking car."

I say it hard, but in a low tone. Need to move.

Still looking in the eyes.
Break contact.
Now!!!
Turning back and running...
Hopping not to hear the boom...
Not seeing, not looking, not breathing, just running.
I know the direction.
I see my friends running toward me...
I heard the car driving way...
"Are you okay?"
Can't answer . . .
My body is shaking so hard...
I am crying . . .
Something is different . . .
There is no joy of escaping . . .
There is no cop I'm running from . . .
There are just the kids and Dani . . .
And
Fear
So big so intense
And
Anger
So big so intense
Fast
Many voices
"Are you crazy? What were you going with your door open? Look like a gringo. Just don't act like one. You're not in Champaign. Have you forgotten that?"

Finally able to speak

Yes, I have. It's my first night out in Brasil.

I forgot . . .

Finally able to laugh

Too American, my senses kicked in late. That Champaign of mine is making me soft.

And then . . .

The sexist end

I'm a wuss.

Act 3: Life 3—Fieldwork

After that, I stayed three days without leaving the beautiful house of my in-laws. It happened a week or so before my planned "fieldwork" in the *favela* of Parque Oziel.

Act 4: Life—Living in Champaign

Scared
I Am Scared
I'm gonna tell you
But, it's a secret

I AM SCARED
I am scared that
In the end
I stop caring!

Yeah, you heard it
In the end I might not care
I might forget the pain
Sorry hooks
I might forget Freire's hunger:

> "It was a real and concrete hunger that had no specific date of departure. Even though it never reached the rigor of the hunger experienced by some people I know, it was not the hunger by those who undergo a tonsil operation or are dieting. On the contrary, our hunger was of the type that arrives unannounced and unauthorized, making itself at home without an end in sight. A hunger that, if it was not softened as our was, would take over our bodies, molding them in angular shapes. Legs, arms, and fingers become skinny. Eye sockets become deeper, making the eyes almost disappear. Many of our classmates experienced this hunger and today it continues to afflict millions of Brazilians who die of its violence every year." (1996, p. 15)

But, can I ever, ever forget my own?

Act 5: Life 5—Living over There ... in Memory

Scared
Can I forget when I read Freire for the first time?
'Cause now, with my moving fingers, I cannot forget that ...
The first time I read Freire, I thought he was talking to me about my life and struggles even if some of his concepts were hard to grasp. Funny ...

I can recall reading his concept of "banking education" and understanding what was going on in my school.

One of my epiphanies happened when I was being punished for a fight in my so called "good school."

I did not attend the poor elementary school of my poor neighborhood but rather went to an elite school downtown.

The principal, Mrs. Iracema, was telling me, among other things, how glad I should be that the school was not only providing my formal education but also teaching me good manners, that of course, I could not have learned with the kind of life I have. God, once that woman started to talk, she would never shut up . . .

At that moment, I had my head down staring at my feet, like a good boy.

And I was really angered.

No, I wasn't angered.

"Angered" is a today word.

I?

I was pissed.

I was mad.

Hey, Mrs. Iracema? Do you think I really beat that boy? Wait and see . . .

I was saying to myself that that woman has no idea about my life.

That I have to deal with a drunken father whose presence I have not figured out, if I want him to be close or far away from me.

That I've been working since I was child.

That when I get home, my grandma would be working in candlelight because we did not pay the power bill.

And what is the big deal?

The big deal was that, I was getting some kind of relief, recalling Freire's words . . .

Words about him being a young teacher, telling the peasants that they should not beat up their children, when a peasant interrupted him to say that they love their children, but sometimes, after a full day of work in the field, they just want to rest when they got home.

Cannot recall the exact words.

Sorry, I will not stop writing to check the exact quote. I will not!

It was something like:

"Mister Freire, we got so tired that when kids do what kids are supposed to do, we lose it. Kids . . . they pay the price."

After that, Freire wondered about what happened to his life that made him forget about his own poverty.

All those things were in my mind while Mrs. Iracema was lecturing me . . .

And they are still with me,

Here . . . now!
I might forget this

Act 6: Life 6—Living in Ethics

Scared
I might forget this
Yeah, I'm scared
I'm scared that in the end
I'm gonna
I'm gonna
PLAY BALL
Even when I know I play some
But remember
Remember
It's a secret

I'm scared
That wind comes and blows away the ethical line I draw in the ground
And then?
Gone! Gone, gone, and gone!

Act 7: Life 7—Living in the U of I

Scared
Denzin's office, someday in December.
Cláudio: I need help to schedule my exams.
Denzin: Sure. Let's do it.
C: Yes. I need to move on . . . The worst that can happen is that I don't pass. If I fail, do I get another chance?
D: Do not worry. It never happened.
C: You know what? Never take things for granted. I learned this early in life.
Little Cláudio could not take things for granted.
Where's your father?
I dunno . . .
Where's your mother?
Not here.
What are you hiding in your pocket?
Nothing.
Later in the day, playing with my kids in the living room.
"Analua be nimble

Analua be quick
Analua jump over the candlestick."
"Francisco be nimble
Francisco be quick
Francisco jump over the candlestick."
Little Cláudio be nimble
Little Cláudio be quick
Little Cláudio jump over the candlestick.
Not so sure. Let's try again.
Cláudio be nimble
Cláudio be quick
Cláudio jump over the candlestick.
Hmmm . . . Still not sure.

Act 8: Life 8—Living in . . . Living in . . .

Scared
I'm scared that
That in the end
I stop caring

Rainy day
Cold
Dark library
Looking at old dissertations
"Black teenagers girls want to be pregnant because they do not have anything of their own."
Really?
Come on, you could have asked Grandma.
Rainy day
Cold
Dark Library
Looking at old dissertations

Stopping caring
Forgetting stuff
Erased/ing memories
Forgotten people
Lost scholarship
Fake commitment
Empty words
Oppressive discourse
Asking for help

Don't wanna be scared
Don't wanna forget
Don't wanna make sense
Why?
Hell!
If you don't know
It might be too late

I AM SCARED
I am scared that
In the end
At the very final moment
I just
I just
Don't care anymore!

Act 9: Life 9—Living in Threat

Many voices
I like your work, but I never meet a junior faculty doing this.
People might be moved by your prose, but they will not hire you.
You have to be flexible as scholar.
Don't let the anger get the best of you.
It's nice, but why do it here in academia?
A Brazilian with a chip on his shoulder.
There are more,
    voices
        but I am too tired.
What is this? Am I not able to land a job because I do not behave, do and think, do not ask/answers, and do not write/research/perform the same questions like the others?
SILENCE
A different voice
Cláudio, go home and tell Dani that you will find a job. You will find a job because of what you do.
BREAK
Norman's office is a good place. I feel safe here. He is working with Giardina. I interrupt them.
"Hi, Norm, do you have a minute?"
"Sure."
"I got the idea for this new performance, and I want to you look at it. I got the title, and the first act and the last. Can you look at it now?"

After some time . . .
"Am I going too far? I mean, I wanna make sure . . ."
"Never." Says Norman.
"Never in this office." Says Giardina
We all smile.
BREAK
The theoretical being.
The doctoral student.
The human being.
The thug

Act 10: Life 10—Disconnected(ing) Reflection(s) from the Thug and the Scholar; A Very Long Act and Life with Breaks and Silences

The Scholar

> "The white man is always trying to know into somebody else's business. All right, I'll set something outside the door of my mind for him to play with and handle. He can read my writing but he sho' can't read my mind. I'll put this play toy in his hand, and he will seize it and go away. Then I'll say my say and sing my song." (Zora Neal Hurston, 1990 [1935], p. 3)

I do claim to be a whole. The fragments are how I experience/live life. They are also the representation of (my) life/body. I try to position my scholarship as a way to reclaim my wholeness even if I cannot possibly re-present my whole body. I try to exercise my own form of "oppositional consciousness" (Sandoval, 2000).
BREAK
Anzaldúa calls it "in betweener," and Collins calls it "the outsider within," hence I do not know. My language (or the reading of it) might show a desire for the colonizer's body, because I am using it in a colonizer institution and also I am re-present among other things the colonizer/colonized.
SILENCE
When reading Sandoval's reading of Jameson's model of the postmodern, I was thinking that of course Jameson would have this kind of reading, because he situates his citizen-subject as a part of modern enlightenment project. Jameson himself inhabits that space.

For the first world well-placed subject (including "intellectuals"), it was a first time of what I call "life in uncertainty," or "to live in contradiction without forgetting —or not being able to forget it," where "first world culture has traded depth for surface, the possibility of egalitarian transformations for the excitement of constant but superficial change, feeling for an indeterminate sense of euphoria and intensity, alienation for fragmentation, style for technological reproduction, and life for death." (Sandoval, 2000, p. 25)

I was saying to myself, how about all these other people who only had experienced life under such conditions? Oppressed people have survived oppression.
Then . . .
Then . . . came happiness when, in the next pages, Sandoval started to say the same things I was saying. Jameson forgot that there are other forms of being. Jameson could not overcome his own position.
SILENCE
That . . . this uncertainty was/is presented in everyday life, living/alive from experience to experience, creating actions for "those who hold out against conditions of hunger, deprivation, humiliation, colonization, and social subjection" (Sandoval, 2000, p. 28).

"Such citizen-subjects often do not lay claim to any single healthy linguistic normality from which to speak and act, because doing so might impair one's chances for survival." (pp. 28–29)

It is finding/using devices in the way they appear, out of necessity, in order to negotiate, confront, or speak to power, and then "moving to new forms, expression, and ethos when necessary" (Sandoval, 2000, p. 29).
BREAK
Caminante no hay puentes, se hace puentes al andar ("Voyager there are no bridges, one makes them as one walks")—Gloria Anzaldúa, 1983, p. v

What I am saying is that I am using my survival skills, I am exercising my own form of "oppositional consciousness" (Sandoval, 2000), where I transform, move, study and theorize *La Facultad* (the skills), locating them inside my theoretical framework as part of my body (they/skills has been there). Again, I repeat in a different format that it is interesting that my idea of fragments was not much more than a sort of gut feeling, and I find some of it on Latina/chicana/native Third World women scholars. That was not an accident. There have been many accounts of process like this, many of these subjects surfaced in many disciplines, when persons who have these experiences in the position of an "outside within" in academic settings.
And BREAK again!

A voice from above
I do not understand . . . why these breaks? Oppositional consciousness and breaks. Don't get it.
Scholar
You know what pal. I am too tired. You better ask the thug.
Thug
It's a smell
That's all
You can smell the cops, can't you?
Smell, smelling, stinking nose, smelling smell.
You cannot smell it, can you?
A story
See the street kid on the corner by the traffic light?
Man, you can't see either, can you?
It's a cold night in Campinas. The Kid is wearing a pair of shorts. He is playing with the cold. He is playing with the catholic faith. He is playing you
Not so simple . . .
I can say that he is "playing." I can use the metaphor cause I'm not him.
He knocks on the car's window. Next move? Depends . . . But I bet he can smell it.
Will the window be opened?
By whom?
Look at the faces
The beggar and the giver
Can you tell me the next move?
Smelling/stinking little trump
Depends
On the smell
Sniff kid
Smelling short life
Smelling extermination
Smelling food
Smelling glue
Smelling everything
Just hope he doesn't catch a cold
BREAK
The distinction between "as" and "is" when/where the do and the doing collide! (Denzin, 2003, p. 9)
BREAK
Thug as scholar
You can't see and smell . . .

Another story
This view of the performative makes it "increasingly difficult to sustain any distinction between appearances and facts, surfaces and depths, illusions and substances. Appearances are actualities." (Schechner, 1998, p. 362, quoted from Denzin, 2003, p. 9)

Anzaldúa sees these survival skills as "*La facultad*, the capacity to see in surface phenomena the meaning of deeper realities" (1999, p. 38).

Lorde say that marginality "whatever its nature, . . . which is also the source of our greatest strength" (p. 53).

One of my own understandings of oppositional consciousness, my incomplete reading of Sandoval/Third World feminism, is that once one consciously brings politics and ideology to these ways of survival he/she develops the oppositional consciousness. That is what women of color brought to table in their fight in academia in their response to the white feminism. Hence, Third World feminism refuses to accept the idea of one ideology as the final answer (as other social movements), instead moving for one form of resistance to another, recognizing "the current situation of power and self-consciously choosing and adopting the ideological stand best suited to push against its configurations, a survival skill well known to oppressed peoples" (Sandoval, 2000, p. 60).

Feel the words . . .

"We survive war and conquest; we survive colonization, acculturation, assimilation; we survive beating, rape, starvation, mutilation, sterilization, abandonment, neglect, death of our children, our loved ones, destruction of our land, our homes, our past and future. We survive, and we do more than just survive. We bond, we care, we fight, we teach, we nurse, we bear, we feed, we earn, we laugh, we love, we hang in there, no matter what." (Allen, 1992, p. 190)

It's a run
Face body
Way of from
Escape
Redemption?
That's not for me to say
I'm a thug who can use metaphors
Scholar
It's my house. Kinda home. It has VCR, TV, and microwave. First time
Me living in a place with all these things.
2000

I finally made IT in grad school
Kinda home
Da home of da brave
Living room
White rice
Black beans
Cheap GROUND beef
All MIXED
Brasilian food in
The land of the free
Kinda home
Titanic on TV
Sinking ship
Gonna die in that boat

Marcelo Diversi, friend, brother, mentor, all the good stuff. It has been so many years without seeing him. Celebration. The verb *to help* cannot describe what Marcelo did (has done) for me last year. Now, I'm a master student. And us? We are watching *Titanic*, eating good food and talking cheap. By the way, Marcelo got married. Yes, he married Emily, can you believe this? But you probably do not know Marcelo. This is a nice story. Hope that in one long night he would tell me the details. We all need nice stories . . . I love you cumpa!

Man, I would die in that boat.

Nope. Not you. You smell life. Your father in-law said you're a winner. He's wrong. You're a survivor. You and this big nose of yours. You would smell a way out of the ship.

Hey, I'm better than Leonardo.
Big hug
2006
Ph.D. student
Gonna die in that boat
Am I?
How about the ones that have not survived?
Thug

I am feeling that my point here—if I ever had one—is slipping through my fingers. I am positioning myself as ally other to the Third World feminism, borrowing and learning from it, transforming/reusing my survival skills as tactics, as forms of resistance and writing theory to fight for more egalitarian forms of social relations. Third World feminists have advocated an ethics of caring, essential to bind these works/women together.

This oppositional/ differential consciousness can be possible only under Anzaldúa's idea of "between and among" that unifies women/people who do not share the same culture, race, sexual orientation, religion, or even the same ideology. In her concept, "differences do not become opposed to each other" (Anzaldúa, 1981, p. 209).

Scholar as thug

I understand Anzaldúa's call to be similar to Butler (2004). When I write this:

Fragments comes from betweenness
ambiguity
or
how this feeling of fragments (living and seeing life as such) comes from people born in this "in between position"
having to deal with the diasporic body, losses of home (land)
internal/external colonization
slavery-past/present
plus race/gender/religion/
you name it . . .
provoking destabilization (de-center) identities
then sometimes oppositional identities . . .

I tried to answer Anzaldúa's call. She asked me to be at the border of what I know. To create an epistemology from and for the borders I have crossed. She pushes me to take risks in a quest for other ways of knowing, and surviving. To rethink, reinvent my masculinity and whiteness expanding my capacity of imaging the human. To work "between and among" academic and nonacademics spaces, with the disrupting/rupturing body, unifying differences (bodies) to make a more inclusionary movement.

> "We are the queer groups, the people that don't belong anywhere, not in dominant world nor completely within our own respective cultures. Combined we cover so many oppressions. But the overwhelming oppression is the collective fact we do not fit, and because we do not fit we are a treat. Not all of us have the same oppressions, but we emphasize and identify with each other's oppressions. We do not have the same ideology, nor do we derive similar solutions. Some of us are leftists, some of us practitioners of magic. Some of us are both. But these different affinities are not opposed to each other. In *El Mundo Zurdo* I with my own affinities and my people with theirs can live together and transform the planet." (Anzaldúa 1981, p. 209)

This is how I see my person into the world, embodied written performing community. This is how I live life as human being, father, and husband. This is how I play scholar. This is how I share, negotiate, and disrupt the power dynamics among people and between the borders I cross to the places I live and labor.

I am performing community.

Multiple Cláudios grounded in one body, in my embodied bleeding epistemological/theoretical position.

Thug as scholar

Multiples Cláudios grounded in one body, in my embodied bleeding epistemological/theoretical position. Butler has this to say about Anzaldúa's call:

> "What she is arguing, then, is that it is only through existing in the mode of translation, constant translation, that we stand a chance of producing multicultural understanding of women or, indeed, of society. The unitary subject is the one who knows already what it is, who enters the conversation the same ways as it exits, who fails to put its own epistemological certainties at risk in the encounter with the other, and so stays in place, guards its place, and becomes an emblem for property and territory, *refusing self-transformation, ironically, in the name of the subject.*" (2004, p. 228

The place I am trying to arrive here is open, fluid, provisory, and temporary. I am not negating that my language might be another way of desiring the colonizers' body/existence/description or that it can be read that way. Instead, I am saying that my goal is different. In doing/being/speaking/embodying my work I try not to forget, overlook, or worse, take for granted that:

> "Given the history of the missionary, of colonial expansion that takes place in the name of 'cultivation' and 'modernity' and 'progress' and 'enlightenment,' of 'the white man's burden,' feminist as well, must ask whether the 'representation' of the poor, the indigenous and the radically disenfranchised within the academy, is patronizing and colonizing effort, or whether it seeks to avow the conditions of translation that make it possible, avow the power and privilege of the intellectual, avow the links in history and culture that make an encounter between poverty, for instance, and academic writing possible." (Butler, 2004, p. 229)

Pretty good for a thug, hum?

BREAK

Not what I would expect from a serious scholar.

SILENCE

Performances are embedded in language (Denzin, 2003). Clearly, my words are trying to do or achieve things. The performative returns to meanings that *were* already rooted in language and culture (Butler, 1993, 1997, 2004; Denzin, 2003). A friend once joked to me, after hearing me whine, that I exert my agency everywhere but in academy. Through my work/

language I seek, or better do and be, enact a performative behavior (Denzin, 2003). Schechner, when talking about performative behavior, gives the gender example on "how people play gender, heightening their constructed identity, performing slightly or radically different selves in different situations" (1998, p. 361). According to Butler, performativity is the "power of discourse to reproduce the phenomenon that it regulates and constrains" (1993, p. 2). How do I play scholar????

Can I play scholar???

Scholar as thug

Can I play scholar???

Denzin says that it, performativity, is the place where the doing and the done collide. When I confront knowledge and experience, I try to build on Denzin's (2003) idea that "hermeneutics is the work of interpretation and understanding. Knowing refers to those embodied, sensuous experiences that create the conditions for understanding. . . . Thus performed experiences are the sites were felt emotion, memory, desire, and understanding comes together" (p. 13). Again, how do I play scholar?

SILENCE

Thug as scholar

Again, how do I play scholar?

Lately, I've been using the word "desire," in my writings. I desire to be a scholar. Butler, in her analysis of gender, tells me that according to the Hegelian tradition, desire is linked with recognition, and only through this recognition I can "become constituted as socially viable being" (2004, p. 2), and yes, I do want to be recognized as a scholar. However, Butler also tells me that this tradition forgets to mention that the terms that allow me to make this recognition are "articulated and changeable." Even more, the terms that give one her "humanness" are sometimes the same that negate the other. These terms become/are sites with power. Recognition becomes a site of power by which the human is differentially produced. (p. 2)

Human and less human; scholar and less scholar.

Look at Butler's questions. Make them my questions. Just substitute the word "gender" for "scholar."

> "If I am a certain gender, will I still be regarded as part of human? Will the 'Human' expand to include me in its reach? If I desire in certain ways, will I be able to live? Will there be a place for my life, and will it be recognizable to others upon whom I depend for social existence?" (2004, p. 3)

I am trying to articulate my own desire to be a scholar, without being recognized by a set of norms that go against my ethical position. If my options are loathsome I use my sense of survival to challenge these norms. I follow Butler's analysis as a possibility of another way to get recognition, developing a "critical relation" with these norms, trying to defer the need for them, even if I need norms that let me be human, let me live. Butler teaches me that this ability, always collective, lays on the articulation of an alternative minority version, which allows me to act; in other words, my differential oppositional consciousness.

"Between and among," "living life in in-betweenness."

I need more time to articulate Butler's ideas in my own words. I am a thug, remember. For now, I present another long quote:

> "If I am someone who cannot *be* without *doing*, then the conditions of my doing are, in part, the conditions of my existence. If my doing is dependent on what is done to me, or rather, the ways which I am done by norms, then the possibility of my persistence as an 'I' depends upon my being able to do something with what is done with me . . ." (2004, p. 3)

My capacity to develop my survival skills—

> "This does not mean that I can remake the world so that I become its marker. The fantasy of godlike power only refuses the ways we are constituted, invariably and from the start, by what is before us and outside us. My agency does not consist in denying this condition of my constitution. If I have any agency, it is opened up by the fact that I am constituted by a social world I never chose. That my agency is riven with paradox does not mean it is impossible. It means only that paradox is the condition of its possibility." (2004, p. 3)

That is not easy, because the "I" has to live life in uncertainty. I need recognition that does not make my life unlivable. How can I play scholar, get my Ph.D., decolonize inquiry/academy while criticizing and refusing (some of) the norms that make my life unlivable?

Scholar as thug and thug as scholar

How can I play scholar, get my Ph.D., decolonize inquiry/academy while criticizing and refusing (some of) the norms that make my life unlivable? I remember, one day when a friend drove me home and I said to him that I did lots of shit jobs in my life, but for me to live in academia,

I need to believe,
I need to love
And
Trust
What
I
Am

Doing
And
Being.
I am obsessed with -ING.

And this does not mean I want to be the marker. I do not. My and others' ways to do this is to disarticulate, expose, challenges the mechanisms, the rights that legitimate these norms of recognition, in a way that being a scholar might have some of the practice and even symbols, that one who chose it can recognize it (taking place in universities for example), and yet the mechanisms and rights of recognition that take other forms.

In some ways, I see my work as an effort to resist the process of assimilation. I do not want to play ball, even if I know I have to play some. My work is an effort to relate the problematic of scholarship production, knowledge, experience, the essence of what is to be a scholar, to the tasks of persistence and survival (Butler, 2004).

First my own, and then for my bunch.

Or for me and my bunch at the same time.

There are no stories to be told, in a chronological sense. My "scholarship"—or whatever name it might have—within its framework does not move from one place to another, from me to the others, or from critical ethnography to performance autoethnography.

> There are no stories to be told because they are not in the past.
> They are happening and overlapping blurring concepts of time and space.
> Overlapping blurring concepts of ethnography and autoethnography.
> They are the place where the done and the doing collide.
> Anzaldúa is dead but her story is still happening now through my own.
> Performativity situates performance narrative within the forces of discourse. (Langellier, 1999, p. 29)

And again . . .

Lorde says that marginality,

"whatever its nature . . . is also the source of our greatest strength" (1984, p. 53).

I am stopping here.

BREAK

SILENCE

A voice from above

Wait a minute. You cannot stop like this. This text is messy. All those facts, breaks, life 1, life 2 . . . How about that street kid that was never there? Who is the thug, and who is the scholar?

The thug and the Scholar
Does this matter?

Act 11: Life 11

And then,
There is none . . .
There is no fucking nothing . . .
There is no fucking anything . . .
And you . . .
Probably not the audience/reader
You
That probably will never
Ever
Acknowledge my body, unless the thug beats you up
Listen to my voice
Share the same space
You
Who never WILL
   Be
     Able
       To
         Acknowledge
My people
Your maids, drivers, caretakers, workers, killers, thieves, robbers
And even if for a few times,
Your teachers . . .
You
Who will probably never read my words
Pick up the better English
                    If there is one.

Part III

METHODOLOGICAL ACTS/DETOURS AND POSTCOLONIAL RESISTANCE: DECOLONIZING SCHOLARSHIP FOR SOCIAL JUSTICE IN THE 21ST CENTURY

Chapter 9

METHODOLOGICAL ACTS AND DETOURS

"*Somos filhos do Paulo Freire!*" Cláudio says in a rising intonation.

"*Bastardos, que ele nunca conheceu,*" Marcelo adds.

We are children of Paulo Freire. We never had a chance to ask him in person for this blessing. But we like to believe he would have approved of our unilateral claim of intimacy. Freire's *Pedagogy of the Oppressed* (1970) gave us language to name and grasp a strong yet confused sense of mission in life. His call for awareness-raising with the purpose of empowering social transformation resonated with our individual desires to act on the world in meaningful ways. Freire's call for liberation seemed to speak volumes to us because of our shared culture of origin. Even though Freire belonged to an older generation of Brazilians than we do, we felt as though we understood some of his central concepts at a visceral level. Freire's concepts of conscientization, humanization, dialogical pedagogy, and the duality of oppression housed in the minds of both the oppressor and the oppressed, to name a few for now, came from the same colonial dehumanization we have experienced as a younger generation of Brazilians. In addition, Paulo Freire's interdisciplinary use of such European theories as phenomenology, Marxism, and critical theory validated our own sense of worldly betweeners wanting to engage in an ever-evolving dialogue about systemic criticism and education *against* colonial ideologies of domination and *for* a continuation toward a pedagogy of hope in Brazil, the United States, and beyond.

Existentially speaking, we feel that the stories in Part II stand alone as slices of lived experience shaping and being shaped by resistance against colonial forces, where all of us—writers, youths, street and sugar-cane workers, and soccer fans—live as betweeners jostling for a pleasant space in the sun. We believe that the stories are, themselves, the *analysis* of the postcolonial struggle of everyday life among the more obviously oppressed and privileged—at least from our performer-ethnographer experiential angle. Unlike the traditional approach to scholarly analysis of lived experience, with its codes and pattern-seeking tendencies, our stories do the analyzing by representing instantiations of visceral encounters with dehumanizing ideologies. In our best effort, our stories attempt to raise issues of colonizing power and resistance agency so that the reader can engage with us in at least two main points: (1) getting a glimpse into the harshness of being stuck, at the micro-level intensity of everyday life, with the sharp end of the rope, and (2) continuing to imagine possibilities in advancing scholarship that treats the more oppressed Others as equal partners in the production of knowledge within the social sciences. Thus we hope the stories stand as problematizers of current ontological, epistemological, methodological, and ethical concerns with voice, authorship, and situatedness. We hope our stories stand as scholarship that treats the Others not as objects/subjects of study but as co-constructors of decolonizing acts and performances. We present the stories as sites of individual and collective struggle and dialogue and not as packaged interpretations of (auto)ethnographic findings. We see the stories as representations of a Sartrean singular experience that is shaped from the outset as agents in the universal ideology of domination. We are comfortable with the open-endedness of our stories, our analyses, reassured by the Rortyan notion that we are all stuck in a perpetual discussion about what the reality of oppression means to each and all of us.

"I read that Rorty said that 'time will tell, but epistemology won't.' I love this phrase," Marcelo says.

"How does it fit here?" Cláudio asks.

"That we shouldn't pretend we have a final answer to questions of decolonizing methodologies. Instead, we should promote and be comfortable with an ever-evolving dialogue about how to represent our efforts in advancing scholarship that includes the Other in decolonizing knowledge production."

"Nice big words," says Cláudio, the Thug-Scholar. "But explain what you mean by decolonizing knowledge production."

"The production of knowledge that makes visceral knowledge of oppressive ideologies of domination central to scholarly discourse, whereby theory becomes a more democratic tool of analysis and further discourse and not a barrier for those with 'bad English,' and whereby the researcher refrains from unilateral analysis after the fact, alone in the office, in favor of a more egalitarian collaboration that produce knowledge that is inevitably open-ended, about possibilities of being more for more people."

"And one where theoretical expertise is valued only as it works as an instrument to value the visceral expertise from the streets," Cláudio completes with a wink.

"I can't see any other way to advance an ideology of humanization to replace the ideology of domination shaping human life as far back as I can see," Marcelo says.

"Big words again. . . . What do you mean by 'humanization' here?" Cláudio asks, playing devil's advocate. "Aren't we naturally in a state of 'humanization' by the very fact of being human?"

"I mean 'humanization' as defined by Paulo Freire, as the conscious search for justice, egalitarian social rights, individual sense of dignity and integrity, cultural space for the exploration of identities that transcend oppressive representations, and ultimately, the search for *conscientização*, a Portuguese word that has been translated as 'consciousness-raising.' According to Paulo Freire, as you know, conscientization is an essential process of self-understanding directed at uncovering and challenging internalized notions of inferiority (Freire, 1970)."

"And, don't forget, uncovering and challenging internalized notions of superiority as well!" Cláudio quickly adds. "Ideologies inhabit the everyday life of dialogical relations. So if feelings and mythologies of unearned privilege aren't uncovered and challenged, also by those who benefit from unearned privilege, then *conscientização* becomes confined to individuals and segments of society."

"And we stay stuck with the Us—Them grand narrative! *Conscientização* doesn't end at the individual level. To be fully realized, it needs to become a collective imaginative endeavor," Marcelo says thinking of Paulo Freire.

"Unconditional humanization," Cláudio says jumping in.

"Not just for my bunch, but for all bunches," Marcelo adds.

"That's a hard one to sell," Cláudio says.

"Of course, it doesn't mean it's possible as everyday practice by all individuals. This concept of humanization is an ideal, a vision, an imagination, a hope that has been around for a long time," Marcelo says.

"Not just a hope, but a concrete hope, as Paulo Freire says. Every time we perform the past in a hopeful way, every time we perform libertatory texts, every time we recreate memories that have been squashed by the dominant men, then we offer concrete hope," Cláudio says.

Marcelo nods, feeling like he is understanding Freire's pedagogy of hope for the first time.

"And we know how well this has worked, right? Turn the other cheek, everyone is a child of God, we are all brothers and sisters, all men and women are created equal. Yeah, right! One of the most translated documents in history, the United-Nations-ratified Universal Declaration of Human Rights, says that 'All human beings are born free and equal in dignity and rights. They are endowed with reason and conscience and should act towards one another in a spirit of brotherhood.' A mighty statement, embraced by most of UN countries in 1948, twenty years before Freire would be writing about it," Cláudio says, his eyes wide and intense.

"That's why we are not claiming to have an original idea for decolonizing scholarship and methodologies. But we are still very distant from living in that world, where all humans are born free and equal in dignity and rights. Race, class, and gender, social constructs at the center of our stories and scholarship, continue to be sites of inequality and indignity here in the U.S.A., in Brazil, and most of the world. We are not trying to reinvent the wheel, or take credit for an original decolonizing idea. But we are suggesting yet another version of decolonizing methodology, one that builds on the poststructural, interpretive, feminist, postcolonial movements, and adds our notion and experience as betweeners as common ground for dialogue," Marcelo says.

"Yeah, and for us to keep pushing Anzaldúa's call for the status quo to come meet us half way. It seems like in order to translate the idea of unconditional equality into everyday practice, consistently, people need to relate to the Other at some emotional level. And the grand narratives of equality don't seem to do the job for most people. That's where I think performative methodologies, like the ones we have in Part II, can help us go to the next level," Cláudio says.

"I agree! Here is where critical (auto)ethnography, or performance autoethnography as you probably prefer to call it, can play a role in promoting and advancing this notion of unconditional humanization. In any case, I feel that critical (auto)ethnography is an inevitable methodological approach for us, given the onto-epistemological framework we embrace and describe in Chapter 2. We don't need to present a formal methodological section, with review of literature, name-dropping, or displays of intellectual prowess. But it's important, in my view, to share with the interested reader the architectural structure sustaining our stories."

"So we still need theory and methodology," Cláudio says with a tinge of irony.

"So that we can continue to expand the discourse on the possibilities of decolonizing scholarship," Marcelo says in the same tone of voice.

"Let's talk methodology, then," Cláudio, the Thug-Scholar, says with a sigh.

"Where another ethnographer might 'see' a particular social event as worth relating because it illustrates how conflict was resolved or provides an interesting case for a discourse analysis of language interaction . . ., the critical ethnographer will consider an event worth recording and reporting because it exemplifies a hegemonic practice." (Brodkey, 1987, p. 71)

"For the naive thinker, the important thing is accommodation to th[e] normalized 'today.' For the critic, the important thing is the continuing transformation of reality, in behalf of the continuing humanization of men [sic]." (Freire, 1970, p. 73)

"The white man is always trying to know into somebody else's business. All right, I'll set something outside the door of my mind for him to play with and handle. He can read my writing but he sho' can't read my mind. . . . I'll put this play toy in his hand, and he will seize it and go away. Then I'll say my say and sing my song." (Hurston, 1990, p. 3)

A Dialogue on (Auto)Ethnography

"To begin with," Marcelo asks, "Why do you call your method autoethnography?"

"That's easy," Cláudio says laughing. "I learned my method as autoethnography with Norman Denzin. It came to me with a name. Seriously, I follow Norman's model. And so I called it performance autoethnography. Doing it situated within the intersections of cultural studies, critical pedagogy, and Third World feminism works to disestablish/subvert the supremacy/division of mind and body often represented in academic settings. While this method explores the singularity of the experience, when performed by the oppressed it gives name '...to experiences of many through the experience of one.'[1]

"It works like this . . . allow me to perform my model," Cláudio says taking some paper from his bag and starting to read:
"Past
Memory(ies)
That
Universalizes in its particularity[2]
I ask the questions:
How did this thing happen?
How these circumstances did come in place, in that way, to articulate these positions of
oppression?
Not why; not causal
But
A set of interpretative narratives
Structuring the model this way, allows me to imagine a model of performance that is

Representational in its art and creation
That is built in
Conquergood's 'i's[3]
Imagination, inquiry, intervention
Conquergood's 'a's
Artistry, analysis, activism
Conquergood's 'c's
Creativity, critique, citizenship
The much talked

Mimesis	imitation	analytic
Poesies	aesthetic	resistance
Kinesis	movement dynamism	activism

From that historical moment in a cultural space
I create analytic answers to how
The analytic is performative
Performatively, making visible, exposing the mechanism of oppression
The poetics creates and re-creates the moment
And then . . .
The space for critique
Through the apparatus of poetics I create
Activism and critique
A citizen who resists the hegemonic articulations in and from the space in the past
Empowerment and *conscientização*
From the event that already happened
Then, when the performance happens, the performance itself articulates and transforms what did happen.
It shows what hasn't happened before.
Always different from what it was . . .
From the being before . . .
The performative
The transformative apparatus of performance, frees me to move around the "pieces" of history and culture.

"I create a performative structure that allows us to do a critical, cultural and political critique in a way which permits the advocacy of a particular moral position (a moral position made visible through the poetics). A moral position for Andre, Roni, me, parents, teachers, and any adult who claims to care about justice, equality, fraternity. The performance, the performative, should contain all the materials that are necessary to bring the co-performer to that space:

"My job is not making the co-performer agree with me.
My job is to articulate a clear text of my moral position that contains in itself all the arguments needed to understand the event.
Showing not telling
The tools to the co-performer to follow the move
The critique of the configuration of class/race/gender in a specific moment, overtly
creating a dialogic moral
I am not doing pieces that reproduce the struggles of the white middle class in late-capitalism society
I move to that racialized, gendered space to set up a counter-hegemonic form of resistance

"I think of Holman Jones: 'Autoethnography is a blurred genre . . . a response to the call . . . it is setting a scene, telling a story, weaving intricate connections between life and art . . . making a text present . . . refusing categorization . . . believing that words matter and writing toward the moment when the point of creating autoethnographic texts is to change the world' (2005a, p. 765).

"Kindness and honest (re)presentations of my history, which proposes alternative ways of being and knowing in and into/of the world

"I want to change the world by writing from the heart

"But where does my project, my participatory action research, take us?

"My project is anchored 'in the worlds of pain and lived experience and is accountable to these worlds' (Denzin, 2003, p. 237).[4] I interrogate and criticize cultural narratives that make the victims responsible for the violence they experience thus blaming and revictimizing them. I am not trying to celebrate the life struggles of persons in raw violent environments; persons who lived through violence and abuse. I am not spitting in the reader's eyes. The narratives I create 'must always be directed back to the structures that shape and produce the violence in question' (Denzin, 2003, p. 239).[5] The performative is political, and pedagogically used, it is putting in check the producers of power and knowledge."

"And how do you think your version of autoethnography advance decolonizing production of knowledge in the social sciences at this particular historical junction?" Marcelo asks.

"In this sense, my project works outward the university and its classrooms, treating these spaces as critical public spheres. My voice, both angry and loving, sees these academic spaces as sites for resistance and empowerment in a performative way, which permits the discourse created there to be transferable to other classrooms and universities, keen on other pedagogical spaces, where a militant utopianism is imagined and experienced. It is an act of doing, being, and knowing, in a concrete moment, constructed in local subjugated knowledges at the bottom of social hierarchies.

"From the position described above, my intent is to work in academic and nonacademic spaces using my performance model as pedagogy of freedom to create better, more just societies, in specific communities. It shows that it is through performances that persons represent, disrupt, interpret, engage, and transform the ideological and material circumstances that shape their lives.

"My work, as cultural performer, cannot be separated from power, knowledge, politics, and identities. It inhabits the performative spaces, in concrete life, where identity is formed, agency is negotiated, and the grand narratives of nation, gender, race, class, religion, and sexual orientation are shaped and confronted. I present myself as a radical urban autoethnographer, committed to participation and performance *with* and for a specific community," Cláudio says and pauses for a while.

"I want to help to mold engaged critical intellectuals, future and past teachers, who will be able to develop an embodied reflexivity of lived experience as a specific cultural site for struggle, resistance, and transformation." Another pause.

"Did I answer your question?" says Cláudio smiling.

"You did. I wanted to know how *you* articulate autoethnography. I think your approach to it shows how deeply misguided the common critique of autoethnography can be—that it's navel-gazing, self-serving, biased. If I understand you right, you are saying that, yes, autoethnography is all these things. And that's okay. There is no reason to panic. Anything written/performed by anybody anywhere anytime will be self-centered, in the sense that knowledge is always produced by a body. Whether an autoethnographic text is also selfish is a different story. So it seems, then, that critical ethnography, with its intense basic tenet of self-reflexivity about issues of power, race, gender, etc. is a form of autoethnography?" Marcelo asks.

Cláudio raises his eyebrows for a moment. "I am not sure . . . I don't think in these terms, with this linearity. . . . I would say that for me autoethnography comes from critical ethnography, as a possibility to address the crises of representation in a way that satisfies me more. . . . How about you? I'm curious to see how you would answer this question."

"My methodology came through critical ethnography," says Marcelo. "But now I think, like you, that there is no ethnography without 'auto' at the epistemological level. I think I understand the nuances that the autoethnographic movement has intended to highlight, such as making the personal a political site of resistance and libertatory praxis. In my mind, Carolyn Ellis's ethnovel, *The Ethnographic I: A Methodological Novel about Autoethnography* (2004), is one of this movement's most moving and evocative examples. But I digress. Like you, I am not interested in creating more narratives of methodological boundaries. . . ."

"Sorry to interrupt your train of thought," Cláudio says. "But you still insist on describing our methodology as critical (auto)ethnography. Isn't this a way of creating methodological boundaries? Why not just call it autoethnography, or ethnography, for example?"

"Perhaps I am unwittingly reifying these methodological barriers. But my intention in describing our methodology as 'critical (auto)ethnography' is to indicate to the reader that our version of ethnography is informed by critical theory and interpretive paradigms. The intention is to signify that, even though we aren't including a handbook-like lit review about methodology in this work, we are standing on the shoulders of many critical theorists, feminists, postcolonialists, and poststructuralists. It's a way, I think, to situate our own knowledge production about life in-between static narratives of Us X Them, about being betweeners, about representations that evoke our human communality in the both/and, in-between, spaces."

"Okay, but why write (auto)ethnography, with the 'auto' part in parentheses?" Cláudio wants to know.

"To signify that our methodologies privilege the view that knowledge about the Other is always produced by a situated body as it, the body, interacts with other bodies and the surrounding environment. It's a way, in my view, to point out where the ethnography's navel is. It's also a way to share with readers that we think all ethnography is autoethnography, as opposed to the most current view that autoethnography is a branch or type in the larger tradition of ethnography," Marcelo says.

"Fine. I suppose I can live with that," Cláudio says with a friendly nod. "But, unlike me, you are more invested in the theory behind the method."

"Perhaps it's because I arrived at critical (auto)ethnography more through theory than through visceral experience of oppression. It was through the discovery of critical ethnography that I felt for the first time empowered to write about street kids, the self, at the intersection with more oppressed Others. It made me believe that I could help transform personal troubles into public issues, as Mills (1959) inspired me to long for. The list of influential authors here is dissertation-long and not part of our project here. But I can vividly remember when bell hooks *gave* me words to explain the central goal of social sciences for me. Let me read this passage to you," Marcelo says to Cláudio over the phone.

> "To me feminism is not simply a struggle to end male chauvinism or a movement to ensure that women will have equal rights with men; it is a commitment to eradicating the ideology of domination that permeates Western culture on various levels—sex, race, and class, to name a few—and a commitment to reorganizing U.S. society so that the self-development of people can take precedence over imperialism, economic expansion, and material desires." (hooks, 1981, p. 194)

Marcelo continues on without a pause: "One of the foremost themes of bell hooks's work, in my opinion, is her concern with a more generalized ideology of domination. hooks (1981, 1990, 1994) has argued that groups that complain about and challenge oppressive social norms often exercise, themselves, domination over other groups. She cites the case of oppressed African-American males who violate, subjugate, and repress African-American women's quest for humanization, for instance. She makes the point that true emancipation is possible only when any, and all, forms of domination are equally opposed. Otherwise, the struggle becomes only for a (racial, gendered, economic) shift of positions in the hegemonic hierarchies."

"And how does that relate to your methodology?" Cláudio asks.

"I thought, still think, that critical (auto)ethnography is a methodology with unique guidelines for scholars concerned with resisting and challenging ideologies of domination. In particular, I am moved by the notion that a critical ethnographer is not above the historical and ideological time from which he or she experiences and writes the world. Calling myself a critical ethnographer keeps me in a constant state of authorial awareness as I try to create language that represents the Other in nondeterministic ways. To be more specific, critical ethnography has given me intellectual tools to write about street kids from the perspective of my interaction with the kids, aware of my position as a betweener (Brazilian like the street kids but from a more privileged class, race, and, sometimes, gender and sexual orientation) trying to resist deterministic narratives of hopeless criminality (street kids as pickpockets uninterested in or incapable of redemption) by presenting narratives that represent street kids living in the space between childhood and survival."

"And in short?" Cláudio quips.

"Critical (auto)ethnography," Marcelo says, deadpan.

"Or autoethnography," Cláudio says. "Much has been written about this. If one writes from a traditional standpoint, he or she may think that he or she is the pure ethnographer. It depends on the paradigm the person writes from. . . . I agree with Guba and Lincoln that paradigm comes first. Norman Denzin told us that when he wrote the ethnography of AA, he was really writing an autoethnography. Norman says that the line between ethnographer and autoethnographer is at least blurred. . . . My personal opinion is that a critical ethnographer has always the auto part. It will depend in how much she/he will disclose it in writing. It's like the trap of insider/outsider."

"Conquergood suggests that we do not write about them—the Others—but with and for them. Studying and preparing for this academic life, but especially in the process of writing, a pattern emerged that the Other is nowhere in the academic space." Cláudio pauses to think.

"How can I express myself better . . . ? I do not believe in a theory/method that the possibility of the other or a community of others being the ones that control/produce/do the research is not there. The Other is always at the end side of the gaze. Those questions are thus ultimately about positioning. It seems to me that one needs to erase ones' Otherness, to become unmarked, using Donna Haraway's term, in order to become the professor, researcher, or philosopher. I can use your words when you said the 'view from nowhere' a little while ago. My point here goes beyond the trap of the insider/outsider. It is about considering the works of Narayan (1993), and Bishop (2005), who explain that 'it is no longer useful to think of researchers as insiders or outsiders; instead, researchers might be *positioned* "in terms of *shifting identifications amid a field of interpenetrating communities and power relations*"' (Narayan, 1993, p. 671; quoted from Bishop, 2005, p. 113, italics added).

Cláudio carries on. "Hence, this positionality of the research demands accountability when it asks for the position of the bodies of everybody involved in the processes of constructing a situated knowledge, and again, I'm using Haraway's term. In this sense, it destroys the binary trap presented by the notion of the insider/outsider. Instead of looking for insider/outsider status, auto/non-auto, what Narayan does, as Haraway does, is ask for accountability. So if we agree with them, which is my case, from a critical and interpretative point of view, there is no way one can be the ethnographer without the auto."

"I'm with you, *meu irmão*," Marcelo quickly agrees.

But Cláudio isn't done yet. "Before moving on, it is important explicitly to note, and I know Marcelo that you are aware of this, that these questions are about 'those people,' men and women of different races, ethnicities, gender, backgrounds, who live and labor not only outside but also inside academia. And here we can even expand our dialogue. The point is not about establishing an identity and a home place as suggested by colonization and decolonization, but rather displacement. Let me read you something that Trinh T. Minh-ha wrote:"

> 'The reflexive question asked . . . is no longer: Who am I? But When, where, how am I (so and so)? This is why I remain skeptical of strategies of reversal when they are not intricately woven with strategies of displacement. Here the notion of displacement is also a place of identity: there is no real me to return to, no whole self that synthesizes the woman, the woman of color and the writer; there are instead, diverse recognitions of self through difference, and unfinished, contingent, arbitrary closures that make possible both politics and identity.' (1990, p. 157)

"This is where I think we take our methodologies to slightly different places. I think I focus more on the messiness of displacement, of having no place or coherent self to return to, where I can create an academic space where I can be both Thug and Scholar, where visceral experience counts just as much as theoretical sophistication, if not even more. I think you focus more on using ethnography to shed light on instantiations of everyday life oppression shaped by deterministic discourse about identity, as in street kids imagined as little criminals. Would you agree with that?" Cláudio asks.

"Fine by me, as long as I can make it clear that I attempt to write against ideologies of domination that essentialize street kids as hopeless delinquents, and that I write as a betweener, aware that I am criticizing dominant narratives (that I judge to be dehumanizing) while also imposing my own top-down narrative (that I judge to be humanizing)."

"I fear you may be interpreted as an ultrarelativist," Cláudio says with some concern.

"I hope not. What I am trying to point out is that critical (auto)ethnography, as I imagine it, is an epistemological tool that allows me to be mindful that it's not for me to decide whether my ethnographic account is more humanizing than the dominant narratives of delinquency. Of course I believe it is. I hope it is. But in a Bakhtinian sense, of meaning always being co-constructed between agents, I want to leave that judgment entirely to the readers of my short stories. And critical (auto)ethnography is my lighthouse in that journey."

"Now that you mentioned short stories as part of your concept of critical autoethnography, tell me again why/how you decided on this type of representation?" Cláudio asks.

"Many times during my field work among street kids in the downtown area of Campinas, Brazil, I wondered how I was going to be able to represent the experience without losing their voices, the multidimensionality of their humanity, and the mystery that surrounds their lived experiences. Early on I decided that I did not want to represent these street kids' experiences from a theoretical perspective, for that would inevitably bury their voices beneath layers of analysis (Denison, 1996, p. 352). Therefore, following alternatives endorsed by epistemological and methodological debates, I decided to transgress the boundaries of traditional forms of writing social sciences, to build one more bridge between the social sciences and the humanities (Denzin, 1997; Ellis, 2004; Ellis and Bochner, 1996, pp. 13–42; Freeman, 1993; Jessor, Colby, and Schweder, 1996). So I decided to represent the kids I met in my fieldwork through short stories.

"Based on my reconstructions of my shared lived experiences with the kids, I employed short story techniques such as alternative points of view, dialogue, unfolding action, and flashback to attempt creating the tension, suspense, delay, and voice that compose a good short story—and that are inseparable from lived experience."

Cláudio smiles, and Marcelo can't stop now.

"I believe," continues Marcelo, "that the short story, as a writing genre, has the potential to render lived experience with more verisimilitude (than the traditional realist text), for it enables the reader to feel that interpretation is never finished or complete. Short stories that *show* instead of *tell* are less author-centered, which in turn invites interpretation and meaning-making. This invitation is crucial to avoid authorial omnipotence, the view from *everywhere* (Richardson, 1990), to avoid 'closing off or nailing down an interpretation without allowing alternative views to creep into view' (Van Maanen, 1988, p. 53).

"I see the short stories I wrote here as part of the decolonizing scholarship we have been trying to advance. The stories are based on my understanding of critical (auto)ethnography: critical theory's focus on writing a kind of social science that aims at resisting the status quo by privileging the struggle for humanity over conformity with economic forces; postmodernism's focus on the fluidity, uncertainty, and fragmentation of social reality; poststructuralism's focus on language as *the* medium through which social reality is both mirrored and constituted; feminism's ethics of caring and struggle against ideologies of domination; action research's focus on the researcher's participation in the experiences being studied. Performative texts attempt to go beyond strict intellectual communion—they try to invite the reader, through emotional and moral involvement, to co-participate in their struggle for liberation.

"To be sure, I *am* the author of these stories, and as such have made important choices in the writing process that both carry my own interpretations of the lived experiences and limit the possibilities of the reader's interpretations. However, the view from *nowhere* is impossible from an epistemological standpoint that is founded on the social construction of reality (that is, reality can be understood only through consciousness, through symbolic systems created by humans), and, therefore, the view from *somewhere* is the closest an author can get to a polyvocal text.

"While I am the one who spent time and shared lived experiences with kids living in downtown Campinas, I wanted to represent them in ways that allowed interpretations of their realities beyond—in addition to, in contrast to—my own. I am the one, through these short stories, opening up windows into a world of lived experience currently unrepresented in the academic and public debates about street kids, but the gaze that interprets and makes sense of the narratives is, inevitably, also yours as reader. My own interpretations and deconstructions, as a researcher and writer, are already all over the stories, starting from my ontological stance and the writing genre I chose. But they are also present in my descriptions, positions as a character in the stories, in my questions and silences. I hope the windows I have tried to open are big enough for readers to gaze in and their own interpretations.

"Also, in my view, the short story format has a unique potential to bring lived experiences unknown to the reader closer to his or her own struggles for humanization, to touch the emotions of people whose only channel of access to street kids' lives is the ascetic representations of printed and televised media. Dialogues and descriptions of places, smells, looks, which are integral parts of short stories, have the potential to move readers from abstract and sterile notions to lively imagery of otherwise distant social realities. Well written short stories, which create tension and voices that sound real, have the power to allow readers to see themselves in the human dramas being represented—even if the specific circumstances shaping these human dramas are different from the circumstances shaping the reader's own dramas (Polkinghorne, 1988). My most optimistic goal, then, is that these stories will emotionally connect, however briefly, human beings living in extremely different social contexts," Marcelo, at last, finishes.

"Do *you* see a difference in our methodology in the way we represent our experiences?" Marcelo then asks Cláudio.

"Yes and no. We came from the same space in theory and method. Really, you were my first mentor. And I read your stories as autoethnography. The difference that pops in front of my eyes is the writing of theory. I don't divide theory and the story. I try to look for an aesthetic format where both are intertwined together. I play more with forms of writing looking for the impossibility of embodiment in my writing . . . what's more . . . my stuff is messy, and I am not sure, but I believe you put more importance in the theory than I do in the process of writing. Again, I am not sure. What is your take? Again, I'm throwing the question back at you. How do you think our methodologies differ from each other?"

Marcelo says, "I don't think there is much of a difference. But yes, I am certainly more interested in articulating a decolonizing theory in the formal sense than you are, as you have often pointed out. I believe it's very important to talk about how Freire's methodology of participative inquiry allowed us to be here in academia in the first place. We need to spell it out, in my view, for the praxis, the action, and the change that participatory action research imagines."

"Are you talking about Freire's concepts of duality of the oppressed and dialogue?" Cláudio asks.

"Yes. I think these two concepts can give us useful cognitive tools to problematize the individual and collective construction of meaning that a research act tries to capture. The duality of the oppressed refers to their internalization of the oppressors' values and beliefs, especially those referring to the opinion of the oppressors about them. This internalization occurs through processes such as the 'banking' concept of education and 'false generosity.' The 'banking' education refers to the act carried by the teacher who deposits information (received knowledge) into the students' minds, who in turn have little choice but to patiently receive, memorize, and repeat it (Freire, 1970, p. 53). As Freire puts it, 'In the banking concept of education, knowledge is a gift bestowed by those who consider themselves knowledgeable upon those whom they consider to know nothing. To project an absolute ignorance onto others, a characteristic of the ideology of oppression, negates education and knowledge as process of inquiry' (p. 53). As a result, the oppressed experience their lives with the oppressor's mentality housed inside themselves. Thus, at the same time that they loathe the oppressors, the oppressed want to be like them, have what they have, experience what they experience. The oppressed, then, can see only the difference between *being* and *nothingness*, rather than the libertatory frontier between *being* and *being more* human.

"This process of internalization of inferiority also occurs through false generosity, which is the oppressors' practice of occasionally giving minute parts of their possessions (including time) to the less privileged. This practice reinscribes the oppressive worldview about the essential materialistic concept of existence, in which the oppressed have little chance of fulfillment. The result is that the oppressed receive nothing more than *things*. And *things*, objects, cannot replace humanity, which is the dream of all human beings. According to Freire, true generosity is based on dialogical communication between subjects and not between subjects and objects, as it tends to happen between (subjective) oppressors and (objectified) oppressed."

"And how does Paulo Freire define dialogue as pedagogical and research projects?" Cláudio probes.

"He wrote that dialogue is the only way to liberation. And I know you and I agree with that. Transformative social organization and resistance will never occur as long as the oppressed are told what their problems are, told how their lives are oppressed. They need to learn to identify by themselves, *with* their leaders and *through* dialogue, what is denying them fuller humanization. Radical change requires courage and commitment; but these come only when one realizes that beyond *being* there is the possibility of *being more* human, the possibility of negating *nothingness*."

"Give me an example from your research with street kids," asks Cláudio.

"When a street youth says something like, well, you are wasting your time talking to us about education. School is for normal kids, not for us street kids. We are don't have school smarts. We won't even live long enough to finish high school. What's the use? I think that is a clear example of how many of the street kids I worked with internalized the prescribed *lesser-being* so prevalent in the deterministic, dualistic, either/or dominant discourse about who street kids are," Marcelo says.

"It seems like Freire is advocating that dialogical relations, with its focus on the co-construction of meaning, make it possible for the oppressed to reclaim the right to speak their word,[6] transforming the world by renaming what had previously been named by the essentializing dominant discourse," Cláudio chips in.

"The premises of participatory action research add important points to our critical (auto)ethnographic project, I think. Freire's concept of banking education is useful in examining how local institutions interact with the street children, which I perceive as interactions marked by a projection of ignorance and incompetence onto the children. False generosity is also enacted in the form of charity that limits its actions to giving things instead of co-creating, with the kids, space for critical reflection and action.

"Anyway, I find it important to discuss theory and methodology in addition to writing short stories, because I want to make my onto-epistemological standpoint as transparent as possible so the reader can have a richer interpretive context. As you know, I am not claiming this is the best or the only way of doing critical (auto)ethnography. But I find that methodology is a constructive ground for dialogue among scholars doing research based on divergent paradigms. My immediate interpretive community, the traditional social sciences, operates under the logical-positivistic paradigm. I am mostly evaluated at work by scholars and administrators who subscribe to logical-positivism. And not only do I want to continue to work in my immediate interpretive community, I also want to engage in productive dialogue with these folks about transformative ways of generating knowledge about the Other. I find methodology, the theory behind methods, to be a constructive site for this dialogue. It's an intellectual landscape to identify and clarify misunderstandings about interpretive methodologies, to try and reach for a shared meaning about examining personal and subjective experiences as a site of systemic power struggle. To me, theory talk is a positive way to reach across cultural and paradigm chasms."

"Suit yourself," Cláudio says with a shrug. "But how did these rather abstract ideas about participatory action inform your critical autoethnography methodology?"

"To me, Freire's participatory inquiry approach were central to the crucial aspects of entering the street scene, acceptance by the kids as someone trustworthy, and ethics. I talk about these issues in detail elsewhere (Diversi, 1998). The short version is that participatory inquiry gave me guidelines to transform my idea of critical (auto)ethnography into practice. I don't mean to say here that these two methods are necessarily different from each other or in any sort of hierarchical relation. This is just how it worked out in my mind. I first thought of critical (auto)ethnography as the method I wanted to pursue, probably because I learned about it before I ever heard of participatory inquiry. . . ."

"Quite ironic, no? That we both discovered participatory inquiry through American scholars who incorporated Freire's ideas into their version of critical ethnography," Cláudio chimes in.

"It seems only appropriate for two self-proclaimed betweeners like us, I suppose."

"Can you give a few examples of how participatory inquiry helped your work with the street kids?" Cláudio asks.

"I couldn't quite ask the street kids or their tribal leader if I could camp out with them while I quietly observed and took notes of their lives. More seriously, though, I took the Freirian model of trying to become a contributing participant in the street kids' lives, at least long enough for me to be of use to them. I worked hard to convince a local grassroots organization that I wanted to be trained as a street educator for them. I was upfront about my project and that I would later write about my experiences with the kids. There was some resistance against my request as I was seen as an outsider and, thus, viewed with suspicion. I was told that researchers, in particular researchers from rich nations, were not welcome. '*Basta de exploração!*' Enough colonial exploitation, I was told in the friendliest manner."

"Another instantiation of being a betweener!" Cláudio says shaking his head a little.

"The negotiation of identity was very intense at that initial stage. I am grateful to the folks at the Movimento Nacional dos Meninos e Meninas de Rua, National Movement for Street Children, for being willing to continue the dialogue with me. Had they not been able to relate to me as a betweener, I don't think they would have taken the time to reconcile my apparent contrasting identities as an upper-class Brazilian associated with an American university claiming to embrace a Freirean approach to working with the oppressed. Eventually they decided to let the kids have the final word about my ability to become a Freirean street educator. I was trained and mentored by Magali, a fabulous street educator who enjoyed the admiration and trust of all the street youth we encountered. It was a stroke of luck for me, as I was extended trust by association. And as a street educator, no one ever questioned my sudden appearance in the street of downtown Campinas. From there, I did what I could as an advocate for the kids during the day and furiously wrote notes at night, from the comfort of my sister's home."

"Is that, your so-called fieldnotes, where your short stories come from?" Cláudio asks.

"Mostly," Marcelo responds, aware that Cláudio thinks the use of the term "fieldnotes" perpetuates the disembodied position from which knowledge about the Other is produced. "I changed identifying features such as names and physical appearance for safety and confidentiality reasons. Standard IRB and common sense stuff. But I also used memories from conversations I forgot to write down in my notes but remembered vividly as I started to write the short stories. But I wasn't concerned with verbatim modernist requirements, as you know."

"The fiction-versus-fact dichotomy isn't part of our methodology," Cláudio adds with the ease of shared understanding.

"Yeah, the idea was to create a sense of being there that rang true to me," Marcelo says.

"How did you actually write the stories?" Cláudio asks.

"I thought of Denzin's (1997) words about the state of ethnographic writing then: 'The preferred strategy has been to stand outside, as critics, or to take up the structural approach to narrative, learning how to dissect rather than how to write stories' (p. 158). I felt I had already learned how to analyze narrative. I wanted to learn how to write stories.

"I had already gone through my fieldnotes many times, trying to add every detail to my recollections and sensations of the kids and the lived experiences we shared. I decided to follow my advisor's suggestion and write several stories, each centered on one or two of the kids I got close to during fieldwork. I wrote their names down as they came to mind, with no conscious order. I then started to write about the first things that came to my mind about the central character, with no particular theme or purpose. I felt that, by portraying the kids in the multidimensional ways I had experienced them, themes and important aspects of their realities would come naturally to the stories—including my own reactions, reflections, and subjectivity. I also felt that the stories would take unpredictable directions and turns along the writing process, which they did. So I tried to let go of occasional temptations to give an unnatural, positivistically informed order to the lived experiences I was writing about and tried to embrace the unpredictability, contradictions, tensions, communions, multiple interpretations, fluidity, frustrations, and messiness inherent in lived experiences and in new ways of writing social sciences."

"And how did you do that?" Cláudio says pushing further.

"I closed my eyes, felt a story coming to me, and wrote," Marcelo finally says.

"How did you write yours, amigo?" Marcelo asks.

"You know I love you, *Lindão*, but your questions . . . First word comes to mind . . .

"Desperation
Did not have a plan B
Did not fit
Rage so intense
If I'm going down I am not going quiet
Survival
This thing that follows me like a curse, a bad spell that I've tried for so many times to terminate and fortunately couldn't.
I hang in there like a cat that always falls on its four paws. A curse and a gift at least for the time being

Or somewhere in-between, like the poeta '*a vida que não pedi tão sofrida mas não perdir por ganhar*'
Once a very good friend wrote this for me and about me:
'. . . and I don't
Think I am nearly as threatening as a Brazilian with a chip on his shoulder.'
Yes, I am a Brazilian but I do not have
A chip on my shoulder . . .
I have many!
And I am feeling the burden
From their weight on my shoulders, fighting hard not to get smashed and
Smashing . . . the persons I love most in the world
Dani, Analua, and Francisco
I played and replayed this plot in my head many times
The day I plead my case in front of you . . .
And it always goes wrong . . .
And going wrong I say to
Myself
Cláudio, you know when you do things that
Very few could replace you
Because you survived
And you learned from Audrey Lorde that
'Survival is not an academic skill'
Very few would be here, standing still, as you're defending
You and yours
Yes, I know this shit, but . . . don't you see
do I really know this? If I KNOW, from where does this knowledge come from?
Power and/is knowledge . . . Experience maybe?
Because of
What I do, How I am
The instability of this messiness we call life
And the love of it
Love for others
Unconditional hope 'cause life is sacred and should be livable, and as an autoethnographer I say to you that it never has been about only me
Acknowledging, understanding, and theorizing the betweenness

"Thug and Scholar refusing the dichotomy that slash my body making me as you said 'the prescribed *lesser-being*' or as I prefer, a being almost human. And Marcelo, I know you have a problem with this, but I demand to be met halfway, and ain't apologizing for this . . . at least, not for now. I am not as a good as Anzaldúa, and my love, hope, and indignation is too exposed in my skin for that. There are others out there that want to and fight for the possibility of being more human, and we care not for the white stuff, for the 'leaders,' we care for comrades. You know, Marcelo, someone needs to say this, in the institutional space, in print and with capital letters. I'm giving the Thug the green light. SUBJUGATED KNOWLEDGE MY ASS! The everyday realization that we are not alone and couldn't possibly be that dumb. You teach me.... We learned how ... and I don't let my writing be controlled. This keeps me moving.

"As an addict
I feel the craving to write
I first wrote it as 'Fragments for Cole.' Now, changing a word here and there, I am writing:
Fragments for Us All
I've tried to move from our dialogue to this (non) space
Fragments as skill for survival
Mobility
Oppositional consciousness
Situated knowledges
Self consciously grounded through the racialized, gendered body
To act (methodology of the oppressed)
Creating/inventing roots
Performing
Co-performing
Community
Using our life as source (Dimitriadis and McCarthy, 2000)
As in this paper/space
Where differences are being negotiated/power in many ways is re-presented
As it has been through our work
By me and you ... as collective
By me and you as different individuals moved toward a shared goal that does not mean without conflict and differences
What kind of knowledge will be the outcome at the partial end of this, our project
As performers and co performers
What will be the un known consequences/precedents/open doors of this legitimation
What we ask, though, is that it
Must be accountable
Embodied, performatively written
In how it would affect me and Us
This sense of the collective Us
But also the sense of me against and with you without exclusion
Not allowing the disembodiment of our work
Live/living in how it would affect
Our lived experience/action now

Our knowledge un production
As scholars, Latinos, partners, straights, males, whatever
People who touched our lives
And lives we hope to touch
With Us and for Us and not about Us
Gut feelings being theorized
Multiple identities shifting as 'I' and 'we'
In my and yours need to survive/to succeed in the many/multiple relationships that are being created by us
To different subjectivism
In the place where we all live and labor
This, among other things, is what our book wants to talk about.
Books do not talk
Bodies do

"Somehow, the mess above, is how I wrote my stories. But in short, Marcelo, I closed my eyes, felt a story coming to me, and wrote," Cláudio, *com uma boa piscada*, finally says.

We share a knowing, long, smile here, as we both know this line intimately, unsure who might have said it first, caring less about this colonizing concern, happy to be writing it together here, inspired by the chance to be constructing a methodology together, in dialogue, in excited cooperation, in ways that we couldn't have imagined alone.

Notes

1. Re: Maya Angelou's autobiographical work, Selwyn Cudjoe explains that "the Afro-American autobiography, a cultural act of self-reading, is meant to reflect a public concern rather than a private act of self-indulgence" (Cudjoe, 1990, p. 275). Lauren Richardson adds to this discussion, advocating the notion that by linking people who share similar experiences, even without knowing one another at a personal level, "the collective story overcomes some of the isolation and alienation of contemporary life" (1990, p. 26).
2. "The autoethnographer functions as a universal singular, a single instance of a more universal social experience. As Sartre describes the universal singular, this subject is 'summed up and for this reason universalized by its epoch, he resumes it by reproducing himself in it as a singularity' (Sartre, 1981, p. ix). Every person is like every other person, but like no other person. The autoethnographer inscribes the experiences of a historical moment, universalizing these experiences in their particular effects in a particular life" (Denzin, 2003, p. 234).

3. "Performance studies is uniquely suited for the challenge of braiding together disparate and stratified ways of knowing. We can think through performance along three crisscrossing lines of activity and analysis. We can think of performance (1) as work of imagination, as an object of study; (2) as a pragmatics of inquiry (both as model and method), as an optic and operation of research; (3) as a tactics of intervention, an alterative space of struggle . . . we often refer to the three a's of performance studies: artistry, analysis, activism. Or to change the alliteration, a commitment to the three c's of performance studies: creativity, critique, citizenship (civic struggles for social justice)" (Conquergood, 2002, p. 152).
4. Denzin, N. 2003. *Performance Ethnography: Critical Pedagogy and the Politics of Culture.* Thousand Oaks, CA: Sage, p. 237.
5. Denzin, 2003, p. 239.
6. In accordance with poststructural views, Freire emphasizes *the word* as the essence of dialogue: "Within the word we find two dimensions, reflection and action, in such a radical interaction that if one is sacrificed—even in part—the other immediately suffers" (1970, p. 68).

Chapter 10

WORDS TO END WITH: DECOLONIZING PRAXIS AND SOCIAL JUSTICE

A former student of Cláudio's sent a video about a visual experiment on street children done in Brazil. The video, directed by Paulo Gandra (2008), goes more or less like this: Streets of downtown São Paulo, February 28, 2008. Hidden cameras. A 5-year-old boy, Matheus Braga, acting as two different children, is shown on a split screen wearing different clothes and levels of personal grooming. On the left screen, the viewer sees Matheus dressed in dirty shorts and tank-top, his face dirty, hair disheveled, shoeless. On the right-hand screen, the viewer sees Matheus sitting exactly on the same spot on a sidewalk in downtown São Paulo, but this time he is looking clean, his hair is combed, he is wearing shoes, and his clothes are well kept. Matheus has the same expression in both situations, his face is serious, and his eyes are looking around as throngs of adults walk by in both directions. Within a few seconds, you can see adults stopping next to Matheus on the right side of the screen. A woman bends down to Matheus's head level and starts talking to him. Soon, there are a dozen adults around Matheus, on the right screen, all with clear expressions of concern, pointing and talking to one another. Then, on the left side of the screen, you see Matheus still sitting alone as people walk by. No one stops. No one seems to look at Matheus in ragged clothes and dirty face. The video ends with the question: "Why are some children our problem and some aren't?".

This question, to us, is at the center of our notion of decolonizing scholarship and education. Matheus represents the visceral experience of betweeners that we have tried to explore in the stories of Part II and in the dialogical co-construction of knowledge informing every step of this book. The experience of Matheus in rags epitomizes the power and pervasiveness of the Us X Them ideology of our (post)colonial times, in this case, a young human experiencing life in between the compassion attached to childhood and the disdain attached to categories of the Other—the poor, the abandoned, the pickpocket street kid. Now imagine this was your child. What would you have liked for adults to do?

As we begin the final chapter of this textual journey, we return to its central metaphor: betweeners and lived experience in-between social categories. Our stories inhabit a space of betweenness and represent, to us, a site of resistance against colonizing production of knowledge about the Other that forces racial, ethnic, class, and gender into categories neater than the Other, and we, actually experience in the world. Our stories are about, and come from, our personal encounters with oppressive ideologies of domination that are sustained by the perpetuation of essentializing narratives of identity, of uncritical narratives of Us versus Them. While our stories are mostly about growing up at the margins of Brazilian society, they are also about the research act and the politics of knowledge production. In and through our stories, we are attempting to resist not only essentializing the narratives of the Other and the Different but also essentializing the narratives of indigenous knowledge.

Let us stop here for a moment and make it clear that we are supportive of the larger postcolonial movement toward creating space for subjugated voices to tell their own stories. But we resist the underlying notion that there is such a thing as a clear distinction between colonizing and indigenous production of knowledge. We, the authors, Brazilian scholars living and writing in the mighty U.S.A., who enjoy the benefits of being perceived in our American universities as indigenous scholars adding a multicultural flavor to higher education, aren't perceived as indigenous scholars in the streets of Brazil. At the same time, we resist the label of colonizer, the label of sellouts working for the oppressive First World, that we sometimes receive from the same indigenous people we are supposed to represent. We are not representatives of the Third World or Brazilian indigenous knowledge. Instead, we are betweeners. Neither here nor there, but in-between. We are not insider-outsiders (Collins, 2000) but betweeners inhabiting the blur surrounding these two identities. We are not the identities on either side of the hyphen (Fine, 1992), Brazilian-Americans, but we live in the hyphen, we straddle the hyphen, we *are* the hyphen.

We are not postcolonial scholars, because we don't make sense of the orderly implication that the world was once precolonial, or the implication that one can ever claim the higher moral ground of having achieved a postcolonial state of being. Instead, we are betweeners aiming for decolonizing performances, reflections, praxis, and narratives of the Other. We continue to embrace the ideal and utopia of postcolonialism, but from the standpoint of embodied betweeners experiencing the world in the space between colonial forces and the postcolonial imaginary, in transition, writing about the journey toward the dream of inclusive, unconditional social justice, but not as if we had arrived at the postcolonial destination ahead of the crowds. For that reason, we prefer the term *decolonizing scholarship* over *postcolonial scholarship*. *Decolonizing* is a term that, to us, signifies action, movement, process, dialogue, and the space between colonial and postcolonial. Decolonizing scholarship, in and of itself, inhabits the space in-between, between being and being more human, between being conditionally free and being free, between being a street child and being a child, between visceral knowledge of subjugation and theories of oppression. We don't put a hyphen in decolonizing, because we embrace it as the hyphen itself.

We believe that creating narratives from the hyphen, from the identity spaces in-between, can become invitations to encounters that demystify the Other and Difference and promote narratives and emotions of unity with all humans and the world we inhabit. Writing from our betweenness is a way to continue forging narrative space for Us to *both* disagree with or dislike fellow humans *and* at the same time respect and honor their indelible right to just treatment. We believe betweenness narratives can contribute to decolonizing movements by bringing visceral and street knowledge to scholarly texts in undiluted forms, without the editorial process of postpositivistic methods of justification/interpretation; by inviting the reader to participate in the making of scholarly "analysis" through our open-endedness and messiness in representation; by creating glimpses into the Other's life that help people see the similarities and brotherhood/sisterhood that we each share even with the most exotic group in our eyes; by revisiting the everyday life of those historically dismissed as individual failures, calling attention to the powerful yet hidden mechanisms of oppression at work in every encounter with the Other in everyday life; by recreating, over and over again, a sociological imagination that inspires the dominant discourse to feel responsible for the humanization of those dealt a rougher hand from birth; by promoting critical decolonizing pedagogies that evoke collective hope instead of individual blaming; by recreating language that allows new generations of thinker-citizens to seek and support systemic possibilities of inclusiveness instead of the current name-calling rhetoric.

At last, we want to return to the decolonizing act of creating narrative space in academia for visceral knowledge. The in-between space from which we write is a constant site of struggle against oppressive forces of colonization. And it's not a metaphorical site but a bodily, visceral site. We want to recover and honor the embodiment of the in-between space, of the physical experience of betweenness. We want to highlight the lived experience of the body, of the flesh in these in-between spaces. And highlight not only the body of the Other but also the body of the narrative maker. The body of the researcher-writer is always present in the research-writing act. And this presence, of course, is always shaped by how the researcher-writer's body is treated in the physical world. Merely claiming to be a postcolonial researcher-teacher-writer isn't enough to achieve a decolonizing praxis. This claim needs to come from an embodied narrative. Show us the scars of oppression on your body. If your scars are in places you can't show, as in the mind, then tell us the story of your scars. Your body, in-between the colonial and postcolonial experience, will then become present in your narrative and praxis.

We hope our stories of betweenness advance Emma Perez's concept of the decolonial imaginary (1999): the embodied space of betweeners who refuse colonization, who not only resist colonization but who cannot be colonized, who long for an imagined decolonial existence. Narratives of the decolonial imaginary can't be told through disembodied analysis, statistics, or group differences, however sophisticated such codified experiences may become in the age of technology. In this spirit, we believe that raising awareness of our communalities in betweenness is one of the new battlegrounds of the decolonial imaginary in the 21st century.

Decolonizing Praxis: The Classroom and Discipline as Renewed Battlegrounds of Conscientização

"So, where do we go from here?" we ask each other often.

"I see my New Battlegrounds as the university classroom and the traditional sites where the production of knowledge takes place, like journals, books, and academic conferences," Marcelo says.

"I agree with you. Our goal is to arrive in the New Battlegrounds: The decolonizing classroom—the territory for struggle moves from memory to the classroom in the making of new memories of resistance, transformation, notions of inclusiveness. The public performance stage—moving from decolonizing discourse toward decolonizing praxis, toward the dream where people come to the academy to do the talking, not the answering; the invasion of the institutional space by the oppressed and marked body, not as object of research but as expert of their own struggle."

"I see . . .," says Marcelo, "but to get there is another . . ."

"We are there, it's not perfect, but we are there . . .," interrupts Cláudio, "and we and others inhabit these spaces of production of knowledge . . . we've been taught and we are teachers . . . we are living betweener bodies in the struggle. . . . I teach about your work in my qualitative class. . . . My students know Grace. What does it mean when we, my students and I, plus you as the author from far way, perform the story? What does it do to us when we see Grace approaching folks walking by the Cathedral Square, cardboard mic in hand, asking what could be done about the street kids' situation in town? Or when she points out a woman who tucks her purse tightly under her arm as Grace walks toward her with the cardboard mic? What is there for us to teach?" asks Cláudio rhetorically.

"The Cathedral Square was full of people walking by, others just hanging out with friends, and parents watching their children chase and feed the pigeons," Marcelo jumps in. "Sitting on the front steps of the Cathedral, I could see how uncomfortable people felt by Grace's comments—made in a loud and clear voice for all to hear. Here was a skinny shoeless street girl breaking a wall of indifference carefully constructed behind religious ('God works in mysterious ways'), classist ('People shouldn't have children they can't care for'), and psychological ('It's not my fault!') rationalizations. Grace was purposefully using the inconvenience of her bodily presence before higher-status adults to challenge the system that creates and sustains such dehumanizing existence."

"And that is now a story, a memory, a retelling that lives in the memories of a university classroom in a faraway land. In that way, Grace's resistance to being essentialized is now heard beyond the moment," Cláudio says.

"It's like her performance of resistance can continue to echo across time, joining other faraway performances of resistance, making a human connection in ways not imagined by students and readers before," Marcelo says.

"And how do you see this performative connection translating into your pedagogical praxis?" Cláudio asks.

"Well, Grace was also challenging each of us to stop pretending to be innocent spectators of this system. Grace makes a public remark that most students in the classroom can't, will choose not to, brush away: by merely observing street kids from a distance, by protecting our purses, by crossing the street away from her, we are all active participants in the creation of the dangerous childhood in which street kids find themselves. With the depth of knowledge about being a street kid that only a, well, street kid can have, Grace was using her flesh and her words to point out that the fear these adults have of her is directly connected to their every-day politics of the Other."

"What politics?" asks Cláudio.

"The politics of blame and separation. Other people's children are not my responsibility. I need to provide for my own. And similar expressions of the Us versus Them ideology."

"And Grace does all that with a sense of humor," Cláudio adds.

"I thought it was an irresistible cultural critique. I doubt, however, many people that day could have overcome their fear long enough to pay attention to Grace's resistance against oppression and dehumanizing narratives of self. Being kids, they are subjected to a social context organized by adults who have not lived through the street experience but who nevertheless have the need to transcend their lack of street experience through cultural expressions that inform them about these kids. That is people's way of experiencing these kids' experiences: through participation in the dominant narratives about street kids (that is, circulated in the media, social interactions, social policies, and economic discourse). And because the local dominant narratives about street kids often represent them as lesser human beings (that is, inherently devious, lazy, lacking morals and ethics, criminals-to-be), most people in Campinas know no other way of imagining and interacting with these kids on a daily basis. At the same time, these kids find few cultural spaces in which to imagine themselves and interpret their lived experiences outside these dominant narratives, thus helping create a vicious circle that justifies and perpetuates these same oppressive narratives and practices."

"A circle you started to break, or hope to break with your story," Cláudio says. "It was the second week of class, the students weren't sure of what to expect. I sat in the middle of them and said that there was no teacher. . . . I asked them what they knew about street kids in Brazil . . . not much was said . . . I took your words and started the performance, each one of us read a piece of your words *for and with Grace*. I cried that day."

"You cry every day," mocks Marcelo.

"Teach what is not supposed to be taught. Dare to teach all your students, but have a special care with the ones that aren't supposed to be there. I thank Yvonna Lincoln often for this line: write what you believe should be written. These are my New Battlegrounds. We live the struggle in so many layers. We're writing this blessed book that we both have been advised not to write together. We were told we should each have our own. We are showing that together, we and our bunches, are a force."

"Inspired by Anzaldúa . . .crossing borders and making bridges," adds Marcelo.

"And yet, especially now in my new job as assistant professor, walking the hallways at U Mass, I have to reassure myself, that even if I still feel that I don't belong, I have the right to teach there. The janitor becomes the teacher," Cláudio says with a mischievous grin.

"The janitor-teacher is in the classroom now," Marcelo retorts.

"And during class, orchestrating critical pedagogy in the New Classroom. Not after class, picking up after the students," the Thug-Scholar chuckles.

"Cheers to that!"

"I'm so grateful to bell hooks for not letting me forget the pain, because the New Classroom can't be sugarcoated, sanitized, suffocated by third-person analysis. Instead, I bring the betweener to the classroom.

What comes from this we cannot be sure, but we have Freire's concrete hope," Cláudio says more seriously now.

"Paulo Freire, betweeners, betweenness narratives. I also see all that as central to my Battlegrounds in the New Classroom and higher learning communities," Marcelo says in agreement.

"Concrete hope that the oppressed also has a place in the New Classroom, and not as merely the subject of study, but present in flesh, blood, and visceral knowledge . . . this can't be taken from us," Cláudio says.

"Still . . . we are not Grace . . . we haven't experienced that intensity of oppression," Marcelo says. "I certainly haven't," remembering the violence felt just in the act of witnessing Grace's performance.

"No, we are not like Grace. No human being should endure this kind of life. And yet so many continue to suffer in our so-called postcolonial times," Cláudio says.

"Acknowledging our privileges and the suffering in the world makes for good starting conversation in the decolonizing New Classroom," Marcelo says with a nod.

"It helps to keep me grounded and ready for the road. It helps me to 'talk back' to the superstructure, to the new corporate model of higher education that wants to call students clients and customers, that would prefer to standardize the *banking* teaching model," Cláudio says.

"I second that, amigo! And in addition to this larger systemic resistance, I think that narratives of resistance help jolt some students out of the torpor often induced by disembodied knowledge about the Other," Marcelo concurs.

"Besides the New Classroom, you mentioned journals and conferences as your decolonizing Battleground. Aren't these Battlegrounds already open to the type of decolonizing scholarship we are advancing here?" Cláudio asks.

"Yes, there are many more journals, conferences, and other scholarly spaces open to decolonizing scholarship now. And thanks to the hard work of others who came before, our hope for a decolonial imaginary feels much more concrete than when I started in the early 1990s.

"But as we've talked about, there is still much to be done even within the most critically inclined interpretive communities for us to reach the next level of emancipation," Marcelo says.

"Like fighting to make visceral knowledge of oppression truly more important to the postcolonial movement than theory and intellectual prowess," Cláudio adds quickly.

"Yes, and I also think we need narratives that turn the mirror toward critical interpretive communities, so that we can continue to resist not only positivistic determinism but determinism of any kind. In my view, it's still a pretty elitist bunch, very status conscious, status proud. It still tends to name the world in an essentializing dichotomous way of Us versus Them.

As bell hooks (1994) alerts, the only thing that such a worldview changes is positions in the hierarchy of the status quo. We need to continue to decolonize the postcolonial academic circles. I need to continue to decolonize myself. I think we have much to gain in our path toward the decolonial imaginary by not putting ourselves above the so-called colonizers, Them. That's what I mean by making journals, conferences, and academic circles one of my New Battlegrounds. Betweeners fighting the elitism within," Marcelo says with a grin.

"I hear you, *cumpa*! It's like the reviewers who rejected my paper 'My Bad English.' My intention here is not to put myself above criticism. I liked some of the comments. But some I did not like at all. I am using this experience here not to talk back to the reviewers about the paper. I'm bringing the comments here to illustrate, again, issues of visceral knowledge we have tried to develop in this book. Two of these comments really left me with a bad taste in my mouth," Cláudio says grimacing.

"Which ones?" asks Marcelo.

"These," says Cláudio starting to read: "(1) To me, it looks like some personal anecdotes with a few scholarly quotes thrown in to give it a bit of a scholarly cachet; (2) And, yes, I am now deploying the rules of a writing system that privilege certain ways of speaking. I would argue that there are some good reasons for holding to those conventional norms. Most often those norms are guided by the desire for communicative clarity.

"Anecdotes? For God's sake. How I am not supposed to be mad? What they call anecdotes I call, as I learned from Haraway, people's lives. To dismiss lived experience as 'anecdote' makes no sense to me. This shows not only ignorance but also intolerance and arrogance of the academic world. The 'ones who know best!' 'Communicative clarity' for whom? Where has this person been?" asks Cláudio.

"A transnational, postcolonial concept of class is there, in the My Bad English story, and it seems to me that it makes people uncomfortable or goes over their heads. It is a matter of writing against the very form of academic writing. Not for the sake of anarchy or nihilism but for the sake of egalitarian inclusion of those less academically sophisticated. More than a syntax issue, it's a class issue that is still being ignored, wittingly and not, in higher learning," Marcelo says in guarded agreement.

"How about the second comment. . . . Excluding ways of knowing, rules of a writing system, communicative clarity—not for me. I position myself against these excluding rules of language. I position myself against the either/or dichotomy of proper language use in academia. I want something more inclusive, as in *both* effort toward clarity *and* effort to understand those with 'Bad English.' It is not about transforming, training and "educating" the oppressed/colonized Other into some white stuff. Clarity? For whom?" asks Cláudio.

"For all," says Marcelo. "I think it's the way the reviewers positioned themselves in their critique, the view from everywhere, as if they could speak for the whole field of performance studies, that is a problem. It all sounds pretty elitist to me. Condescending."

"They could have easily made their points about language clarity, for example, in a constructive way," Cláudio fumes.

"But Cláudio, I also think it's important to work to become more culturally bilingual. We need to be able to speak with and be understood by the street child and the intellectual."

"Marcelo, I know you're trying to get stuff out of me," Cláudio says shaking his head. "We got here from different trails. Even though you came to this country without knowing English, as did I, yours is much better than mine. You can perform this culturally bilingual stuff and . . . I can't, not in this sense. Our stories show how differently our educational paths were shaped by class. It might be, as the second reviewer suggests, that I am lazy or don't do my homework. Or, as I suggest, it may be that we are still silencing the less educated with our hegemonic ways of producing scholarship.

"My point is this: What happens to the one who is not able to be bilingual? Who will be left out of the university walls? I am not able to be one. The academic clarity is confusing. The way I learn, read, and write does not fit in these rules. They don't make sense to me. I am not able to be articulate and so should I be quiet? It's a rhetorical question, of course," Cláudio says recovering his sense of humor.

"Marcelo, you lived this with me. At the beginning of my academic life in the States, I felt lost. Many of my papers came with comments such as: 'It's not a sentence' or 'I do not believe you have the skills, English and otherwise, to succeed here.' I had difficulty in reading and writing theory, small tasks that my classmates seemed to take for granted and move on. I felt dumb. I am not smart enough. Stop pretending . . . who was I trying to fool? See, doesn't this look like a report that a social scientist would write about many high school dropouts?"

"Yes," Marcelo agrees.

"But I wasn't in high school. Most of the classes I took did not speak to me. They were not in one but two foreign languages. English and disembodied theory. I felt desperate. I wanted to give up, but Dani and I were pregnant. I did not have a plan B, so I kept on keeping on. . . . Analua was born, I started drinking, and being good Latinos, Dani and I got pregnant again."

"Will your students, in your New Classroom, understand the criticism to determinism you mean by this last comment?" Marcelo says interrupting.

"Humor and self-deprecation is also part of my New Classroom, as an invitation to decenter the power of the teacher, as an invitation to not taking oneself too seriously. Much of elitism, in my view, comes from scholars taking themselves too seriously, thinking they have arrived at some deserving pedestal," Cláudio says without hesitation.

"Touché," Marcelo says, tongue in cheek.

"As I was saying, I am a stubborn person who has a wife and two children and did not have a plan B. I decide to do what I know/do best, to hang in there no matter what, to survive. I stopped drinking. Not drinking, I had a chance. At the same time, in my 'fieldwork' trips to Brazil I became stronger. The abstract discussions that did not speak to me in the classroom were very far away from the lives I was interacting with in Brazil. Something was wrong, and I decided it wasn't me. In many ways, Jorge Amado's fiction and Chico Buarque's songs have helped me more than the social science writings that I have read, because they spoke of suffering and injustice in embodied narratives. I did not know Foucault or Derrida enough, and I did not have the previous formal knowledge, luxury, or privilege/time—we were four people in a foreigner country living under a thousand dollars a month budget—to learn what I did not think I could.

"But," Cláudio pauses and raises his finger, "I knew how to walk in the *favelas*. I knew how to interact with soccer fans and sugar cane workers. When Justino said to me: 'You know . . .,' I knew it, not with my brains and books only, but with my whole living body. *Conscientização*, it was good to remember that I knew stuff."

"So how will you make your New Classroom different from those grad school classrooms?" asks Marcelo.

"Well, I started to interrogate the reasons it was so difficult to be in grad school. The answer was in front of me. It was for the same reasons it was difficult to make it through high school. It was the familiar feeling of not belonging, not having any friends, a system that wasn't there for me or did not speak to/for me. Marcelo, I am asking you now, in your many trips to my hometown, how many people have you met from my childhood? I recall you have met only two of my friends: Robinho and Gleidson. Did they have the tools in place to go to college? No, and I didn't either. But I got luckier than they did. In a way, if my friendship with you and Claudinho did not save my life, what I believe it did, it gave me, at the very least, a way out. I did make it through high school and beyond in Brazil, as a troublemaker with weak language skills. Familiar, isn't it?"

"It's pure, good ol' Paulo Freire," says Marcelo.

"Anyway, that's how I want to do decolonizing battle in my New Classroom, by trying to make those who feel out of place feel at home, in a place where their vernacular is honored and welcomed as integral part of our critical pedagogy," Cláudio says.

Marcelo, indulge me for a minute. Let's perform this next thing together; we construct it together; each reads a paragraph," Cláudio suggests.

"I start because I'm prettier," says Cláudio.

"The mentality of the oppressed," replies Marcelo. "Fine, go on."

Visceral Knowledge in the New Classroom

(We invite you to read this out loud, with other people if possible.)

"My father is a drunk. Neither my father nor my mother has a college degree, owns a house, a car, or has held a regular job in the last fifteen years. My sister never went to college and got pregnant when she was 17. Am I the product of the colonial rape or just the product of a broken family living in a vacuum? Sociology 101.

"What happens to the one that is not able to be culturally bilingual? Who will be left out of the university walls? Under what circumstances?

'It isn't enough to simply suggest that one's background is responsible for the language one uses—what does a particular language usage reveal?' (Reviewer 1)

"This is a question for you, too.

"I have felt alone in school, basically because I've been. I am in an unfamiliar surrounding because, well, it is. The learning processes for survival in the streets and in scholarship are different. Norman Denzin asked me to write a theoretical chapter in indigenous scholarship, ethics, and decolonizing academy/inquiry for my dissertation. I ended up with 'Unspeakable Transgressions' (Chapter 3). And I wasn't trying to dodge his assignment. Abstractness does not work well for me. I do not look to theory to explain life. I look into life to intervene in theoretical writings.

"Folks like me, without an educated upbringing, enter the decolonizing dialogue through lived experience. I write "some personal anecdotes with a few scholarly quotes thrown in to give it a bit of a scholarly cachet." And I do so for the sake of clarity to those who, like me, are interested in participating in the postcolonial movement in academia not only as subjects of research but also as producers of knowledge.

"I've been called many names. However, if it is my task to name myself, I would call me a teacher; an educator, because I love.

"Now, it is time for the quote, so I can pretend to be a scholar:

'Shortly before his death, Freire was reported to say something to the effect that he "could never think of education without love, and that is why I think I am an educator, first of all because I feel love."' (McLaren, 2002, p. 253)

"It seems to me, that even the quotes I choose do not quite sound very scholarly. Even though I am scared, my intention is to hang in there no matter what. Oh, I almost forget the other quote:"

'When we are faced with concrete fears, such as that of losing our jobs or not being promoted, we feel the need to set certain limits to our fear. Before anything else, we begin to recognize that fear is a manifestation of being alive. I do not hide my fears. But I must not allow my fears to immobilize me. Instead, I must control them, for it is in the very exercise of this control that my necessary courage is shared.' (Freire, 1998b, p. 41)

"Yes, I am hanging in there no matter what.

"The only way to keep me from pointing out the masked disdain for the embodied oppressed in academia, to this very day, is to take your academic knife and cut my disarticulated, untheoretical tongue. But be aware, I might bite your hand and swallow your fingers . . . and looking at your fingerless and bloody hand I will go on, crying in my nothingness, making awful utterances in my tongueless mouth, drinking coffee and smoking cigarettes. . . .

"But this is never going to happen, is it?

"We, academics, work only in abstraction. Unless someone high above, using the rights of the Patriotic Act, decides that I have not behaved well, that I am a threat to the only real democracy in the world, and silences my accented tongue. . . .

"Then, you all, 'who know best,' can make good use of your theories and methods, and study, classify, and represent my silenced body. Because, as I've been told so many times, you have the right tongue and I don't know theory.

"But I am not exchanging places wit' ya.

"I understand that to have a tenure-track position is a privilege for anyone.

"And don't take it lightly.

"I do not write anecdotes with few quotes to give it a scholarly cachet. I write about lives and painfully marked bodies!

"However, in the end, the visceral truth, as painfully as it is to invoke it here, is simple. I might be a poor scholar, but hey, I am a heck of a subject, ain't I?"

"So this is the kind of thing you will teach in your New Classroom?" Marcelo asks in jest.

"Not teach. Perform. The decolonizing classroom is right here in front us. In my case, I've been hired by a prestigious university, even with the tensions surrounding performance autoethnography inside the field of communication, and in performance studies for that matter, where some fellow scholars don't accept my performances as legitimate performances. So it's also a way to show narratives of resistance from within Communications as a discipline. It's a way to talk about the politics of knowledge production, discipline borders, etc. And it's another instantiation of being a betweener, this time as a Communications scholar rejected by the mainstream Communications discipline. I am, with my bad English, a professor of communications," Cláudio says with the largest grin, straightening up his back, standing a tad taller.

"I face similar challenges in my own discipline, Human Development, though perhaps the resistance to decolonizing scholarship is a bit more prosaic than in your field. I think the notion of paradigm has not really sunk in yet. Most folks still talk in terms of qualitative versus quantitative studies, structured versus open-ended interviews, coding, etc. I feel that I have more space now than when I first became a faculty member in the late 1990s. But I still get comments like, 'Well, it's a lovely story. But I missed hearing your analysis of it,' or 'It's very moving, but you can't generalize it.' On a few occasions, I get some more condescending comments, like 'How can you be satisfied with descriptive studies and not go for where social science gets interesting, predictive methods?'"

"It sounds like you are still in the middle of Denzin and Lincoln's 4th Moment of qualitative research, the crisis of representation!" Cláudio teases.

"More like still fighting between the 2nd and 3rd Moments, still being a betweener straddling the transitions and tensions between the modernist, postpositivist and the performative, decolonizing interpretive paradigms," Marcelo says with a sigh. "But the space for critical (auto)ethnography is growing. So hope becomes just a bit more concrete and makes the battle to rewrite silenced memories of colonial oppression a worthwhile scholarship act. We may not be able to change the past, but we can change the colonial interpretation of the past. In this decolonizing act, we have a chance to create cultural plots (Richardson, 1990) that allow us to look at old ideals of equality, liberty, and social justice afresh, mindful of the need to occupy the silenced spaces between Us and Them with narratives of betweenness, where everyone becomes a bit grayer, and more comfortably so."

"We may not be able to change the beginning of our colonial history, but decolonizing acts may still be able to bring about its ending," Cláudio says.

"By relentlessly problematizing and combating racism, sexism, classism, and other forms of determinism in contemporary societies," Marcelo adds.

"By the way of honoring visceral knowledge of oppression in the classroom and performance texts," says Cláudio.

"And keeping on building bridges between academia and community until the distinction between scholars and activists becomes too blurred to be worth mentioning," says Marcelo in turn.

"To engage in decolonizing and polyvocal projects with our students, colleagues and the community where we live and labor," Cláudio completes.

"Okay. So this is our vision for decolonizing classrooms. We want to stand on the shoulders of earlier critical educators without whitewashing critical pedagogy (Darder, Baltonado, and Torres, 2003). We want to use our positions as betweeners, Third World folks teaching at major American universities, to foster Freire's notion of *conscientização* in the very practice of our pedagogy, going beyond teaching *about* critical pedagogy," Marcelo says.

"And that means rejecting, in overt ways, the banking model of teaching so prevalent in American undergraduate studies, in favor of a more democratic form of educational dialogue that problematizes the construction of knowledge about the Other. And bringing narratives of life in-between into the classroom is a way to invite students to consider the commonalities between themselves and the Other," Cláudio says.

"In my teaching experience, students respond with concern about, say, large numbers of children living in the streets of Brazil. But the response is even, and always, more engaged and emotionally invested when they read about the street life of a single individual, a fellow human being, in greater depth. It is in this higher emotional connection with the Other that the decolonial imaginary can become a more concrete possibility in our students' lives," Marcelo says.

"And we each teach hundreds of college students every year. The potential is high for a slow but steady revolution in levels of *conscientização* toward inclusive narratives of the Other. Our students may not agree with us, but they will have to weigh the betweener narratives we share with them against the mainstream push for the positivist narrative of means and averages that stand as the privileged representation of the Other in our times," Cláudio adds.

"As our Muse says, Onward!"

PARTING THOUGHTS . . .

"The colonizers spent centuries trying to impose their language. The colonized people were told either verbally or through message systems inherent in the colonial structure that they did not possess effective cultural instruments with which to express themselves. This language profile imposed by the colonizers eventually convinced the people that their language was in fact a corrupt and inferior system unworthy of true educational status." (Freire and Macedo 1987, p. 118)

"I cannot quite see the next step in my work when I am so dissatisfied with the present, when I feel that what I have done is not enough in the now." (Cláudio Moreira, today, here, now)

In a tribute to Richard Rorty's life and philosophy, Stephen Metcalf (2007) pointed out a Rortyan thought that we think resonates with the driving force behind this book and the stories we are trying to tell: "We are stuck arguing with one another, in order to achieve, not truth, but consensus." Like Rorty, we believe that there is no end to the negotiation of representation, interpretation, and study of social reality. We are seeking, through the stories told in this book, not a truer representation of the social reality shaping the lives of disenfranchised humans but a legitimization of stories that have not yet entered the process of knowledge construction in academic and public spheres. And we believe that the Rortyan consensus we embrace can be most effectively sought out by intimate narratives—that is, narratives born out of personal struggles against oppression and out of relationships of trust between the teller and the oppressed.

When successful, intimate narratives have a way of fostering a sense of Us that challenges the still pervasive sense of Us versus Them that fuels inequality and privilege at the cost of the right of Others. This is far from a novel idea and has been at the center of poignant literature, poetry, and corporate marketing. Think of the recent Olympic Games coverage by American broadcasting companies and its focus on stories of individual athletes' dramas, instead of on the actual sporting events, as a strategy to attract female audience/consumers.

But even in the wake of postmodernism and postcolonial critique in academic circles, we have found much resistance at the gates of social science venues. Fictionalized representations of ethnographic studies are deemed fluffy even if they succeed in bringing to the text visceral lived experience otherwise lost in favor of objectivity. Autoethnography is still dismissed as self-serving and navel-gazing even if it succeeds in representing situated, bodily experience, going beyond illusory *means* and *averages* that represent not even a single human's real experience of life. And visceral knowledge of oppression is still seen in academic circles as an inferior stance to theoretical analysis of oppression. Our joint venture, this book, is our way of creating a discussion piece to continue the dialogue about how the self-proclaimed resistance social sciences can escape the ivory tower and write a bit more from the trenches. We, the authors, will continue to study the theories and the English language, but let us, all of us, also write from visceral experience in the process. Besides turf, there is nothing to lose and much to be gained.

Into the Future

We are both irreparably romantic and optimistic. We believe in the dream that everyone's children can, one day, be judged by the strength of their character and not by the color of their skin or other symbols of unearned (under)privilege. But we have been in and around human misery too long and too deep to dream that we will see this in our lifetime. Our visits to Brazil, for fieldwork and family time, are striking reminders that the ideology of domination sustaining a world of blatant inequality is hardly losing steam. While writing this book, we both read intimate narratives of life in the *favelas* of São Paulo[1] and Rio de Janeiro,[2] the two largest urban centers of Brazil, that portrayed the inconsequence of humanizing cultural plots in face of extreme inequality and violence with such force that we were pushed close to despair. We struggled to recover a sense of historical perspective.

But we did. We recovered perspective and concrete hope by thinking, reading, and talking to each other about the progress we feel we have made since the end of government-sponsored slavery, legislated patriarchal absolutism, and separate-but-equal laws. We talked with passion about the power that the writings of Gloria Anzaldúa and bell hooks have had in our lives. We talked with hope about the fact that a boy-soldier such as Ishmael Beah (2007) can tell his own story nowadays, and with such evocative emotional pull that readers will never again be able to think that Sierra Leone is not part of their own world.

We came out of this introspection with a renewed sense that intimate scholarship, that is, scholarship formed within the visceral knowledge of oppression and resistance, can and must play a role in the expansion of our individual and public notions of social justice. And we believe a more inclusive notion of social justice, however gradual in a historical scale of time, can be extended by creating representations that allow readers to see themselves in the plight of others, by texts that invite connection through emotional resonance with the Other. With more than 6 billion of us spread over a vast and varied planet, sustainable social investment depends on emotional resonance with the concept of the Other as one of Us, and not as one of Them.

We all know every human needs oxygen, food, and water, even if in different quantity, taste, and purity. Within and between cultural communalities abound. We are touched by stories representing humans long gone from earth. We are inspired by the stories of strangers in distant lands finding the same redemption we seek. We shed tears watching fictitious characters overcome familiar odds on the screen. Yet, when it comes to identity, we seem to be transfixed by the differences we attribute to the Other. In our reading of history and experience of the world, humans seem to focus on communality with the Other only after personal emotional connections have been made.

Power struggles within ethnicity, class, caste, religious orientation, disabilities, sexuality, skin color, nationality, and immigration, all have one common denominator: the focus on difference. While we, the authors, have divergent views about its origin, a story for another day, we agree that this attention to difference is global and pervasive. We agree that this attention to difference is mostly evocative of negative emotions and thoughts. We agree that difference is highlighted or created by those with more power to justify privilege and subjugation. We agree that difference, when successfully essentialized as the totality of the Other, becomes the spark and fuel of hatred. We agree that the politics of identity and difference is one of the most contentious battlegrounds for issues of social justice and equality in the 21st century. And we agree that new narratives of betweenness can help us create language about the Other that reaches out for commonalities and shared understanding. Instead of immigrants, we will see New Americans. Instead of illegals, we will see brave humans seeking the same dreams we want for ourselves and our children. Instead of dirty pickpockets, we will see resourceful children managing urban survival without a single caring adult. Instead of being indignant about having to secure our borders or homes, we will engage our imaginations in constructing a new world order where security against ourselves becomes mostly obsolete. To get going toward the utopia of social justice and equality we need, in our view, narratives of identity that are more nuanced, slower to judge, grayer . . .

gray area
noun
    an ill-defined situation or field not readily conforming to a category or to an existing set of rules: ***gray areas in the legislation have still to be clarified.***
    (*Oxford English Dictionary* (*OED*), online, accessed 7/31/20008)

We want to advance narratives of betweenness that help people feel comfortable, not "ill," with fuzzy categories of the Other. We hope narratives of betweenness become so pervasive that any impulse to call the Other some either/or name, as in either good or bad, either with Us or against Us, either legal or illegal, will invariably trigger more complex identifying cognitive processes of both/and. Perhaps, then, we will see a new entry under "gray area" in the *OED*:

gray area
noun
    2. figurative for the space where most human experiences inhabit: ***gray areas in the legislation have yet to be made grayer.***

As we move forward, we want to continue to problematize, challenge, and resist essentializing social constructions of identity, while at same time offering narratives of betweenness from our encounters with the deterministic world. We want to advance Anzaldúa's notion that we are all experiencing life in-between identities, transients seeking fleeting anchors of identity, attempting to hang on to fixed identities we deem worthy, while desperately trying to avoid ridiculed ones, only to be morphed into another identity as soon as the next person comes a-knocking, and often too fast for true composure. Still kicking and screaming, we might have a chance, as aware betweeners, to fulfill dreams of *liberté, égalité, fraternité,* through dialogue, consensus, and common ground. It's this betweenness that unites us and can create a sense of common identity, a sense of Us. And it's harder to hurt one of Us than one of Them.

Each of us, authors, has connected to the children and adults in these stories through a concern for their predicament. We have connected, too, through an admiration for their *joie de vivre* in face of daunting realities. We saw ourselves in their stories and invariably felt a common human struggle to live without much pain. If our representational abilities have matched our ontological and epistemological stances, then it is possible that readers may see themselves in our protagonists and be moved in similar ways. This is our version of Paulo Freire's concrete hope.

> "Hope is ethical. Hope is moral. Hope is peaceful and nonviolent. Hope seeks the truth of life's sufferings. Hope gives meaning to the struggles to change the world. Hope is grounded in concrete performative practices, in struggles and interventions that espouse the sacred values of love, care, community, trust, and well being. ... Hope, as a form of pedagogy, confronts and interrogates cynicism, the belief that change is not possible or too costly. Hope works from rage to love. It articulates a progressive politics that rejects "conservative, neoliberal postmodernity. . . . Hope rejects terrorism. Hope rejects the claim that peace must come at the cost of war." (Freire, quoted in Denzin, 2003, p. 229)

We joined our critical (auto)ethnographic, our performance autoethnographic, work in this book in the spirit of adding to the larger dialogue of possibilities about the meaning and praxis of more inclusive social justice. In the writing process, we have thought ideas and reached levels of understanding about the concepts and stories in this book that hadn't occurred to our individual minds. We believe that this writing collaboration was the kind of dialogue Paulo Freire claimed essential for *conscientização* and critical education. We believe our stories complement each other in telling about the struggle against the dehumanizing treatment that ideologies of domination invariably create for children growing up in our exclusive concepts of social justice—justice for my people even if at the expense of others. We hope this work will stand as an evocative invitation for people to join in Our search for humanization.

At the end,

We are all betweeners
Us, betweeners
Them, betweeners
You, betweener

EveryBody, betweener
Writing from the flesh
Exposing the vulnerability and power
Of our branded bodies
Making visceral knowledge count

We are
Not ready to settle
Willing to struggle for a world without Them
Where everybody is
And should be
Us.

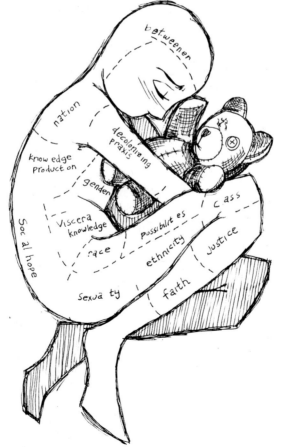

Notes

1. *Manual Pratico do Odio,* which translates into something like "The Practical Manual of Hatred," by Reginaldo F. Ferréz, 2003.
2. *Abusado: O Dono do Morro Dona Marta*, which translates into something like "Audacious: The Ruler of the Santa Marta Slum," by Cacá Barcellos, 2003.

REFERENCES

Agencia Futebol Interior. 2005. *Guerra no Moises Lucarelli*. Accessed October 17, 2005, www.futebolinterior.com.br.

Alexander, B. K. 2005. Performance ethnography: The reenacting and inciting of culture. In N. Denzin and Y. Lincoln (Eds.), *The Sage Handbook of Qualitative Research*. Thousand Oaks, CA: Sage.

Allen, P. G. 1992. *The Sacred Hoop: Recovering the Feminine in American Indian Traditions*. Boston: Beacon Press.

———. 2001. Angry women are building: Issues and struggles facing American India women today. In K. Bhavnani (Ed.), *Feminism and Race*. New York: Oxford University Press.

Amado, J. 1937. *Capitaes da Areia* [Captains of the Sand]. Rio de Janeiro: J. Olympio.

Anzaldúa, G. E. 1981. La Prieta. In C. Moraga and G. E. Anzaldúa (Eds.), *This Bridge Called My Back: Writings by Radical Women of Color*. New York: Kitchen Table, Women of Color Press.

———. 1990. *Making Face, Making Soul/Haciendo Caras: Creative and Critical Perspectives by Women of Color*. San Francisco: Aunt Lute Foundation Books.

———. 1999. *Borderlands / La Frontera: The New Mestiza* (2nd ed.). San Francisco: Aunt Lute Books.

———. 2000. *Interviews/Entrevistas*. In A. L. Keating (Ed.). New York: Routledge.

Anzaldúa, G. E., and Keating, A. L. 2002. *This Bridge We Call Home: Radical Visions for Transformation*. New York: Routledge.

Bakhtin, M. M. 1981. *The Dialogic Imagination*. In M. Holquist (Ed.). Austin: University of Texas Press.

———. 1986. *Speech Genres and Other Essays*. Austin: University of Texas Press.

Barad, K. 2003. Posthumanist performativity: Toward an understanding of how matter comes to matter, *Signs: Journal of Women in Culture & Society* 28(3). Chicago: The University of Chicago Press.

Barcellos, C. 2003. *Abusado: O Dono do Morro Dona Marta*. Rio de Janeiro: Editora Record.

Beah, I. 2007. *A Long Way Gone: Memoirs of a Boy Soldier*. New York: Farrar, Straus and Giroux.

Bernardes, M. 2005. Violencia no Futebol. Ate quando? Accessed October 20, 2005, www.marciobernardes.com.br.

Bishop, R. 2005. Freeing ourselves from colonial domination in research: A Kaupapa Maori approach to creating knowledge. In N. Denzin and Y. Lincoln (Eds.), *The Sage Handbook of Qualitative Research*. Thousand Oaks, CA: Sage, 109–138.

Bochner, A., and Ellis, C. 2002. *Ethnographically Speaking: Authoethnography, Literature, and Aesthetics*. Walnut Creek, CA: AltaMira Press.

Brasil de Fato. 2005. Morte de Cortador de Cana. www.brasildefato.com.br/v01/agencia.

Brodkey, L. 1987. Writing critical ethnographic narratives, *Anthropology and Education Quarterly* 18: 67–76.

Butler, J. 1993. *Bodies That Matter: On the Discursive Limits of "Sex."* New York: Routledge.

———. 1997. *Excitable Speech: A Politics of the Performative*. New York: Routledge.

———. 2004. *Undoing Gender*. New York: Routledge.

Collins, P. H. 1998. *Fighting Words: Black Women and the Search for Justice*. Minneapolis: University of Minnesota Press.

———. 2000 [1991]. *Black Feminist Thought: Knowledge, Consciousness, and the Politics of Empowerment*. New York: Routledge.

Conquergood, D. 1985. Performing as a moral act: Ethical dimensions of the ethnography of performance, *Literature in Performance* 5: 1–13.

———. 1986. Between experience and meaning: Performance as a paradigm for meaningful action. In T. Colson (Ed.), *Renewal and Revision: The Future of Interpretation*. Denton, TX: NB Omega Publications.

———. 1991. Rethinking ethnography: Towards a critical cultural politics, *Communications Monographs* 58: 178–194.

———. 1998. Beyond the text: Toward a performative cultural politics. In S. J. Dailey (Ed.), *The Future of Performance Studies: Visions and Revisions*. Annandale, VA: National Communication Association.

———. 2002. Performance studies: Interventions and radical research, *TDR: The Drama Review* 46(2): 137–141.

Cudjoe, S. 1990. Maya Angelou: The autobiographical statement updated. In H. Gates, (Ed.), *Reading Black, Reading Feminist: A Critical Anthology*. New York: Meridian, 272–306.

Darder, A., Baltonado, M., and Torres R. D. (Eds.). 2003. *The Critical Pedagogy Reader*. New York: RoutledgeFalmer.

Denison, J. 1996. Sport narratives, *Qualitative Inquiry* 2: 351–362.

Denzin, N. 1989. *Interpretive Interactionism*. Newbury Park, CA: Sage.

Denzin, N. 1991. *Symbolic Interactionism as Cultural Studies.* New York: Basil Blackwell.

———. 1994. The art and politics of interpretation. In N. Denzin and Y. Lincoln (Eds.), *The Sage Handbook of Qualitative Research.* Thousand Oaks, CA: Sage, 500–515.

Denzin, N. 1997. *Interpretative Ethnography: Ethnographic Practices for the 21st Century.* Thousand Oaks, CA: Sage.

———. 2000. Aesthetics and the practices of Qualitative Inquiry, *Qualitative Inquiry* 6(2): 256–265.

———. 2003. *Performance Ethnography: Critical Pedagogy and the Politics of Culture.* Thousand Oaks, CA: Sage.

———. 2005. Emancipatory discourses and the ethics and politics of interpretation. In N. Denzin and Y. Lincoln (Eds.), *The Sage Handbook of Qualitative Research.* Thousand Oaks, CA: Sage.

———. 2006a. Analytic autoethnography, or déjà vu all over again, *Journal of Contemporary Ethnography* 35(4): 419–428.

———. 2006b. Pedagogy, performance, and autoethnography, *Text and Performance Quarterly* 26(4): 333–338.

Denzin, N., and Lincoln, Y. 1994. *The Sage Handbook of Qualitative Research.* Thousand Oaks, CA: Sage.

———. 2000. *The Sage Handbook of Qualitative Research* (2nd ed.). Thousand Oaks, CA: Sage.

———. 2005. *The Sage Handbook of Qualitative Research* (3rd ed.). Thousand Oaks, CA: Sage.

Derrida, J. 1978. *Writing and Difference.* Chicago: University of Chicago Press.

Dimitriadis, G., and McCarthy, C. 2000. Stranger in the village: James Baldwin, popular culture, and the ties that bind, *Qualitative Inquiry* 6(2): 171–187.

———. 2001. *Reading and Teaching the Postcolonial: From Baldwin to Basquiat and Beyond.* New York: Teachers College Press.

Diversi, M. 1998a. Street kids in search of humanization: Expanding dominant narratives through critical ethnography and stories of lived experiences. Unpublished doctoral dissertation, University of Illinois at Urbana-Champaign.

———. 1998b. Glimpses of street life: Representing lived experience through short stories, *Qualitative Inquiry* 4:131–147.

———. 2003. Glimpses of street children through short stories. In M. Gergen and K. Gergen (Eds.), *Social Construction: A Reader.* London: Sage.

———. 2006. Street kids in Nikes: In search of humanization through the culture of consumption, *Cultural Studies and Critical Methodologies* 6: 370–390.

Diversi, M., Moraes Filho, N., and Morelli, M. 1999. Daily reality on the streets of Campinas, Brazil, *New Directions for Child and Adolescent Development 85*: 19–34.

Ellis, C. 2004. *The Ethnographic I: A Methodological Novel about Teaching and Doing Autoethnography.* Walnut Creek, CA: AltaMira Press.

Ellis, C., and Bochner, A. 1996. *Composing Ethnography: Alternative Forms of Qualitative Writing* (Eds.). Walnut Creek, CA: AltaMira Press.

———. 2000. Autoethnography, personal narrative, reflexivity: Alternative forms of qualitative writing. In N. Denzin and Y. Lincoln (Eds.), *The Sage Handbook of Qualitative Research*. Thousand Oaks, CA: Sage.

Fine, M. 1992. *Disruptive Voices*. Ann Arbor: University of Michigan Press.

Folha de São Paulo. 2005. *Ribeirao Preto tem 10ª Morte de Boia Fria*. www1.folha.uol.com.br/fsp/dinheiro/fi0410200526.htm.

Foucault, M. 1974. *The Order of Things: An Archeology of the Human Sciences*. New York: Vintage Books.

———. 1978. *The History of Sexuality*, Vol. 1: *An Introduction*, Robert Hurley (Trans.). New York: Vintage Books.

———. 1979. *Discipline and Punish: The Birth of the Prison*, Alan Sheridan (Trans.). New York: Vintage Books.

———. 1980. *Power/Knowledge*. In C. Gordon (Ed.) and C. Gordon, L. Marshall, J. Mepham, and K. Soper (Trans.). New York: Pantheon.

———. 1982. The subject and power, *Critical Inquiry* 8(4): 777–795.

Freeman, M. 1993. *Rewriting the Self: History, Memory, Narrative*. New York: Routledge.

Freire, P. 1970. *Pedagogy of the Oppressed*. 20th anniversary edition. M. Bergman Ramos (Trans.). New York: Continuum.

———. 1985. *The politics of Education: Culture, Power, and Liberation*. D. Macedo (Trans.). Hadley: Bergin & Garvey.

———. 1995a. *Cartas a Cristina*. São Paulo: Paz e Terra.

———. 1995b. *A Sombra Desta Mangueira*. São Paulo: Olho d'Agua.

———. 1996. *Letters to Cristina: Reflections on My Life and Work*. D. Macedo, Q. Macedo, and A. Oliveira (Trans.). New York: Routledge.

———. 1998a. *Pedagogy of Freedom: Ethics, Democracy, and Civic Courage*. P. Clarke (Trans.). Lanham, MD: Rowman & Littlefield Publishers.

———. 1998b. *Pedagogy of the Heart*. D. Macedo and A. Oliveira (Trans.); foreword by M. Carnoy. New York: Continuum.

———. 2004a [1994]. *Pedagogy of Hope: Reliving Pedagogy of the Oppressed*. R. R. Barr (Trans.). New York: Continuum.

———. 2004b. *Pedagogy of Indignation*. Boulder, CO: Paradigm Publishers.

Freire, P., and Macedo, D. 1987. *Literacy: Reading the Word and the World*. South Hadley, MA: Bergin and Garvey.

Freyre, G. 1936. *Sobrados e Mucambos: Decadencia do Patriarchado Rural no Brasil*. São Paulo, Companhia Editora Nacional.

Gramsci, A. 1971. *Selection from the Prison Notebooks*. New York: International Publishers.

Hall, S. 1990. The emergence of cultural studies and the crisis of the humanities, *October 53*: 11–23.

———. 1992. Cultural studies and its theoretical legacies. In L. Grossberg, C. Nelson, and P. Treichler (Eds.), *Cultural Studies*. New York: Routledge, 277–294.

Haraway, D. J. 1988. Situated knowledges: The science question in feminism and the privilege of partial perspective, *Feminist Studies* 14(3).

———. 1991. *Simians, Cyborgs, and Women: The Reinvention of Nature*. New York: Routledge.

Holman Jones, S. 2005a. Autoethnography: Making the personal political. In N. Denzin and Y. Lincoln (Eds.), *The Sage Handbook of Qualitative Research*. Thousand Oaks, CA: Sage.

———. 2005b. Torch singing as autoethnography. In N. Denzin and Y. Lincoln (Eds.), *Turning Points in Qualitative Research*. Walnut Creek, CA: AltaMira Press.

hooks, b. 1981. *Ain't I a Woman: Black Women and Feminism*. Boston: South End.

———. 1990. *Yearning: Race, Gender, and Cultural Politics*. Boston: South End.

———. 1994. *Outlaw Culture: Resisting Representations*. New York: Routledge.

Hurston, Z. N. 1990 [1935]. *Mules and Men*. New York: Harper.

IBGE-Brazilian Institute of Geography. 1999. Anuario Estatisco do Brasil. Rio de Janeiro: Instituto Estatistico.

Jessor, R., Colby, A., and Schweder, R. 1996. *Ethnography and Human Development: Context and Meaning in Social Inquiry* (Eds.). Chicago: The University of Chicago Press.

Jones, J. L. 1997. "Sista Docta": Performance as critique of the academy. In *TDR: The Drama Review* 41(2). Cambridge: MIT Press.

———. 2002. Performance ethnography: The role of embodiment in cultural authenticity, *Theatre Topics* 21(1): 1–5.

Lancenet: O Campeao da Rede. 2001. *Mais uma Cena de Violencia no Futebol Brasileiro*. Accessed September 11, 2001, http://lancenet.ig.com.br.

Langellier, K. M. 1999. Personal narrative, performance, performativity: Two or three things I know for sure, *Text and Performance Quarterly* 19: 125–144.

Lorde, A. 1983. The master's tools will never dismantle the master's house. In C. Moraga and G. E. Anzaldúa (Eds.), *This Bridge Called My Back: Writings by Radical Women of Color*. New York: Kitchen Table, Women of Color Press.

———. 1984. *Sister Outsider*. New York: Crossing Press.

Madison, D. S. 1998. Performance, personal narratives, and the politics of possibility. In S. J. Dailey (Ed.), *The Future of Performance Studies: Visions and Revisions*. Annandale, VA: National Communication Association.

———. 2005. *Critical Ethnography: Method, Ethics, and Performance*. Thousand Oaks, CA: Sage.

———. 2006. The Dialogic performative in critical ethnography, *Text and Performance Quarterly* 26(4): 320–324.

Madison, D. S., and Hamera, J. 2006. *The Sage Handbook of Performance Studies*. Thousand Oaks, CA: Sage.

McLaren, P. 1992. Literacy research and the Postmodern turn: Cautions from the margins. In R. Beach, J. Green, M. Kamil, and T. Shanahan (Eds.), *Multidisciplinary Perspectives on Literacy Research*. Urbana, IL: National Council of Teachers of English, 318–339.

McLaren, P. 2002. Afterword. In A. Darder, *Reinventing Paulo Freire: A Pedagogy of Love*. Boulder, CO: Westview Press.

McLaren, P. 2003. *Life in Schools: An Introduction to Critical Pedagogy in the Foundations of Education*. Boston: Allyn & Bacon.

McLaren, P., and Hammer, R. 1989. Critical pedagogy and the postmodern challenge, *Educational Foundations* 3: 29–69.

Merleau-Ponty, M. 1969. *The Visible and the Invisible*. Evanston, IL: Northwestern University Press.

Metcalf, S. 2007. Richard Rorty: What made him a crucial American philosopher? *Slate*. Accessed June 15, 2007, www.slate.com/id/2168488/.

Miller, L. C., and Pelias, R. J. (Eds.). 2001. A beginning preface. In *The Green Window: Proceedings of the Giant City Conference of Performative Writing*. Carbondale, IL: Southern Illinois University Press, v–vi.

Mills, C. W. 1959. *The Sociological Imagination*. New York: Oxford University Press.

Mohanty, C. T. 2003. *Feminism without Borders: Decolonizing Theory, Practicing Solidarity*. Durham, NC: Duke University Press.

Moraga, C. L., and Anzaldúa, G. E. (Eds.). 1981. *This Bridge Called My Back: Writings by Radical Women of Color*. Berkeley: Third Woman Press.

Moreira, C. 2005a. Words. In N. Denzin (Ed.), *Studies in Symbolic Interaction 28*. London: Elsevier.

———. 2005b. Words, *Studies in Symbolic Interaction* 28: 173–176.

———. 2007. Made for sex, *Qualitative Inquiry* 13(1): 48–57.

———. 2008a. Fragments, *Qualitative Inquiry* 14(5): 663–683.

———. 2008b. Made for Sex, *Qualitative Inquiry* 1: 48–57. Thousand Oaks, CA: Sage.

Narayan, K. 1993. How native is a "native" anthropologist? *American Anthropologist* 95(3): 671–686.

Pelias, R. J. 2004. *A Methodology of the Heart: Evoking Academic and Daily Life*. Walnut Creek, CA: AltaMira Press.

Perez, E. 1999. *The Decolonial Imaginary: Writing Chicanas into History*. Bloomington: Indiana University Press.

Phelan, P. 1995. Performing ends. *The Drama Review* 39: 184–187.

Polkinghorne, D. 1998. *Narrative Knowing and the Human Sciences*. Albany: State University of New York Press.

Pollock, D. 1998. Performing writing. In P. Phelan and J. Lane (Eds.), *The Ends of Performance*. New York: New York University Press.

Richardson, L. 1990. *Writing Strategies: Reaching Diverse Audiences*. Newbury Park, CA: Sage.

Rinehart, R. E. 1998. *Players All: Performances in Contemporary Sport*. Bloomington: Indiana University Press.

Rosaldo, R. 1989. *Culture and Truth: The Remaking of Social Analysis*. Boston: Beacon Press.

Russell, R. V. 2002. *Pastimes: The Context of Contemporary Leisure*. Champaign, IL: Sagamore Publishing.

Sandoval, C. 2000. *Methodology of the Oppressed*. Minneapolis: University of Minnesota Press.

Sartre, J.-P. 1981. *The Family Idiot: Gustave Flaubert*, Vol. 1, 1821–1857. Chicago: University of Chicago Press.

Schechner, R. 1998. What is performance studies anyway? In P. Phelan and J. Lane (Eds.), *The Ends of Performance*. New York: New York Press, 357–362.

Scheper-Hughes, N. 1992. *Death without Weeping: The Violence of Everyday Life in Brazil*. Berkeley and Los Angeles: University of California Press.

Scheper-Hughes, N., and Sargent, C. 1998. *Small Wars: The Cultural Politics of Childhood*. Berkeley and Los Angeles: University of California Press.

Smith, L. T. 1999. *Decolonizing Methodologies: Research and Indigenous Peoples*. Dunedin: University of Otago Press.

———. 2005. On trick ground: Researching the native in the age of uncertainty. In N. Denzin and Y. Lincoln (Eds.), *The Sage Handbook of Qualitative Research*. Thousand Oaks, CA: Sage.

Strawson, P. F. 1959. *Individuals: An Essay in Descriptive Metaphysics*. New York: Routledge.

Trinh T. Minh-ha. 1990 [1989]. *Woman, Native, Other: Writing Postcoloniality and Feminism*. Bloomington: Indiana University Press.

Van Maanen, J. 1988. *Tales of the Field*. Chicago: University of Chicago Press.

Wagner, F. E., and Ward, J. O. 1980. Urbanization and migration in Brazil, *American Journal of Economics and Sociology* 39(3): 249–259.

Weems, M. E. 2003. *Public Education and the Imagination-Intellect: I Speak from the Wound in My Mouth*. New York: Peter Lang.

West, C. 1991. *The Ethical Dimensions of Marxist Thought*. New York: Monthly Review Press.

Yellow Bird, M. 2005. Tribal critical thinking centers, in W. A. Wilson and M. Yellow Bird (Eds.), *For Indigenous Eyes Only: A Decolonization Handbook*. Santa Fe: School of American Research, 9–30.

INDEX

A

"As an addict" 202–203
African-American males 192
aliens 19, *see also* betweeners
Allen, Paula Gum 27
"And then" 179
Angelou, Maya 203n1
Anglos 23
Anzaldúa, Gloria 31, 186, 201; and betweenness 25; *El Mundo Zurdo* of 29; notion of 221; writings of 22–24, 220
autoethnography 186, 187–203, 219
awareness-raising 183

B

Back on the Streets 61–65
Bakhtinian 20, 194
"Because" 45–46
"Being a kid, Sugar Cane" 50–51
betweeners 13, 18–25, 184, 186, 191, 199, 206–208, 211–212
betweenness 22, 24, 25; *see also* identities
Bhabha, Homi, and concept of hybridity 22
binary thinking 23
Bishop, R. 193
bodies 19, 21–23, 31, 32, 44, 59, 62, 123, 174
Brazil 14, 19–21, 31; minority white in 57; poor in 75; social class oppression in 110; street kids in 29
Brazilian-Americans 206–207
Brazilians 18–19, 22, 57
"Bridge" 24
Buarque, Chico 16–17, 214

C

children's lives 21
civil rights 17, 32
Collin, P. H., concept of 22–23
"Conde is dead" 99–100, 145
Conquergood 192
conscientização 185, 214, 218, 222
Cook, Dan 23, 24
cultural performer 190

D

decolonizing 8, 13–14, 20, 28, 142, 184; classroom 28, 208, 216; knowledge 29; praxis 208–214; scholarship 28–29, 33, 186, 195, 206–207
"Decolonizing Inquiry" 114
democracy 32, 46, 143, 215
Denzin, Norman 23, 26, 73–84, 187, 192, 200, 215
"Desperation" 200–201
Dickens, Charles 16

E

education 32; *against* colonial ideologies 183
El mundo zurdo (left-handed world) 24
Ellis, Carolyn's *The Ethnographic I* 190
ethnography 76, 78, 86, 110, 191–192

F

'false generosity' 196
feminism, Diversi on 191
Fire in the Mission 157–161

Freire Paulo 27, 211, 214; "concrete hope" of 222; concept of banking education 197, 198; participatory inquiry approach 198; pedagogy of hope of 29; *Pedagogy of the oppressed* 19, 183

G

Gandra, Paulo 205
Gavroche, 'le Gamin de Paris' 16
gender 186

H

Haraway, D. J. 193, 212
"He is five years old" 131–133
"Hey Gringo" 53–54
human misery 220
human rights 8, 32, 77, 186
humanization, ideology of 185; and Paulo Freire 185
humor and self-deprecation 213–214

I

"I am understanding" 18
"I am We are" 114
"I have a daughter, Analua" 48–49
"I have the duty" 149–154
identities 20
inclusive social justice 32
internalization of inferiority 197
"It is necessary to hope" 59–60
"It's a run" 172–173

J

Jones, Holman 189

K

knowledge production, politics of 206, 208
"Knowledge versus experience" 161–162

L

Latinos 23
"Leg?" 162–163

liberation, call for 183
"Like Anzaldúa, we ask to be met halfway" 27–28
Lincoln, Yvonna 210
"Living in Threat" 168–169
logical-positivism 198

M

Magali, a fabulous street educator 199
Merleau-Ponty, Maurice 31
Minh-ha, Trinh T. 193
Moraga, Cherrie 24
Moreira, Cláudio 31, 102, 186–187
Movimento Nacional dos Meninos e Meninas de Rua, National Movement for Street Children 199
"My questions Who are the Others?" 79

N

Nepantla 25
Newspaper Picture 86–87
Nike Cap 155–156
"No money in the pocket" 61
No More Soccer 115–116

O

Off the Streets 69
Old-Fashioned Nikes 137–138
oppressed, 8, 20–21, 25–27, 146, 147, 170, 184, 197; pedagogy of 19;
oppression 13, 19, 20, 23–27, 29; colonial 217; visceral knowledge of 211

P

"Past" 187–188
pedagogy 183, 187, 190, 210, 214, 218
Perez, Emma 208
performance 70n2,3, 186
performance studies 204n3
Place for Recovery, A 119–133

politics 158, 174, 190, 209; of possibility 80
postcolonial academic circles 212
power relations 20, 193
praxis 19, 28, 190, 196, 207, 208, 222
production of knowledge 28, 184–185
public performance stage 28, 208, see also performance
"Purple Conde" 110–111

R

race 186; American construction of 22
resistance 17, 25, 27, 28, 33, 190
Rio de Janeiro 220
Rorty, Richard 219
São Paulo 220

S

"Scared" 164, 166–168
She Could Be Living in Italy Now... 138–155
social class 22, 33, 49, 102, 110, 186; constructs 186; transformation 183
Stolen Romance 133–135
Strawson, P. F. 32
street children/kids 14–15, 18, 43, 191–192, 209–210; in Brazil 18, 205
Street Life 37–45, 155, 218, see also street children/kids

T

The Streets or Not the Streets 65–68
The Tales of Conde, Zezao, Master Cláudio, and Cláudio 98–114
Third World feminism 23, 146, 172, 173, 178, 187
Too Blond, Too White 92–98
trombadinhas 21

U

Universal Declaration of Human Rights by United-Nations 186
U.S.A, Brazilian scholars in 206; foreigners in 19; see also Brazilian-Americans

V

visceral knowledge 27, 29, 32–33, 184, 207, 211–212, 215–218, 219
"voice from above" 171–172

W

"We're 30 million street kids" 40
"Who are the Others?" 77
"Why?" 49–50
With Grace 71–86
"With my bad English" 84
"Words" 89–92
works of Narayan 193

Y

"Yes, I am an angry man" 59–60
"You know, Gringo..." 58

About the Authors

Marcelo Diversi is Assistant Professor of Human Development at Washington State University Vancouver. He is author of a dozen published articles based on his studies of Latino youth in the United States and street children in Brazil.

Cláudio Moreira is Assistant Professor in the Department of Communications, University of Massachusetts, Amherst. A specialist in performance ethnography, cultural theory, and sport, he has a half dozen published articles.

Both authors are originally from Brazil.